CAN NUMBERS LIE...?

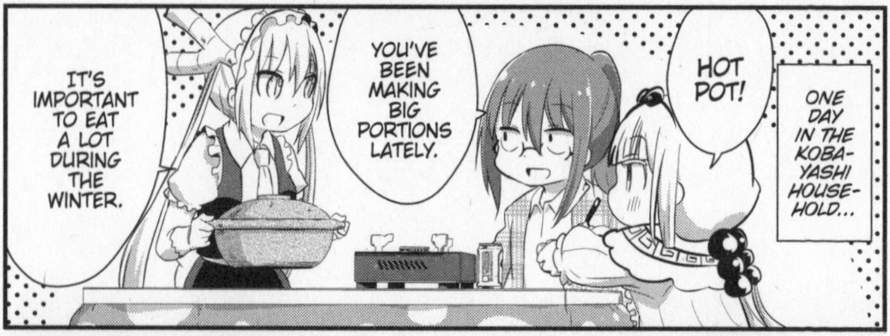
ONE DAY IN THE KOBA-YASHI HOUSE-HOLD...
HOT POT!
YOU'VE BEEN MAKING BIG PORTIONS LATELY.
IT'S IMPORTANT TO EAT A LOT DURING THE WINTER.

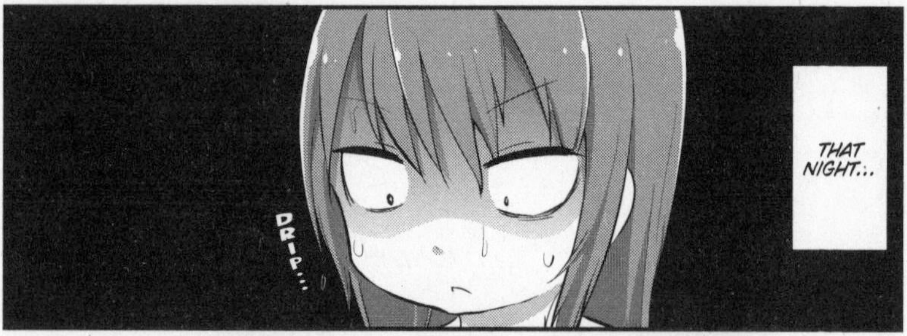
THAT NIGHT...
DRIP...

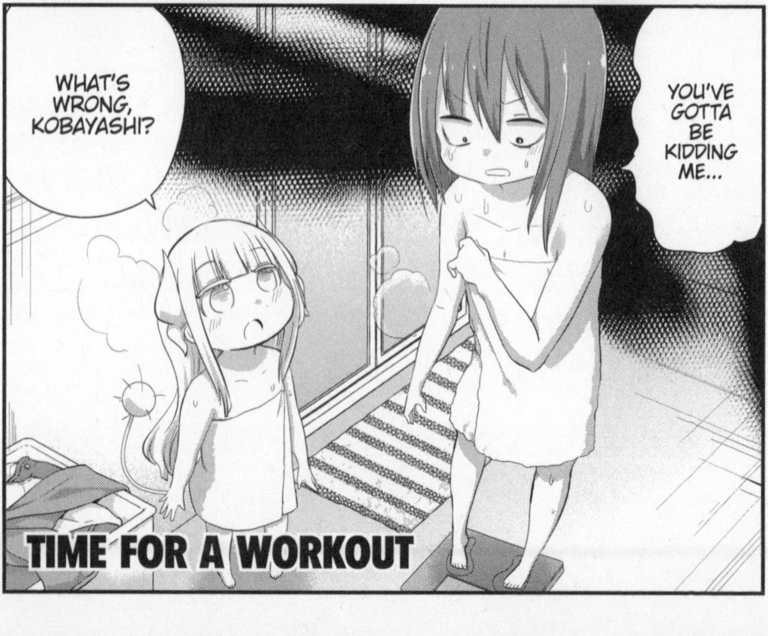
YOU'VE GOTTA BE KIDDING ME...
WHAT'S WRONG, KOBAYASHI?
TIME FOR A WORKOUT

HELLO, SADNESS, MY OLD FRIEND...

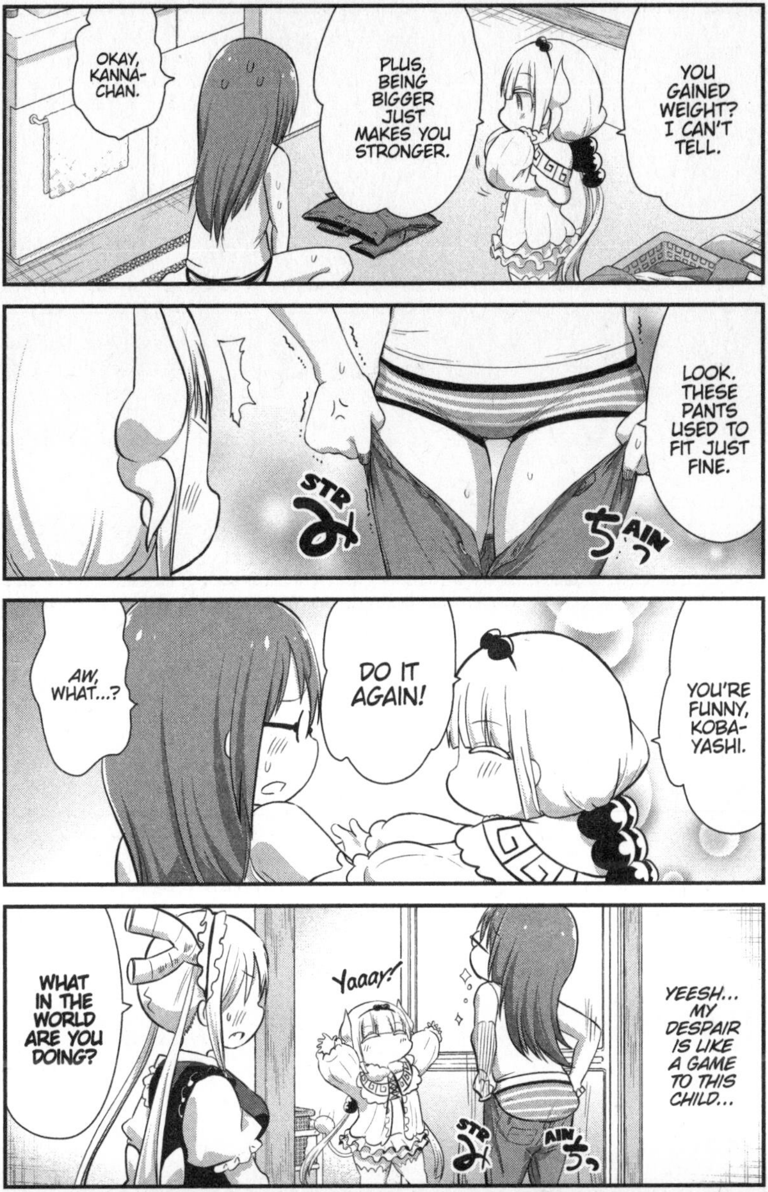

YOU GAINED WEIGHT? I CAN'T TELL.
PLUS, BEING BIGGER JUST MAKES YOU STRONGER.
OKAY, KANNA-CHAN.
LOOK. THESE PANTS USED TO FIT JUST FINE.
AIN
STR
YOU'RE FUNNY, KOBA-YASHI.
DO IT AGAIN!
AW, WHAT...?
YEESH... MY DESPAIR IS LIKE A GAME TO THIS CHILD...
AIN
STR
Yaaay!
WHAT IN THE WORLD ARE YOU DOING?

RARING TO GO

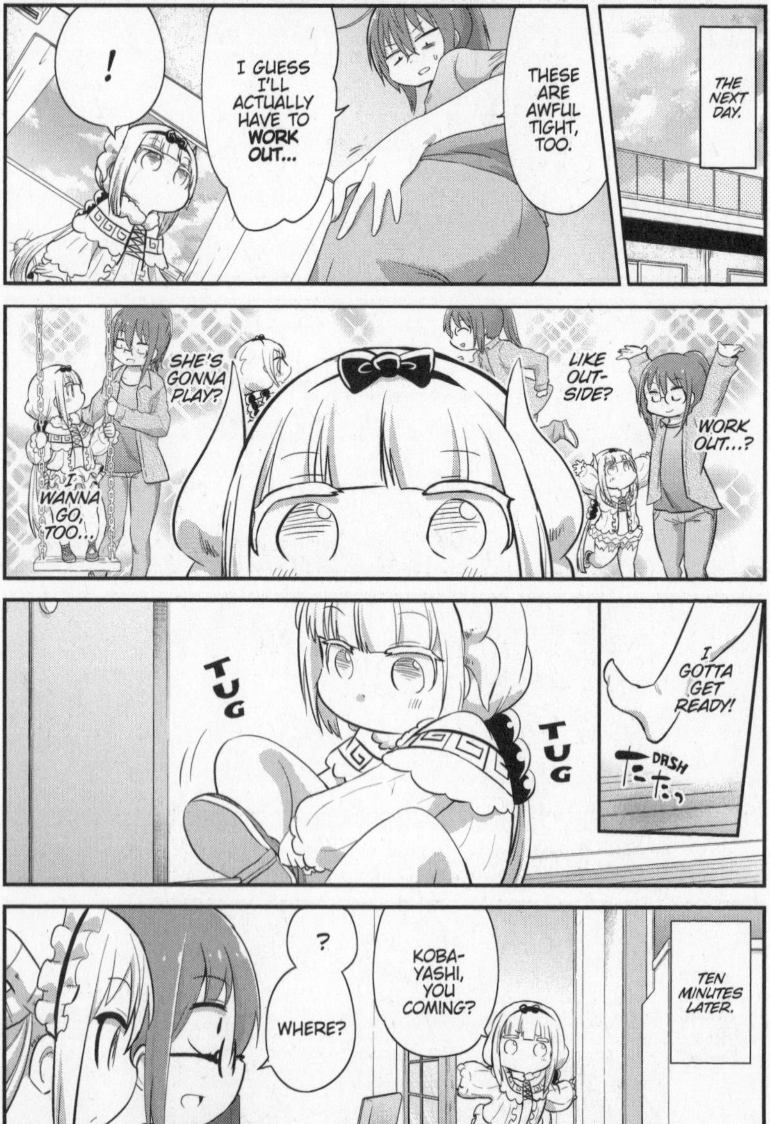
THE NEXT DAY.
THESE ARE AWFUL TIGHT, TOO.
I GUESS I'LL ACTUALLY HAVE TO WORK OUT...
!
WORK OUT...?
LIKE OUT-SIDE?
SHE'S GONNA PLAY?
I WANNA GO, TOO...
I GOTTA GET READY!
DASH
たたっ
TUG
TUG
TEN MINUTES LATER.
KOBA-YASHI, YOU COMING?
?
WHERE?

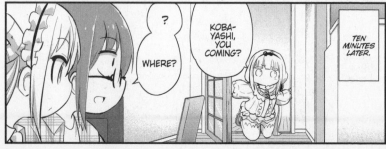

A SHOCKING DISCOVERY

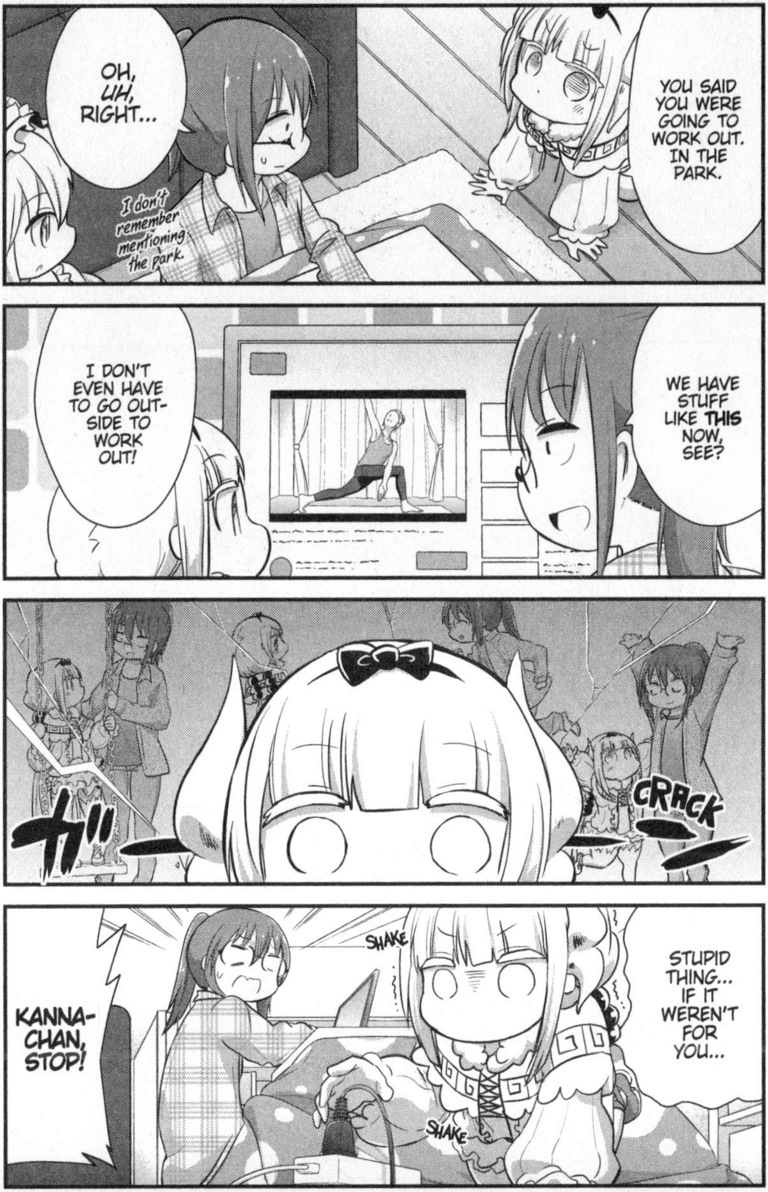
YOU SAID YOU WERE GOING TO WORK OUT. IN THE PARK.
OH, UH, RIGHT...
I don't remember mentioning the park.
WE HAVE STUFF LIKE THIS NOW, SEE?
I DON'T EVEN HAVE TO GO OUT-SIDE TO WORK OUT!
CRACK
ガッ
STUPID THING... IF IT WEREN'T FOR YOU...
SHAKE
SHAKE
KANNA-CHAN, STOP!

THE STRAW THAT BROKE KOBAYASHI'S BACK

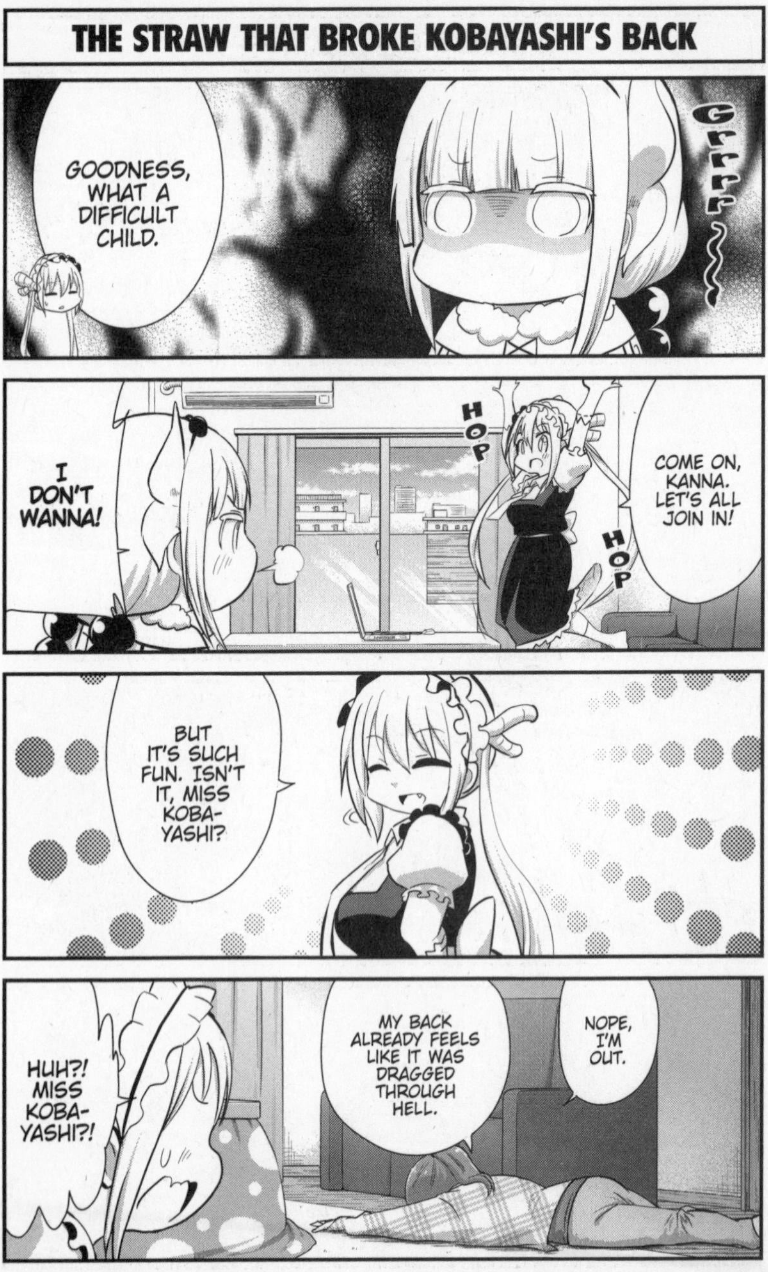
Grrr~~
GOODNESS, WHAT A DIFFICULT CHILD.
COME ON, KANNA. LET'S ALL JOIN IN!
HOP
HOP
I DON'T WANNA!
BUT IT'S SUCH FUN. ISN'T IT, MISS KOBA-YASHI?
NOPE, I'M OUT.
MY BACK ALREADY FEELS LIKE IT WAS DRAGGED THROUGH HELL.
HUH?! MISS KOBA-YASHI?!

A GRAND ADVENTURE

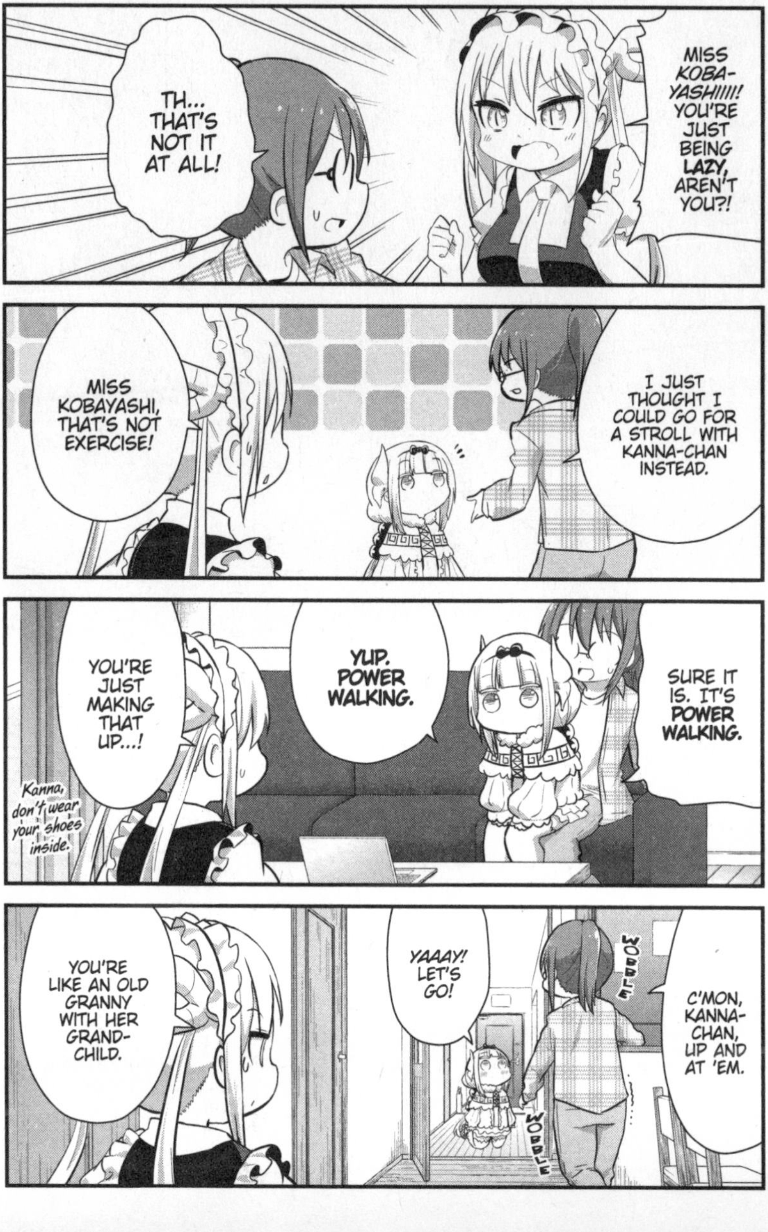
MISS KOBA-YASHI!!!!! YOU'RE JUST BEING **LAZY**, AREN'T YOU?!
TH... THAT'S NOT IT AT ALL!
I JUST THOUGHT I COULD GO FOR A STROLL WITH KANNA-CHAN INSTEAD.
MISS KOBAYASHI, THAT'S NOT EXERCISE!
SURE IT IS. IT'S **POWER WALKING.**
YUP. POWER WALKING.
YOU'RE JUST MAKING THAT UP...!
Kanna, don't wear your shoes inside.
C'MON, KANNA-CHAN, UP AND AT 'EM.
WOBBLE
WOBBLE
YAAAY! LET'S GO!
YOU'RE LIKE AN OLD GRANNY WITH HER GRAND-CHILD.

THE EVER-ACTIVE KANNA-CHAN

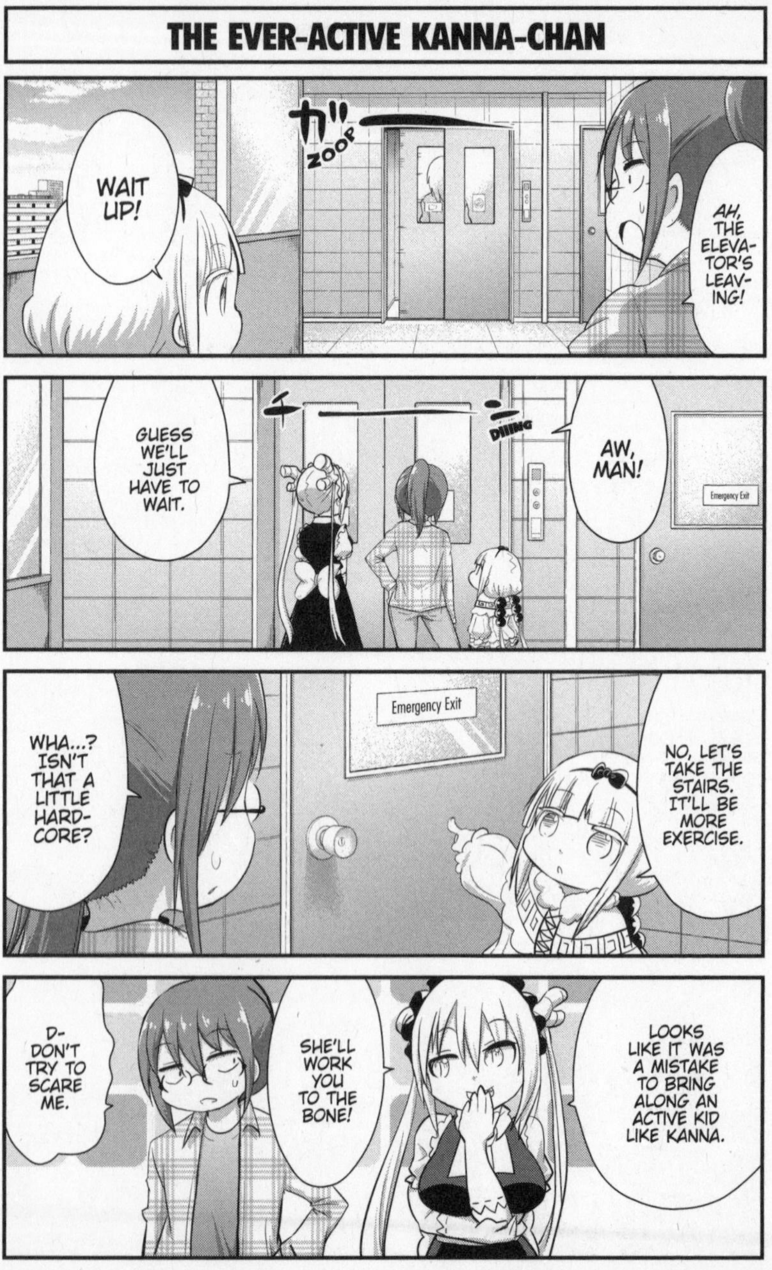
AH, THE ELEVATOR'S LEAVING!
ZOOP
WAIT UP!
AW, MAN!
DIIING
Emergency Exit
GUESS WE'LL JUST HAVE TO WAIT.
NO, LET'S TAKE THE STAIRS. IT'LL BE MORE EXERCISE.
Emergency Exit
WHA...? ISN'T THAT A LITTLE HARDCORE?
LOOKS LIKE IT WAS A MISTAKE TO BRING ALONG AN ACTIVE KID LIKE KANNA.
SHE'LL WORK YOU TO THE BONE!
D-DON'T TRY TO SCARE ME.

OVERCONFIDENT

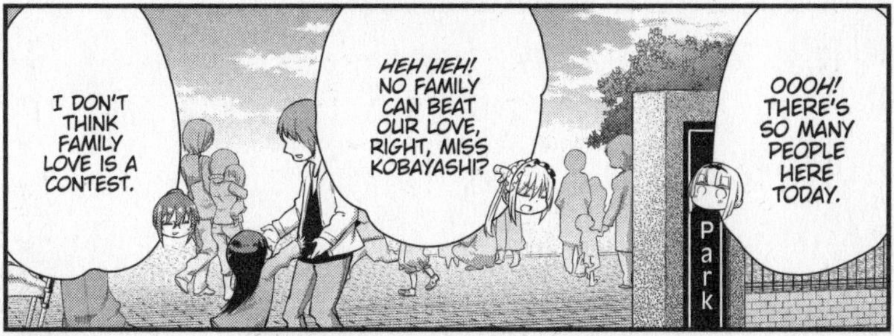
OOOH! THERE'S SO MANY PEOPLE HERE TODAY.
Park
HEH HEH! NO FAMILY CAN BEAT OUR LOVE, RIGHT, MISS KOBAYASHI?
I DON'T THINK FAMILY LOVE IS A CONTEST.

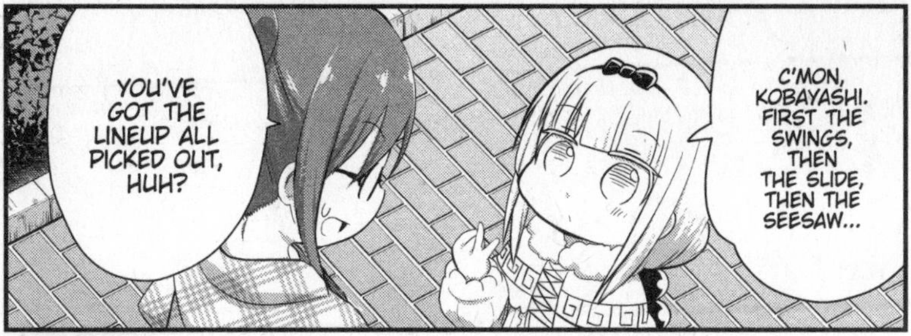
C'MON, KOBAYASHI. FIRST THE SWINGS, THEN THE SLIDE, THEN THE SEESAW...
YOU'VE GOT THE LINEUP ALL PICKED OUT, HUH?

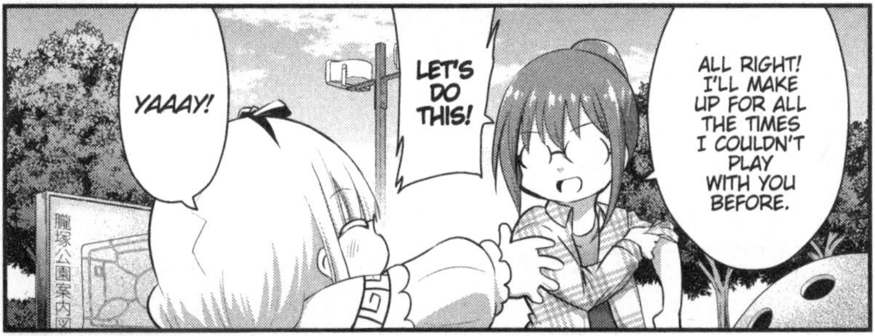
ALL RIGHT! I'LL MAKE UP FOR ALL THE TIMES I COULDN'T PLAY WITH YOU BEFORE.
LET'S DO THIS!
YAAAY!
朧塚公園案内図

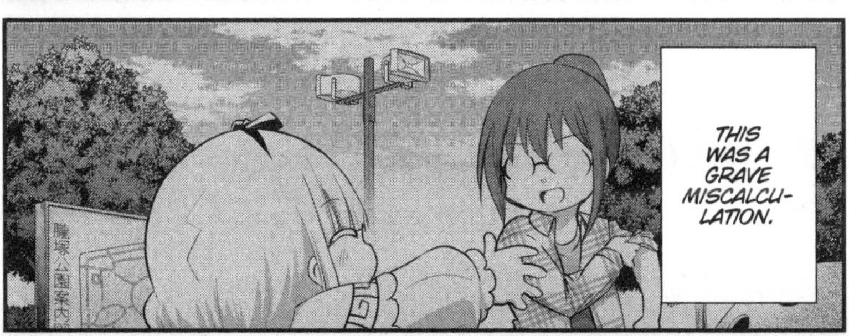
THIS WAS A GRAVE MISCALCU-LATION.

Poster: Oborodzuka Park Map.

FULL STOP

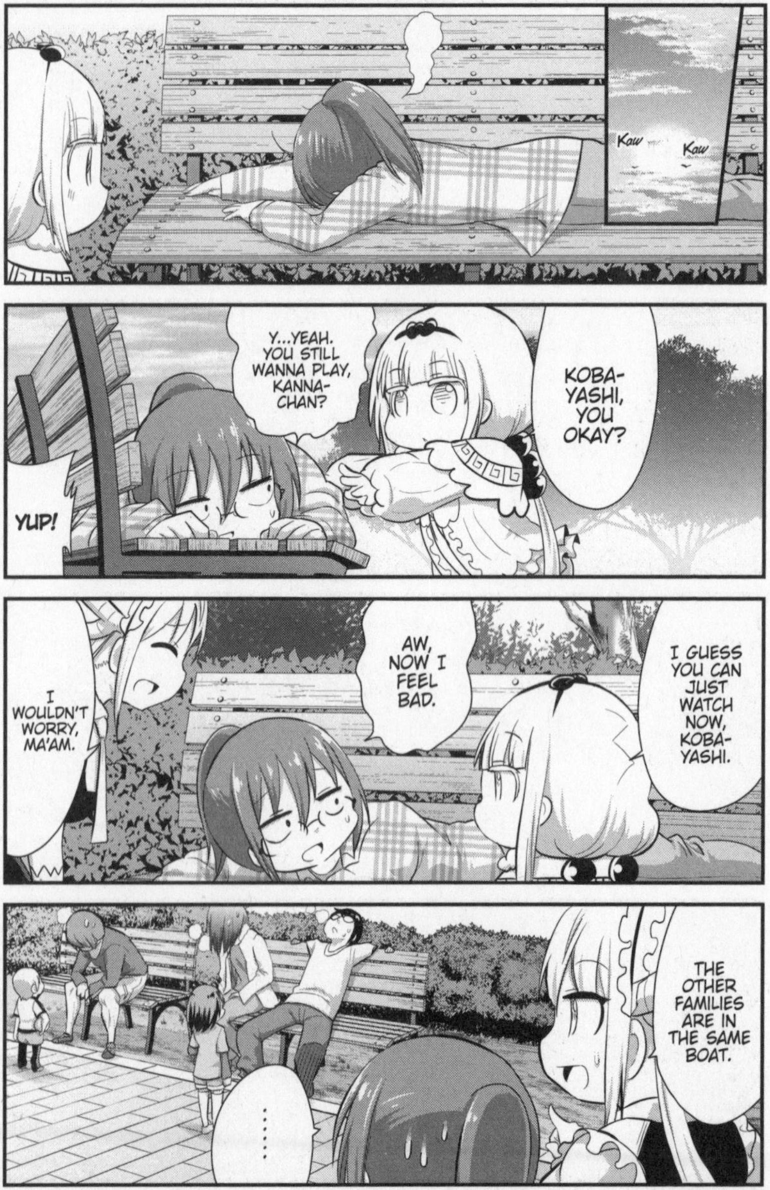
Kaw
Kaw
KOBA-YASHI, YOU OKAY?
Y...YEAH. YOU STILL WANNA PLAY, KANNA-CHAN?
YUP!
I GUESS YOU CAN JUST WATCH NOW, KOBA-YASHI.
AW, NOW I FEEL BAD.
I WOULDN'T WORRY, MA'AM.
THE OTHER FAMILIES ARE IN THE SAME BOAT.
......

MANO A MANA

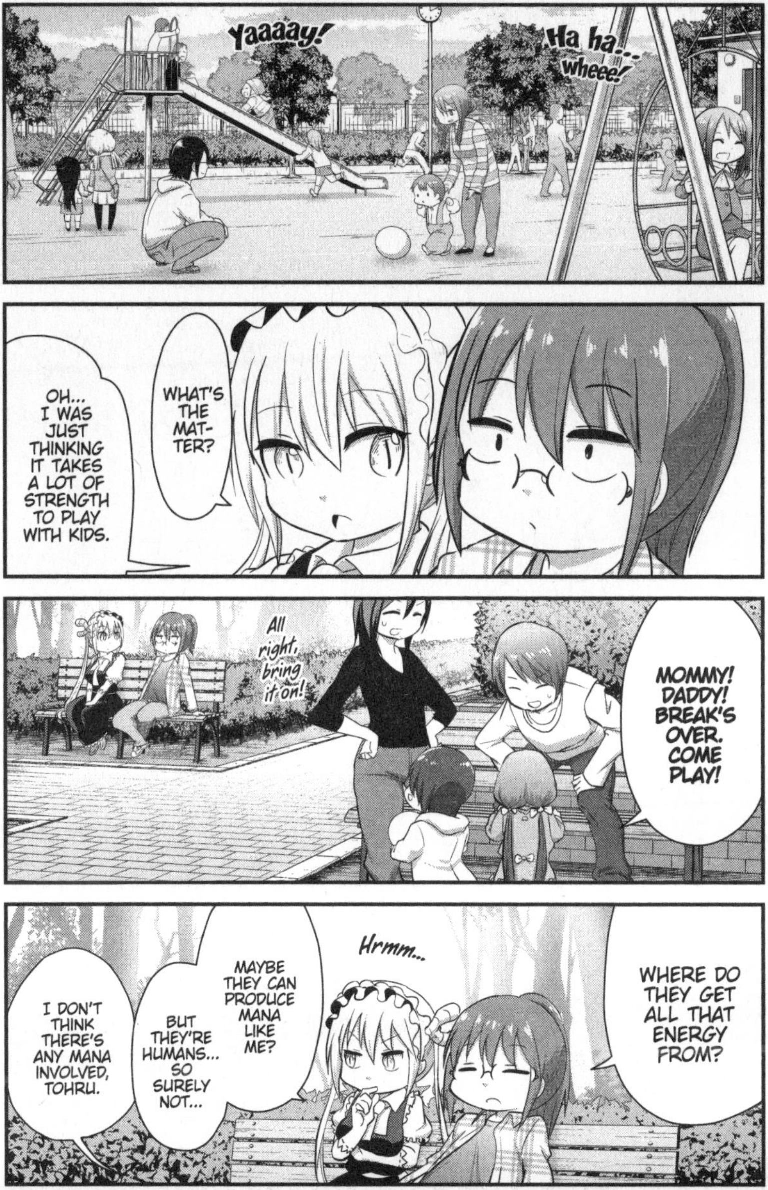
Ha ha... wheee!
Yaaaay!
WHAT'S THE MAT-TER?
OH... I WAS JUST THINKING IT TAKES A LOT OF STRENGTH TO PLAY WITH KIDS.
MOMMY! DADDY! BREAK'S OVER. COME PLAY!
All right, bring it on!
WHERE DO THEY GET ALL THAT ENERGY FROM?
Hrmm...
MAYBE THEY CAN PRODUCE MANA LIKE ME?
BUT THEY'RE HUMANS... SO SURELY NOT...
I DON'T THINK THERE'S ANY MANA INVOLVED, TOHRU.

FLOWER CROWN

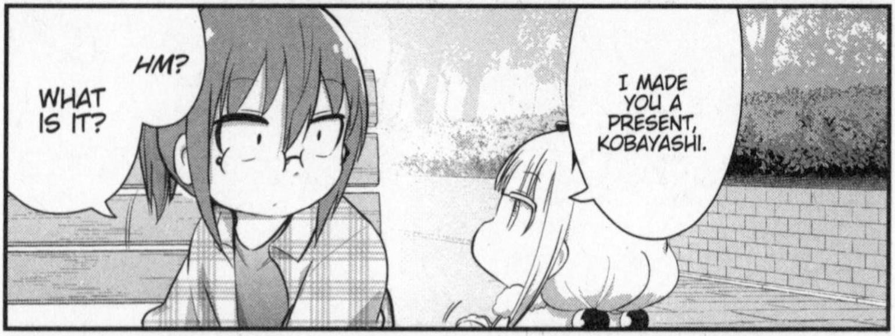
I MADE YOU A PRESENT, KOBAYASHI.
HM?
WHAT IS IT?

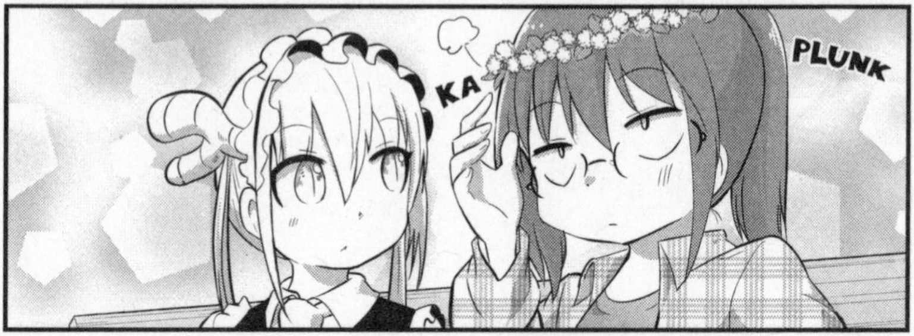
PLUNK
KA

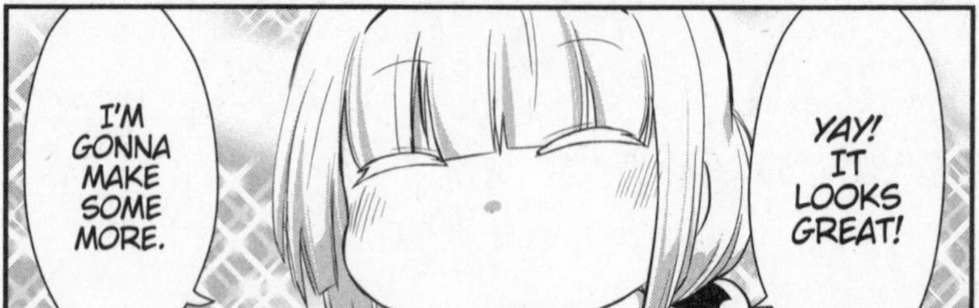
YAY! IT LOOKS GREAT!
I'M GONNA MAKE SOME MORE.

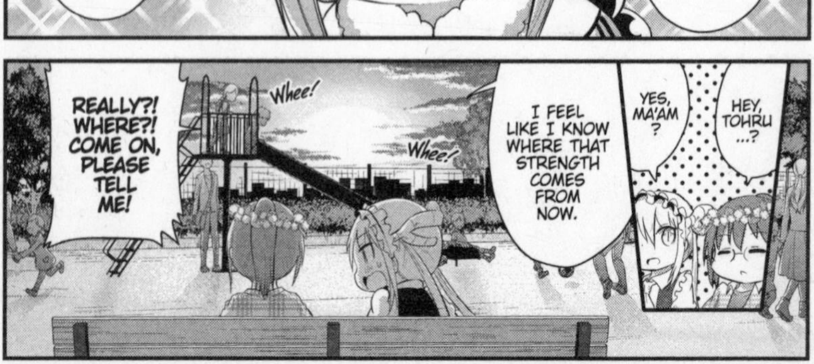
HEY, TOHRU ...?
YES, MA'AM ?
I FEEL LIKE I KNOW WHERE THAT STRENGTH COMES FROM NOW.
Whee!
Whee!
REALLY?! WHERE?! COME ON, PLEASE TELL ME!

IT GETS RESULTS

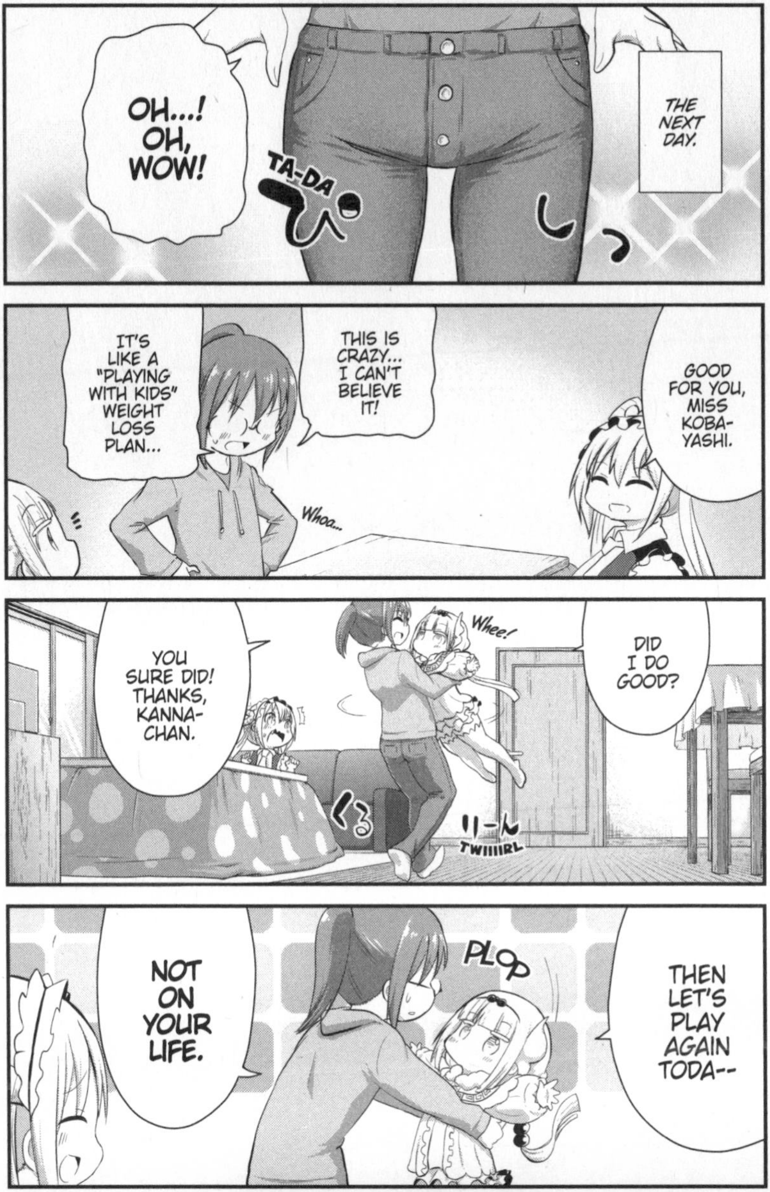
THE NEXT DAY.
TA-DA
OH...! OH, WOW!
GOOD FOR YOU, MISS KOBA-YASHI.
THIS IS CRAZY... I CAN'T BELIEVE IT!
IT'S LIKE A "PLAYING WITH KIDS" WEIGHT LOSS PLAN...
Whoa...
DID I DO GOOD?
Whee!
TWIIIIRL
YOU SURE DID! THANKS, KANNA-CHAN.
THEN LET'S PLAY AGAIN TODA--
PLOP
NOT ON YOUR LIFE.

TIME FOR A WORKOUT/END

Miss Kobayashi's Dragon Maid

Kanna's Daily Life

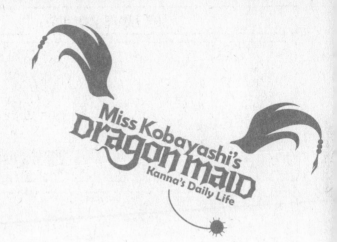

WE LOVE BOOKS!

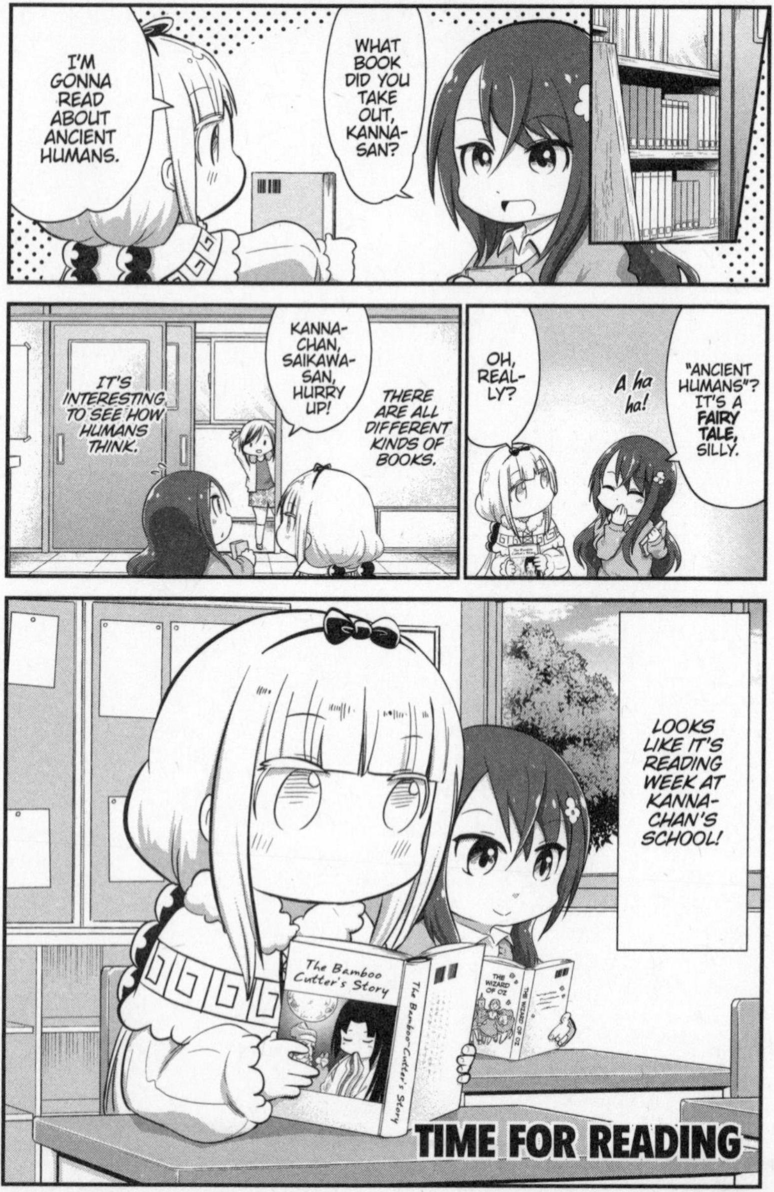
WHAT BOOK DID YOU TAKE OUT, KANNA-SAN?
I'M GONNA READ ABOUT ANCIENT HUMANS.
"ANCIENT HUMANS"? IT'S A FAIRY TALE, SILLY.
A ha ha!
OH, REALLY?
KANNA-CHAN, SAIKAWA-SAN, HURRY UP!
THERE ARE ALL DIFFERENT KINDS OF BOOKS.
IT'S INTERESTING TO SEE HOW HUMANS THINK.
LOOKS LIKE IT'S READING WEEK AT KANNA-CHAN'S SCHOOL!
THE WIZARD OF OZ
The Bamboo Cutter's Story
TIME FOR READING

SPEED-READING, DRAGON STYLE

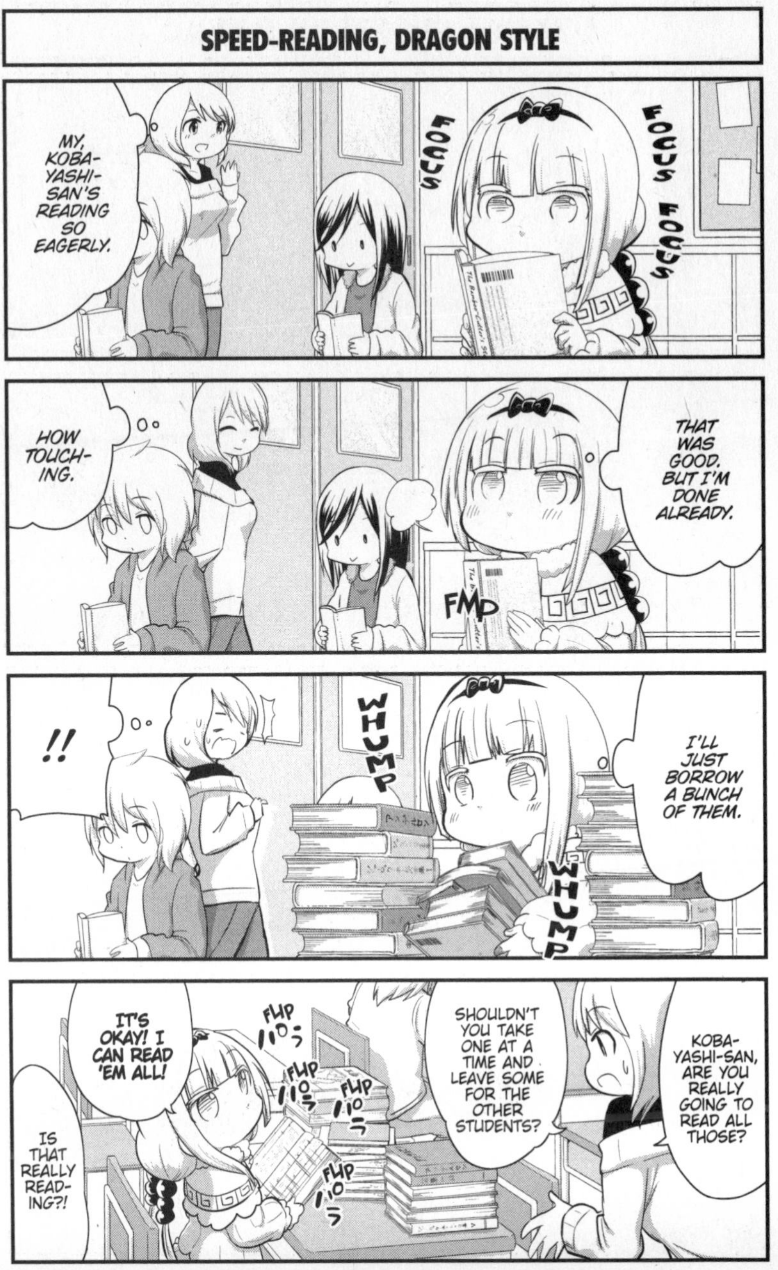
FOCUS
FOCUS
FOCUS
MY, KOBA-YASHI-SAN'S READING SO EAGERLY.
THAT WAS GOOD. BUT I'M DONE ALREADY.
FMP
HOW TOUCH-ING.
I'LL JUST BORROW A BUNCH OF THEM.
WHUMP
WHUMP
!!
KOBA-YASHI-SAN, ARE YOU REALLY GOING TO READ ALL THOSE?
SHOULDN'T YOU TAKE ONE AT A TIME AND LEAVE SOME FOR THE OTHER STUDENTS?
FLIP
FLIP
FLIP
FLIP
IT'S OKAY! I CAN READ 'EM ALL!
IS THAT REALLY READ-ING?!

SAIKAWA-SAN THE WILD CHILD

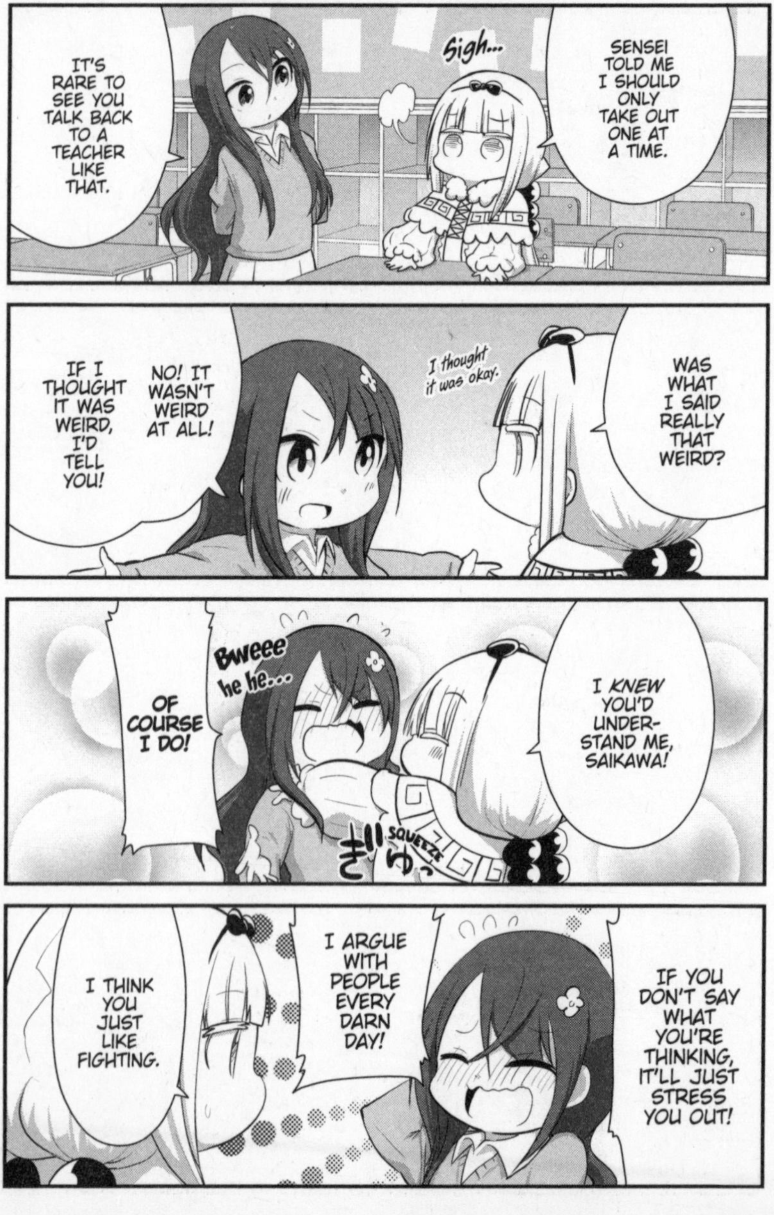
SENSEI TOLD ME I SHOULD ONLY TAKE OUT ONE AT A TIME.
Sigh...
IT'S RARE TO SEE YOU TALK BACK TO A TEACHER LIKE THAT.
WAS WHAT I SAID REALLY THAT WEIRD?
I thought it was okay.
NO! IT WASN'T WEIRD AT ALL!
IF I THOUGHT IT WAS WEIRD, I'D TELL YOU!
I KNEW YOU'D UNDER-STAND ME, SAIKAWA!
Bweee he he...
OF COURSE I DO!
ぎゅっ
SQUEEZE
IF YOU DON'T SAY WHAT YOU'RE THINKING, IT'LL JUST STRESS YOU OUT!
I ARGUE WITH PEOPLE EVERY DARN DAY!
I THINK YOU JUST LIKE FIGHTING.

A LITTLE LIGHT READING?

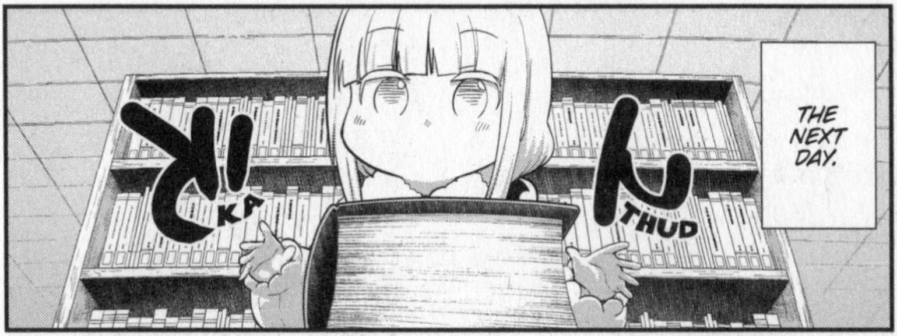
THE NEXT DAY.
KA
THUD

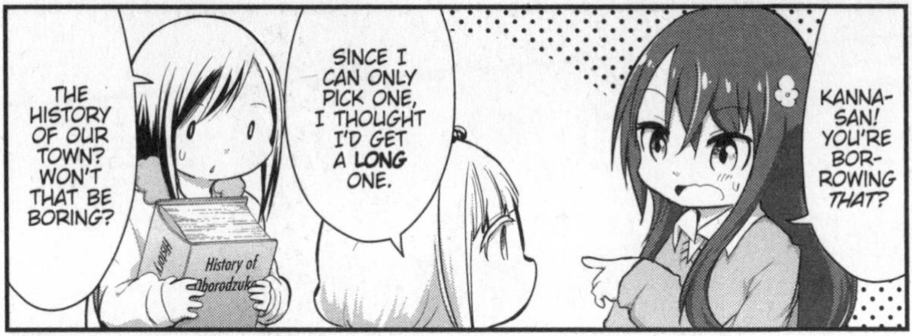
KANNA-SAN! YOU'RE BOR-ROWING THAT?
SINCE I CAN ONLY PICK ONE, I THOUGHT I'D GET A LONG ONE.
THE HISTORY OF OUR TOWN? WON'T THAT BE BORING?

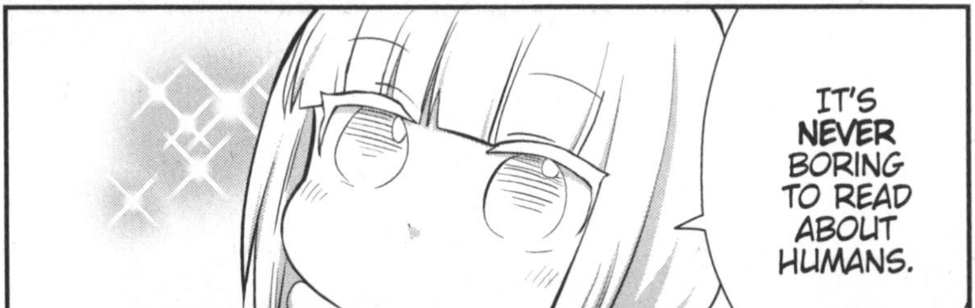
IT'S NEVER BORING TO READ ABOUT HUMANS.

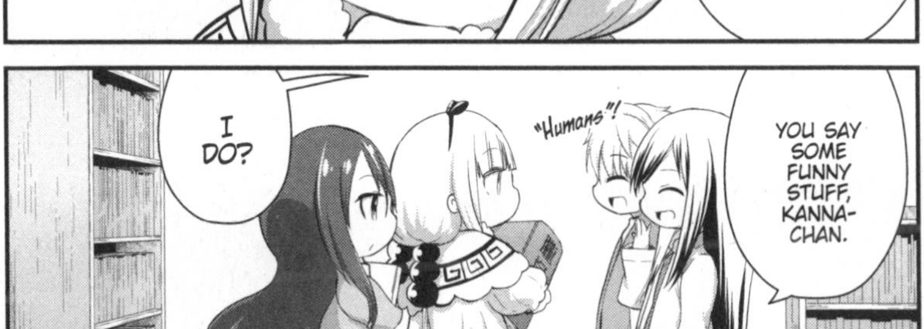
YOU SAY SOME FUNNY STUFF, KANNA-CHAN.
"Humans"!
I DO?

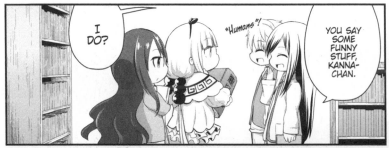

I JUST WANTED TO BE LIKE HER

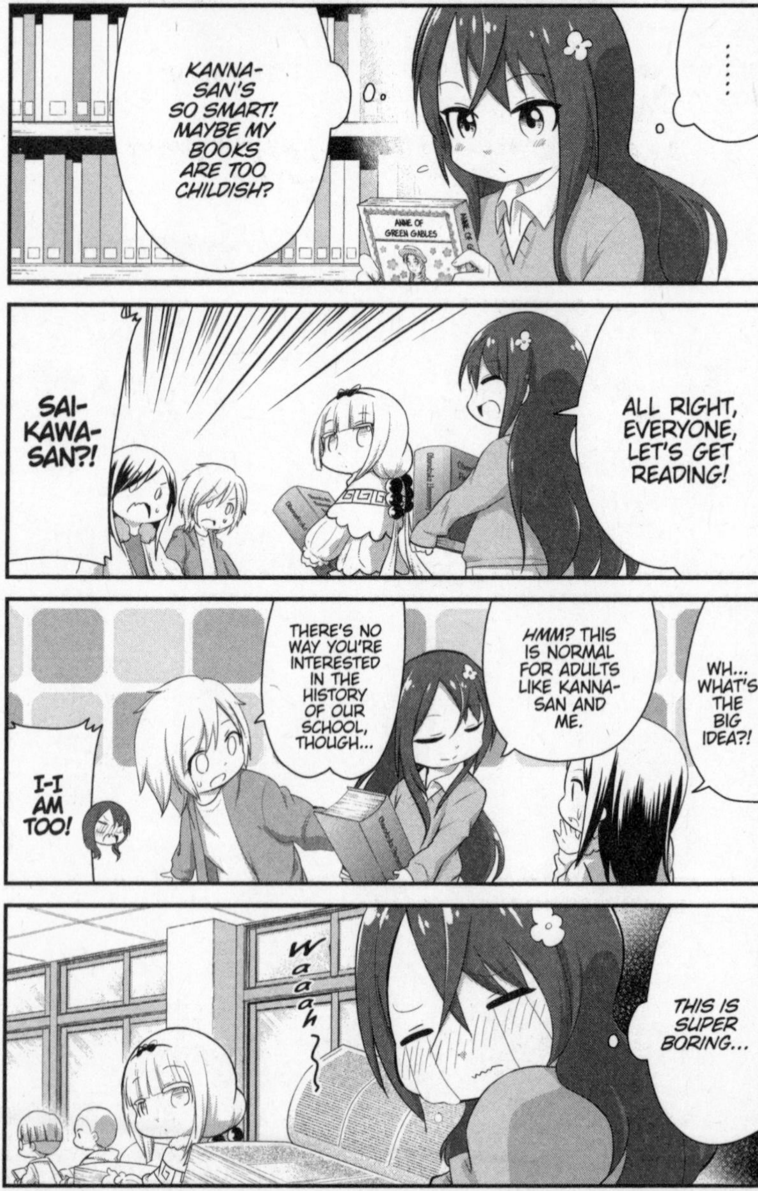
......
KANNA-SAN'S SO SMART! MAYBE MY BOOKS ARE TOO CHILDISH?
ANNE OF GREEN GABLES
ALL RIGHT, EVERYONE, LET'S GET READING!
SAI-KAWA-SAN?!
WH... WHAT'S THE BIG IDEA?!
HMM? THIS IS NORMAL FOR ADULTS LIKE KANNA-SAN AND ME.
THERE'S NO WAY YOU'RE INTERESTED IN THE HISTORY OF OUR SCHOOL, THOUGH...
I-I AM TOO!
THIS IS SUPER BORING...
Waaah~

JUST THE TWO OF US?

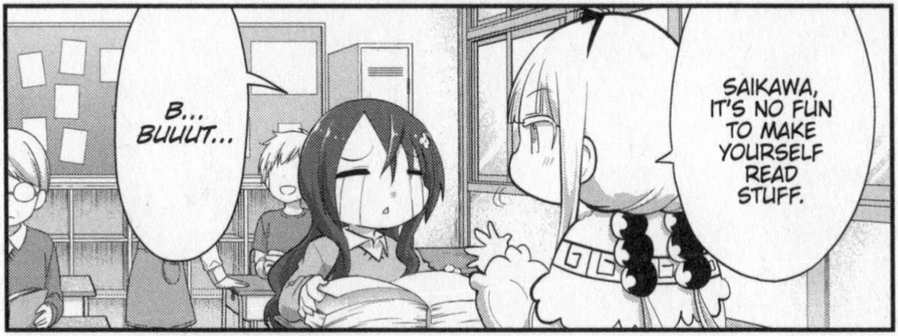
SAIKAWA, IT'S NO FUN TO MAKE YOURSELF READ STUFF.
B... BUUUT...

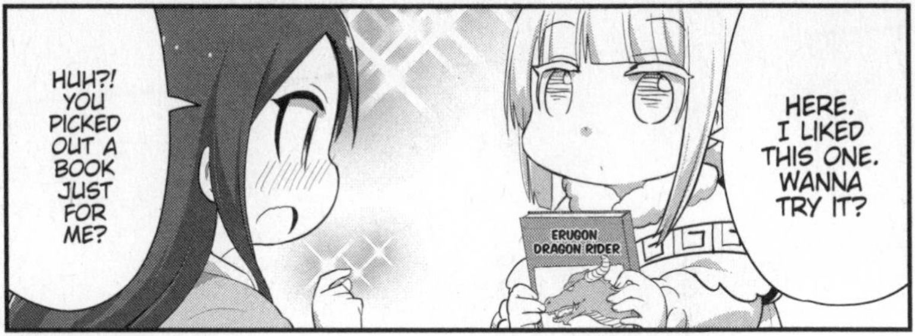
HERE. I LIKED THIS ONE. WANNA TRY IT?
ERUGON DRAGON RIDER
HUH?! YOU PICKED OUT A BOOK JUST FOR ME?

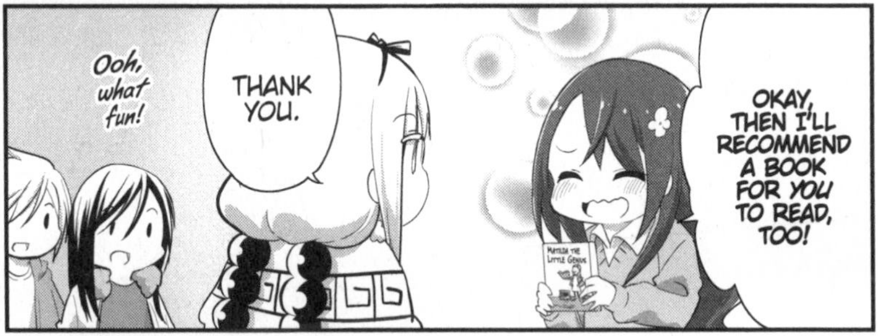
OKAY, THEN I'LL RECOMMEND A BOOK FOR *YOU* TO READ, TOO!
MATILDA THE LITTLE GENIUS
THANK YOU.
Ooh, what fun!

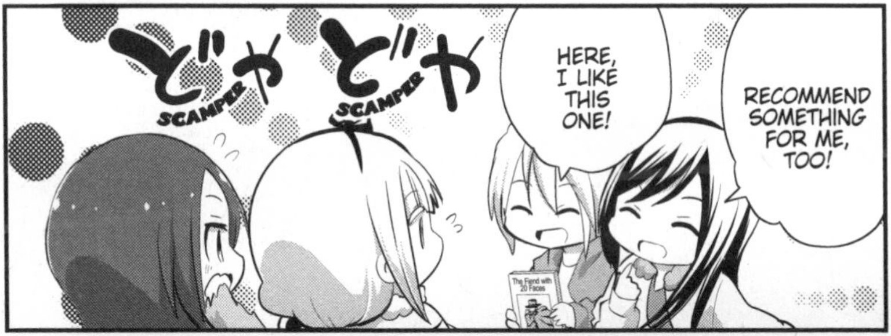
RECOMMEND SOMETHING FOR ME, TOO!
HERE, I LIKE THIS ONE!
The Fiend with 20 Faces
どやどや
SCAMPER SCAMPER

THE CHARGE OF THE BOOK BRIGADE!

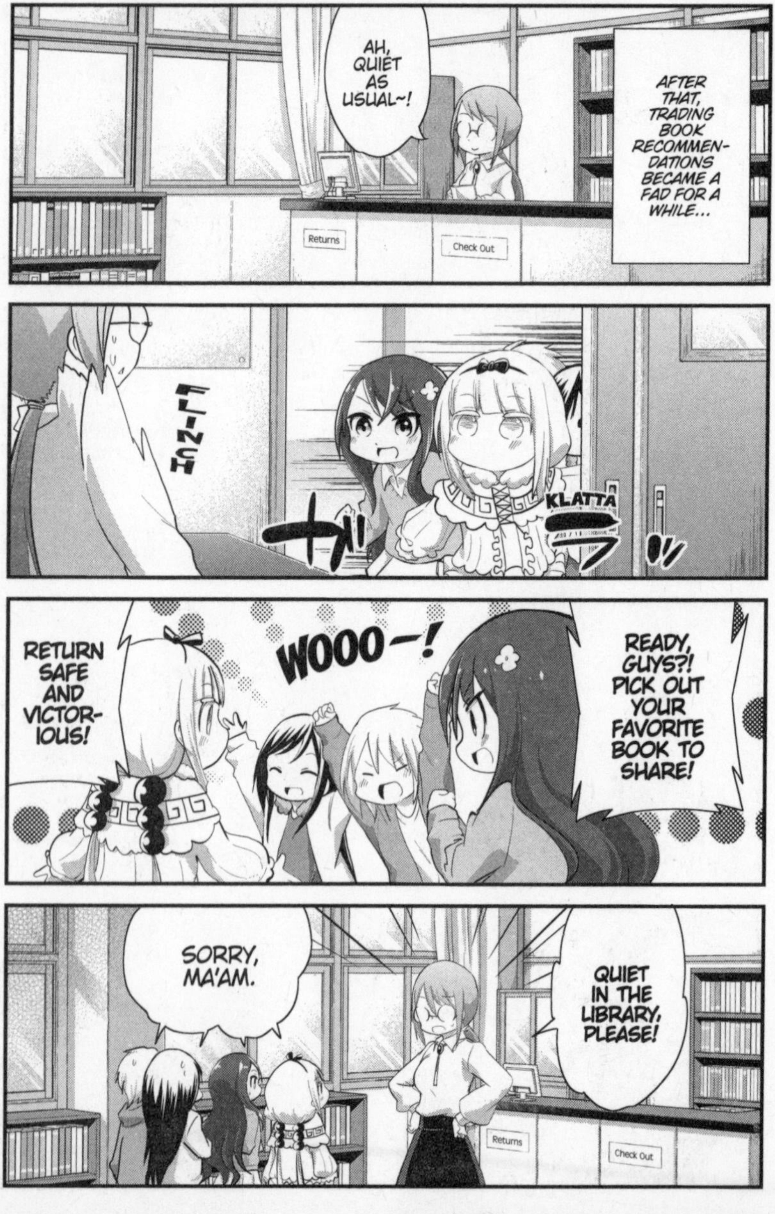
AFTER THAT, TRADING BOOK RECOMMENDATIONS BECAME A FAD FOR A WHILE...
AH, QUIET AS USUAL~!
Check Out
Returns
KLATTA
FLINCH
READY, GUYS?! PICK OUT YOUR FAVORITE BOOK TO SHARE!
WOOO—!
RETURN SAFE AND VICTORIOUS!
QUIET IN THE LIBRARY, PLEASE!
SORRY, MA'AM.
Check Out
Returns

SAIKAWA-SAN IS LIKE THIS...

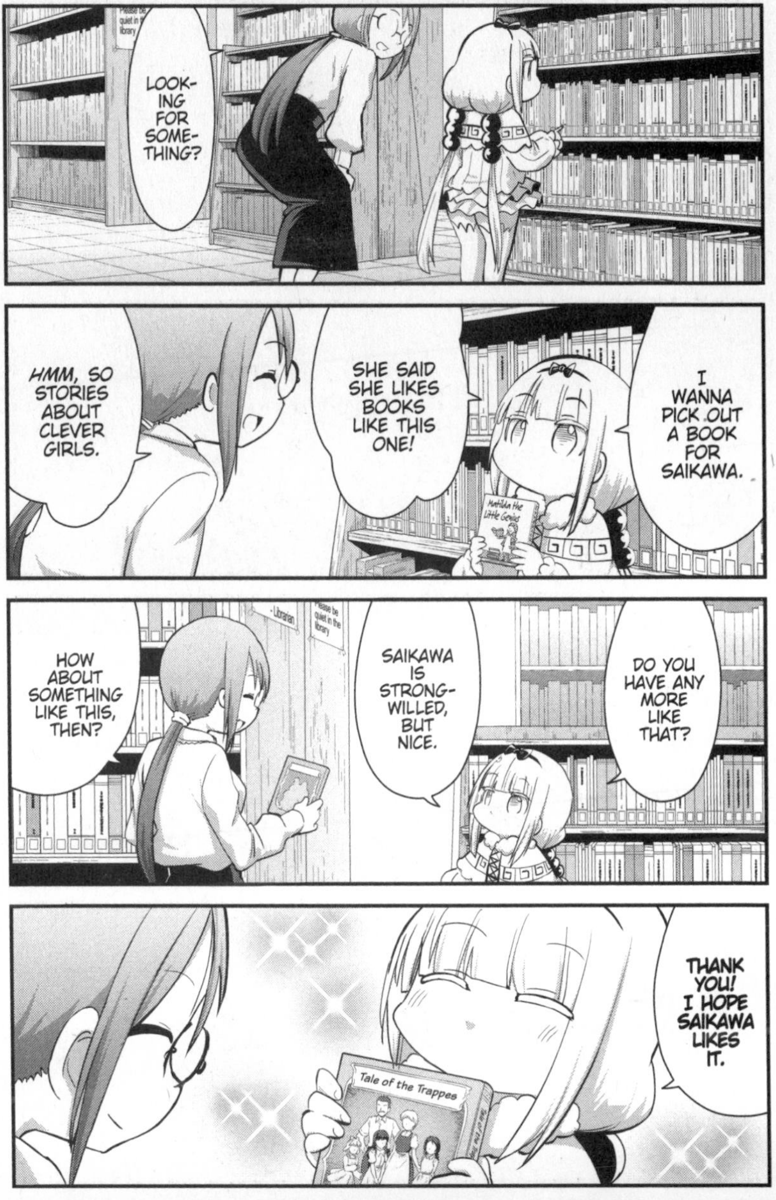
LOOKING FOR SOMETHING?
I WANNA PICK OUT A BOOK FOR SAIKAWA.
SHE SAID SHE LIKES BOOKS LIKE THIS ONE!
Matilda the Little Genius
HMM, SO STORIES ABOUT CLEVER GIRLS.
DO YOU HAVE ANY MORE LIKE THAT?
SAIKAWA IS STRONG-WILLED, BUT NICE.
Please be quiet in the library
- Librarian
HOW ABOUT SOMETHING LIKE THIS, THEN?
THANK YOU! I HOPE SAIKAWA LIKES IT.
Tale of the Trappes

SEE, KANNA-SAN IS...

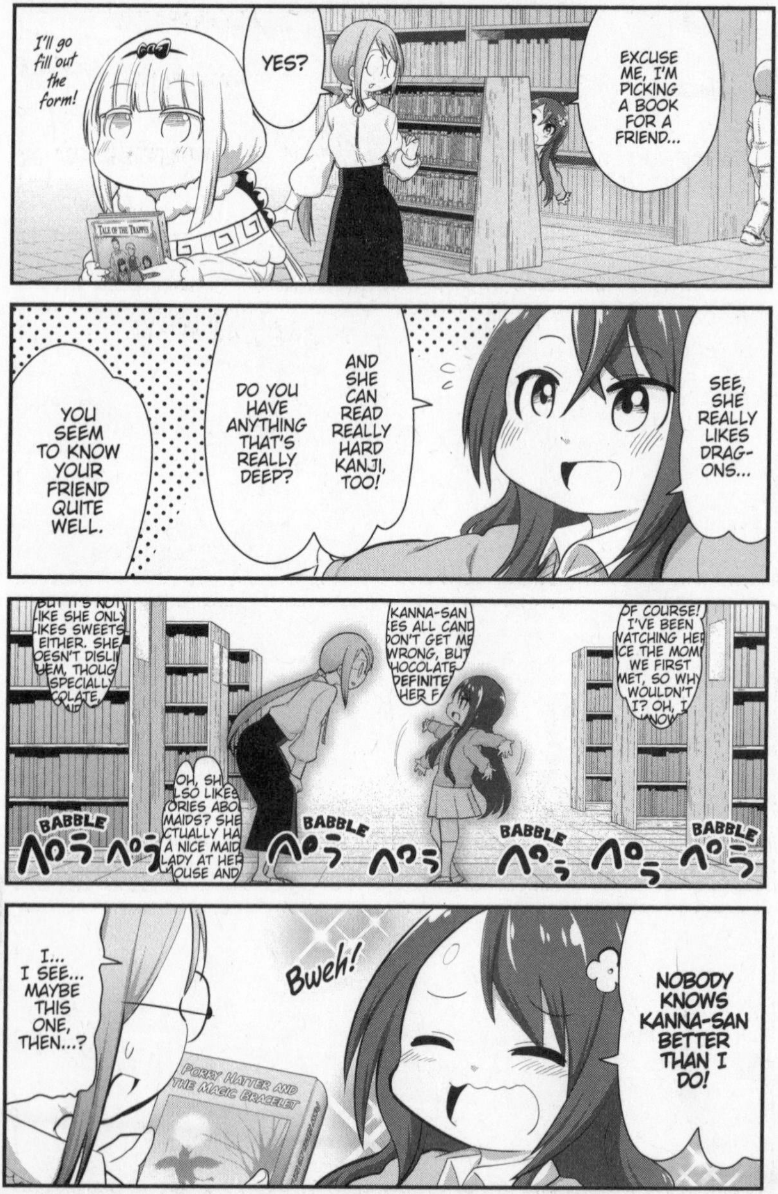
EXCUSE ME, I'M PICKING A BOOK FOR A FRIEND...
YES?
I'll go fill out the form!
TALE OF THE TRAPPES
SEE, SHE REALLY LIKES DRAG-ONS...
AND SHE CAN READ REALLY HARD KANJI, TOO!
DO YOU HAVE ANYTHING THAT'S REALLY DEEP?
YOU SEEM TO KNOW YOUR FRIEND QUITE WELL.
OF COURSE! I'VE BEEN WATCHING HE ICE THE MOM WE FIRST MET, SO WHY WOULDN'T I? OH, I NOW
KANNA-SAN ES ALL CAND ON'T GET ME WRONG, BUT HOCOLATE DEFINITE HER F
BUT IT'S NOT LIKE SHE ONLY LIKES SWEETS EITHER. SHE OESN'T DISLI HEM, THOUG SPECIALLY COLATE,
OH, SH LSO LIKES ORIES ABO MAIDS? SHE CTUALLY HA A NICE MAID LADY AT HER OUSE AND
BABBLE
へらへら
BABBLE
へらへら
BABBLE
へらへら
BABBLE
へら
NOBODY KNOWS KANNA-SAN BETTER THAN I DO!
Bweh!
I... I SEE... MAYBE THIS ONE, THEN...?
PORRY HATTER AND THE MAGIC BRACELET

SO CLOSE, SAIKAWA-SAN!

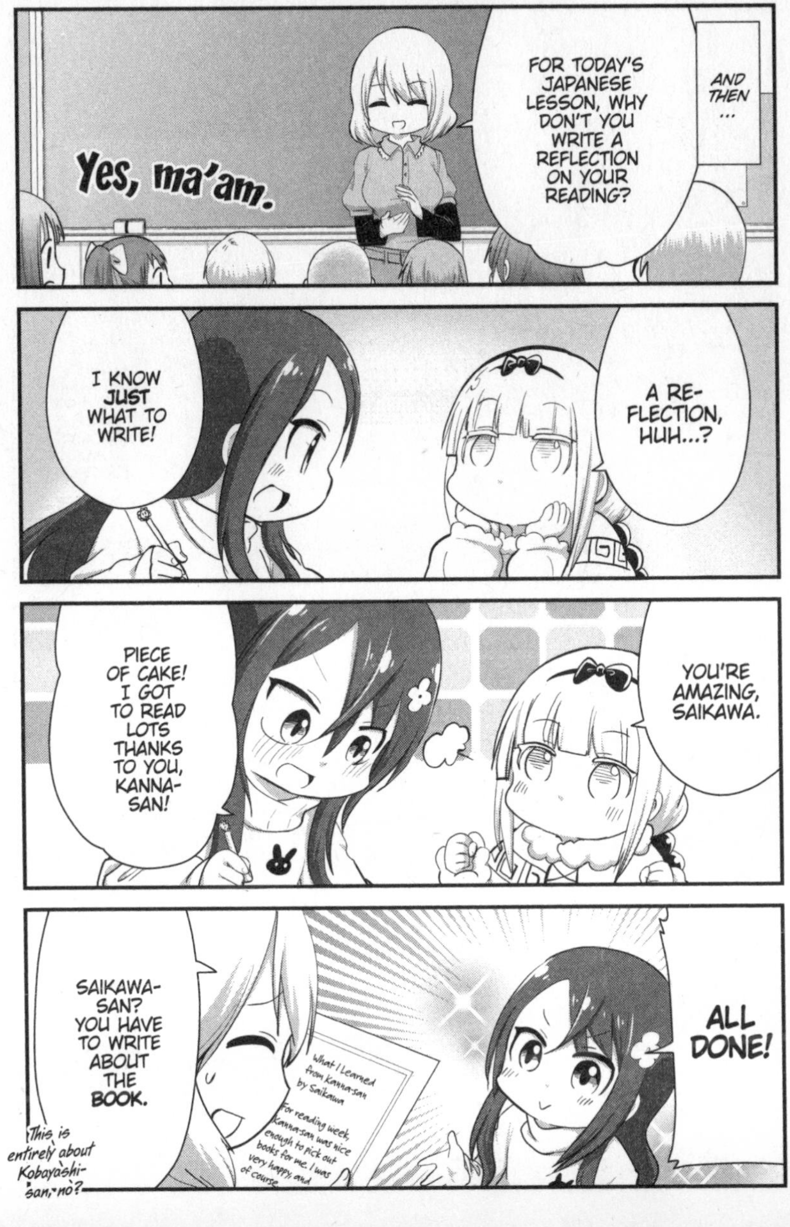

AND THEN...
FOR TODAY'S JAPANESE LESSON, WHY DON'T YOU WRITE A REFLECTION ON YOUR READING?
Yes, ma'am.
A RE-FLECTION, HUH...?
I KNOW JUST WHAT TO WRITE!
YOU'RE AMAZING, SAIKAWA.
PIECE OF CAKE! I GOT TO READ LOTS THANKS TO YOU, KANNA-SAN!
ALL DONE!
What I Learned from Kanna-san by Saikawa
For reading week, Kanna-san was nice enough to pick out books for me. I was very happy, and of course
SAIKAWA-SAN? YOU HAVE TO WRITE ABOUT THE BOOK.
This is entirely about Kobayashi-san, no?

THE JOY OF READING!

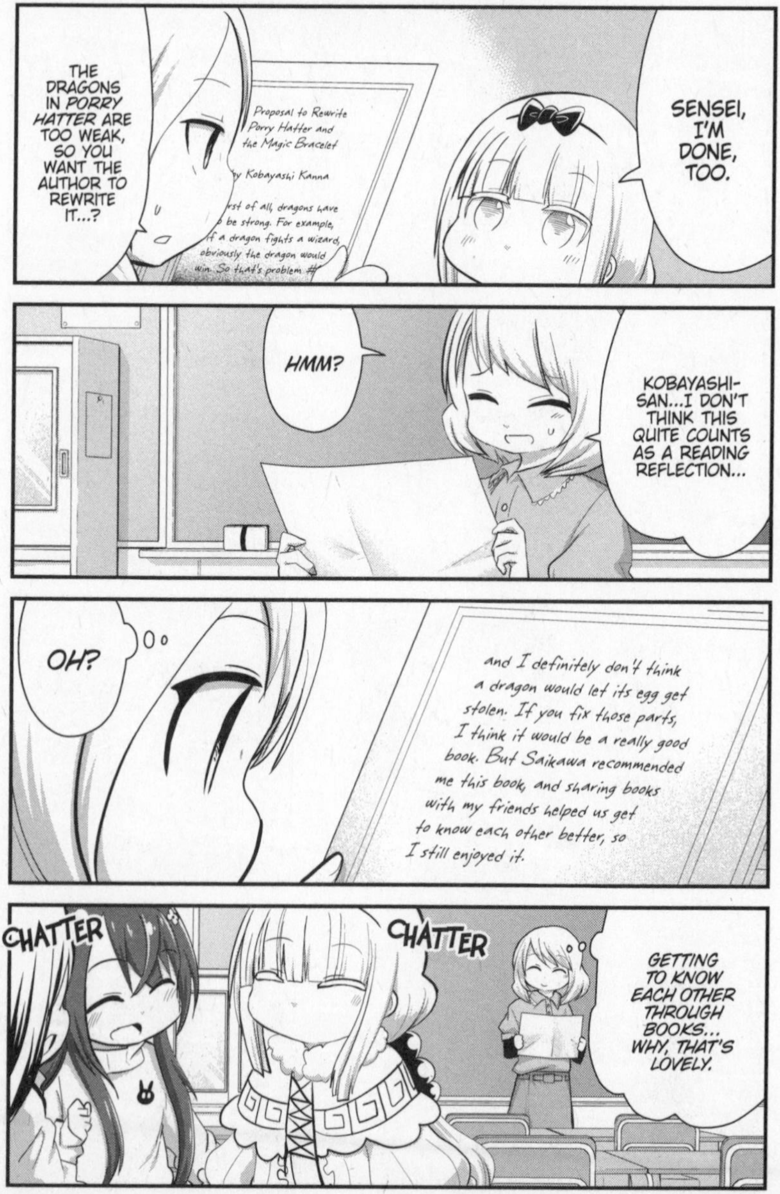
SENSEI, I'M DONE, TOO.
Proposal to Rewrite Porry Hatter and the Magic Bracelet
Kobayashi Kanna
dragons have be strong. For example, a dragon fights a wizard, obviously the dragon would win. So that's problem
THE DRAGONS IN PORRY HATTER ARE TOO WEAK, SO YOU WANT THE AUTHOR TO REWRITE IT...?
KOBAYASHI-SAN...I DON'T THINK THIS QUITE COUNTS AS A READING REFLECTION...
HMM?
and I definitely don't think a dragon would let its egg get stolen. If you fix those parts, I think it would be a really good book. But Saikawa recommended me this book, and sharing books with my friends helped us get to know each other better, so I still enjoyed it.
OH?
GETTING TO KNOW EACH OTHER THROUGH BOOKS... WHY, THAT'S LOVELY.
CHATTER
CHATTER

THE REWARDS OF LEARNING!

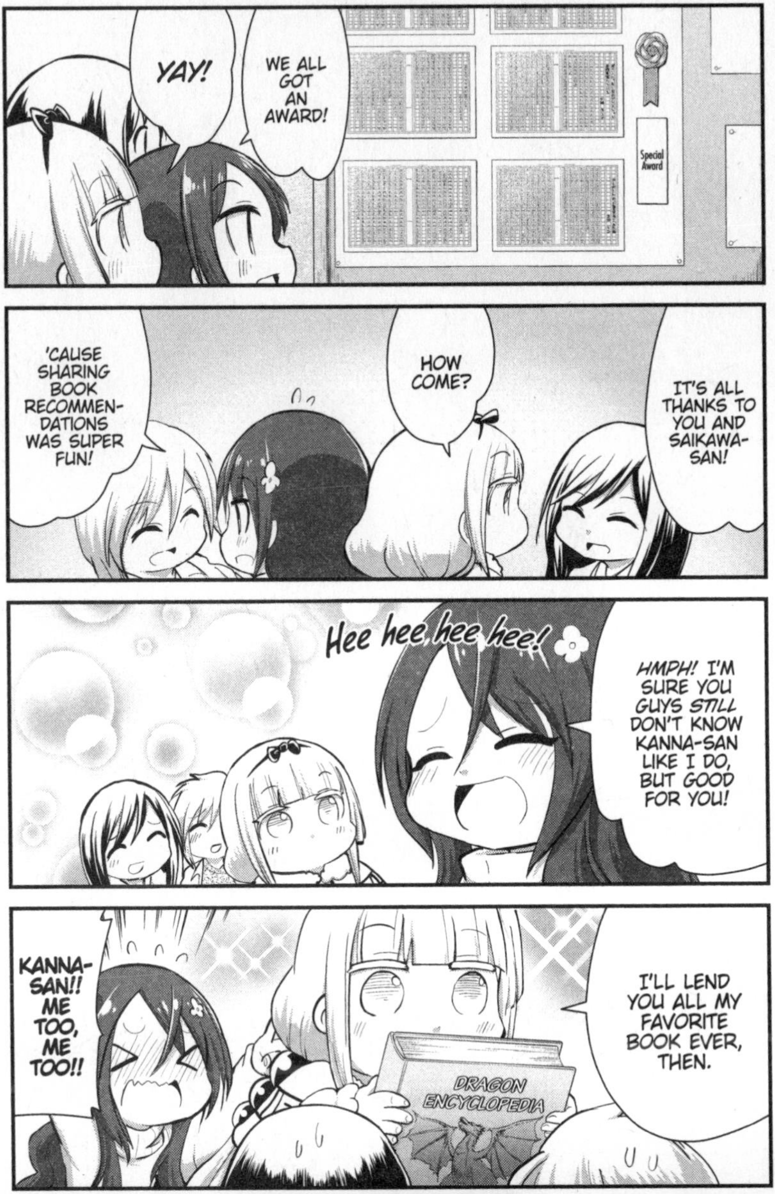
Special Award
WE ALL GOT AN AWARD!
YAY!
IT'S ALL THANKS TO YOU AND SAIKAWA-SAN!
HOW COME?
'CAUSE SHARING BOOK RECOMMEN-DATIONS WAS SUPER FUN!
HMPH! I'M SURE YOU GUYS STILL DON'T KNOW KANNA-SAN LIKE I DO, BUT GOOD FOR YOU!
Hee hee hee hee!
I'LL LEND YOU ALL MY FAVORITE BOOK EVER, THEN.
DRAGON ENCYCLOPEDIA
KANNA-SAN!! ME TOO, ME TOO!!

TIME FOR READING/END

DANGEROUS CHAPERONES

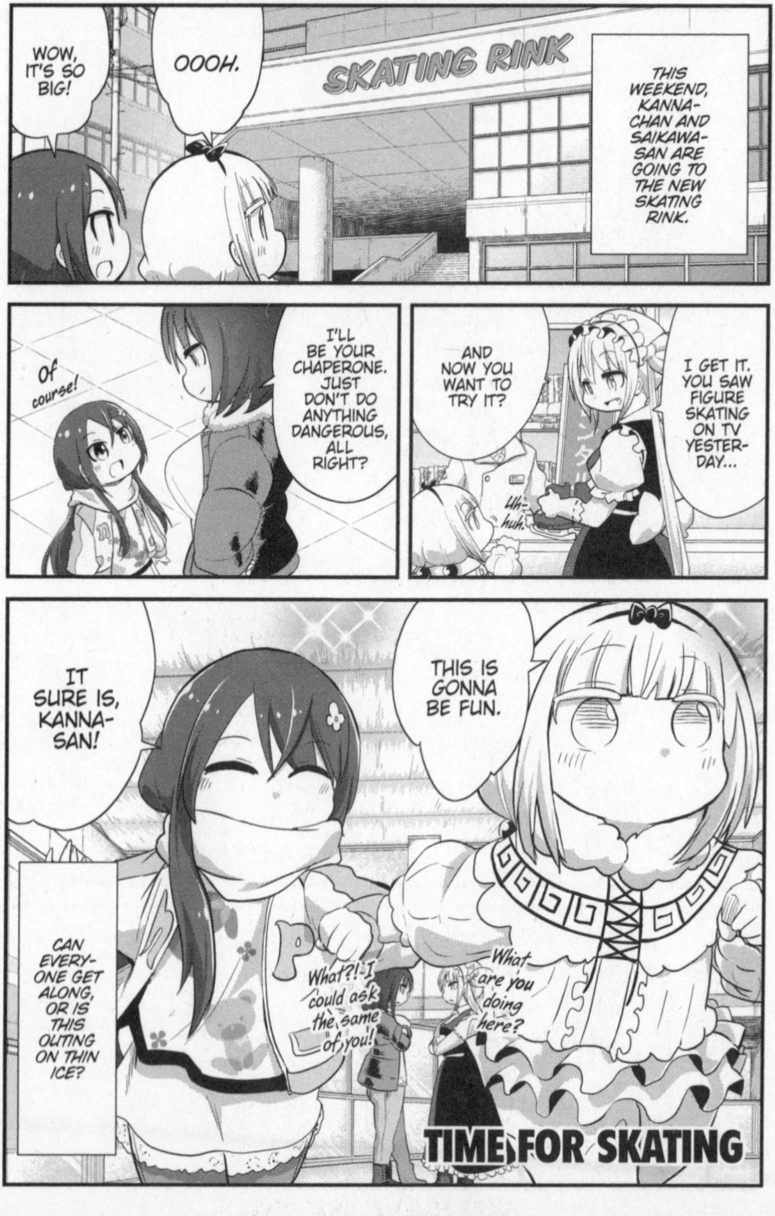
SKATING RINK
THIS WEEKEND, KANNA-CHAN AND SAIKAWA-SAN ARE GOING TO THE NEW SKATING RINK.
OOOH.
WOW, IT'S SO BIG!
I GET IT. YOU SAW FIGURE SKATING ON TV YESTER-DAY...
AND NOW YOU WANT TO TRY IT?
Uh-huh.
I'LL BE YOUR CHAPERONE. JUST DON'T DO ANYTHING DANGEROUS, ALL RIGHT?
Of course!
THIS IS GONNA BE FUN.
IT SURE IS, KANNA-SAN!
What are you doing here?
What?! I could ask the same of you!
CAN EVERY-ONE GET ALONG, OR IS THIS OUTING ON THIN ICE?
TIME FOR SKATING

MELTDOWN

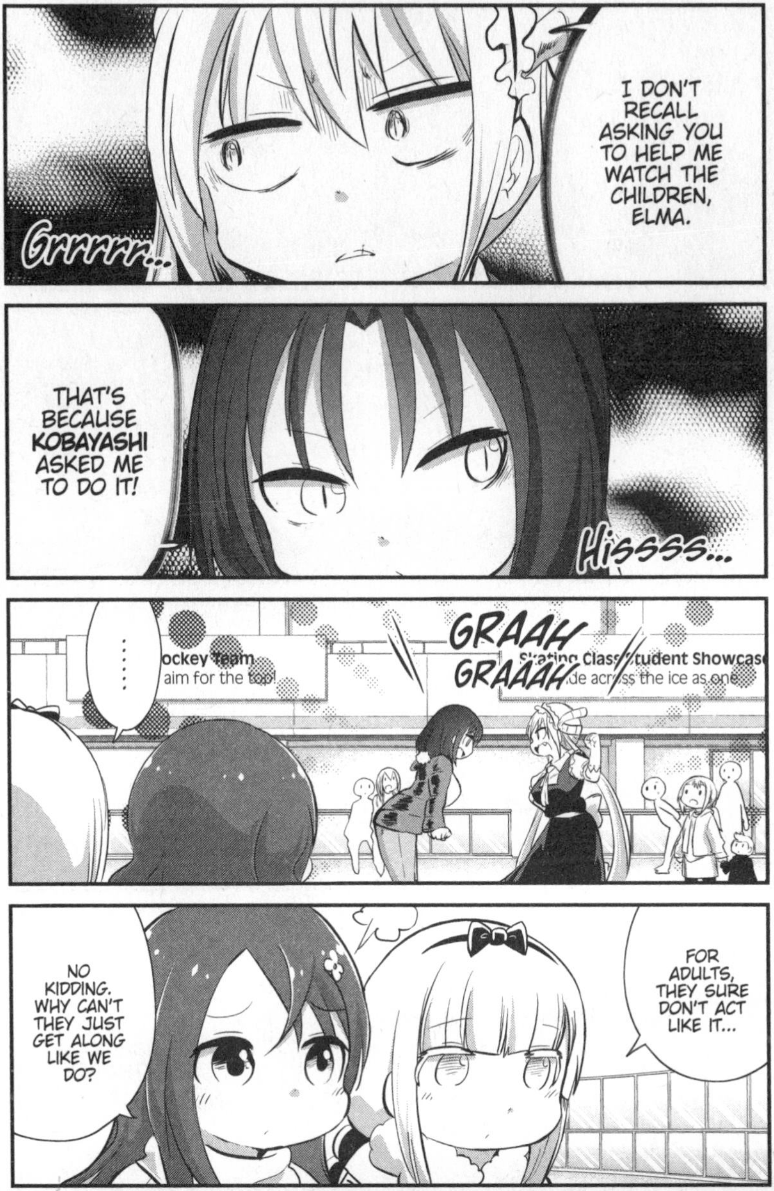
I DON'T RECALL ASKING YOU TO HELP ME WATCH THE CHILDREN, ELMA.
Grrrrrr...
THAT'S BECAUSE KOBAYASHI ASKED ME TO DO IT!
Hissss...
GRAAH GRAAAH
......
FOR ADULTS, THEY SURE DON'T ACT LIKE IT...
NO KIDDING. WHY CAN'T THEY JUST GET ALONG LIKE WE DO?

LANGUAGE BARRIER

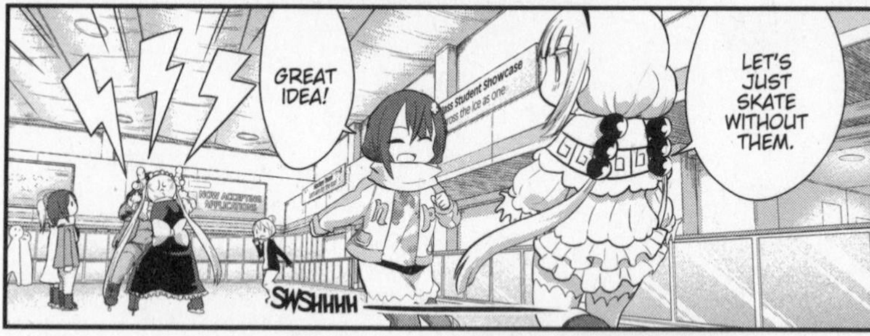
LET'S JUST SKATE WITHOUT THEM.
GREAT IDEA!
SWSHHHH

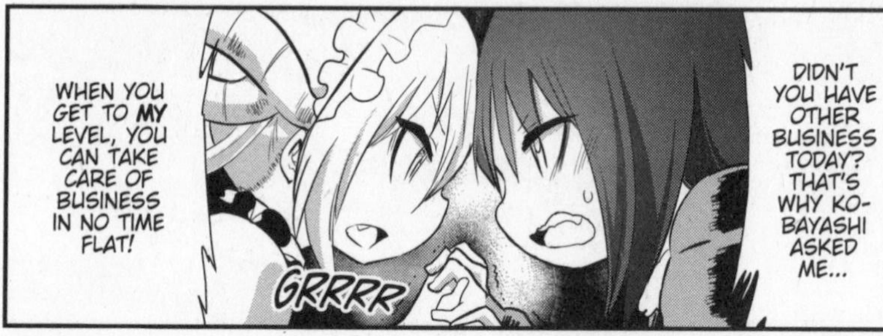
DIDN'T YOU HAVE OTHER BUSINESS TODAY? THAT'S WHY KO-BAYASHI ASKED ME...
WHEN YOU GET TO MY LEVEL, YOU CAN TAKE CARE OF BUSINESS IN NO TIME FLAT!
GRRRR

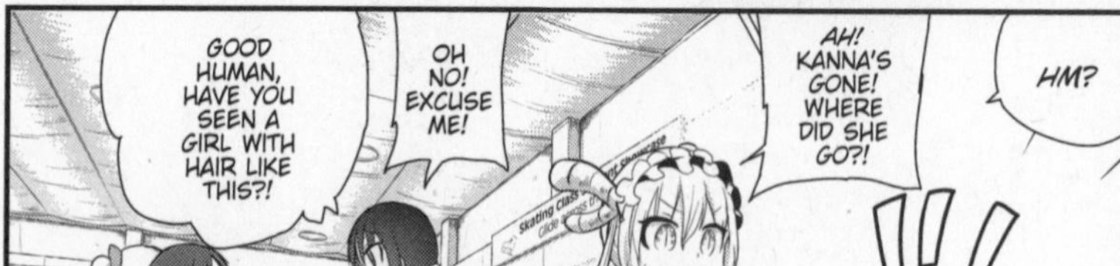
HM?
AH! KANNA'S GONE! WHERE DID SHE GO?!
OH NO! EXCUSE ME!
GOOD HUMAN, HAVE YOU SEEN A GIRL WITH HAIR LIKE THIS?!

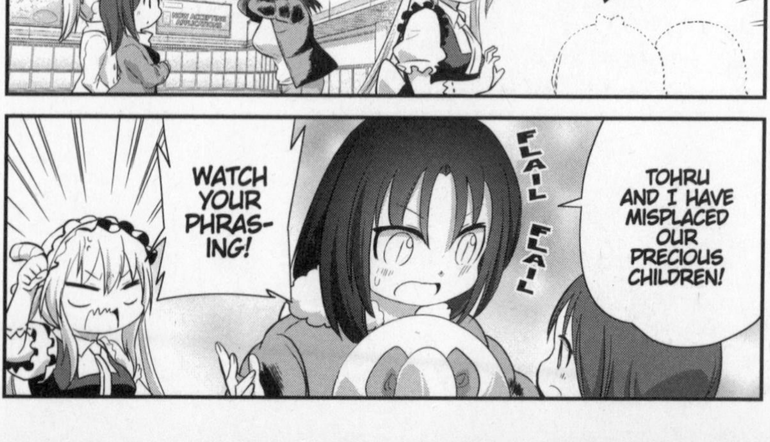
TOHRU AND I HAVE MISPLACED OUR PRECIOUS CHILDREN!
FLAIL FLAIL
WATCH YOUR PHRAS-ING!

LET'S DO IT!

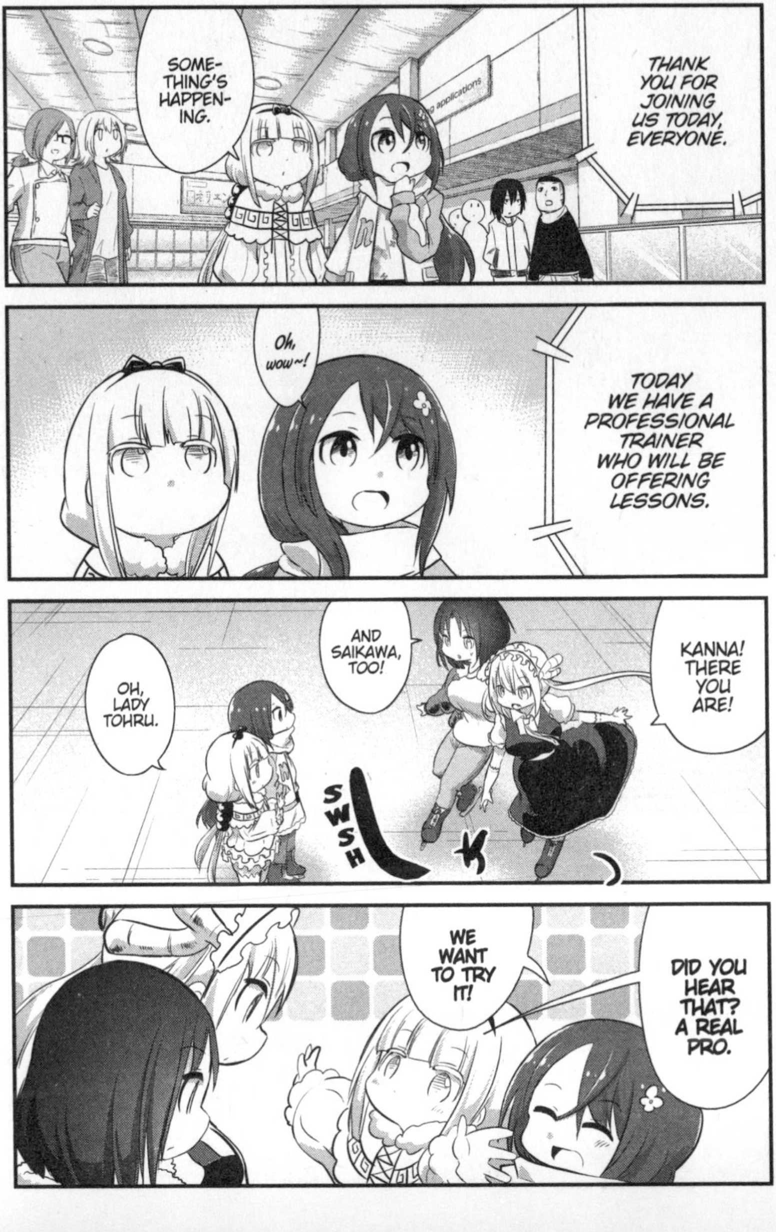
THANK YOU FOR JOINING US TODAY, EVERYONE.
SOMETHING'S HAPPENING.
TODAY WE HAVE A PROFESSIONAL TRAINER WHO WILL BE OFFERING LESSONS.
Oh, wow~!
KANNA! THERE YOU ARE!
AND SAIKAWA, TOO!
OH, LADY TOHRU.
SWSH
DID YOU HEAR THAT? A REAL PRO.
WE WANT TO TRY IT!

ENTER (AND EXIT!) THE SKATING PRO!

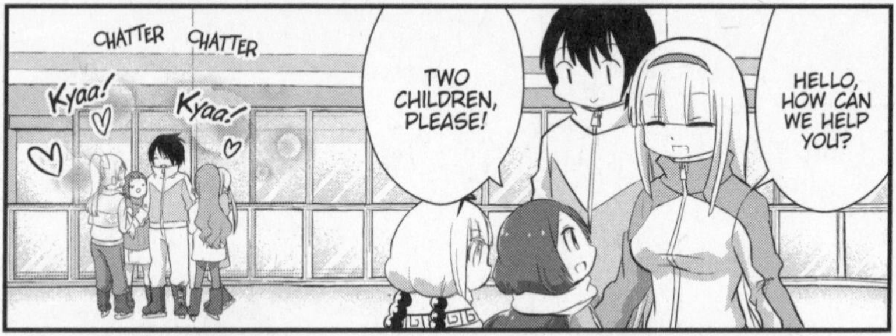
HELLO, HOW CAN WE HELP YOU?
TWO CHILDREN, PLEASE!
Kyaa!
Kyaa!
CHATTER
CHATTER

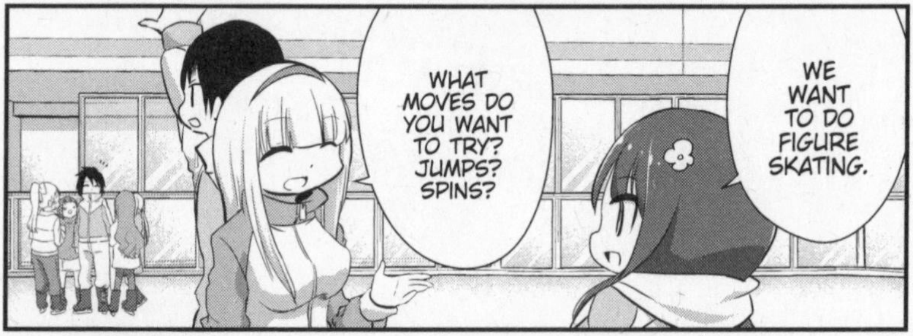
WE WANT TO DO FIGURE SKATING.
WHAT MOVES DO YOU WANT TO TRY? JUMPS? SPINS?

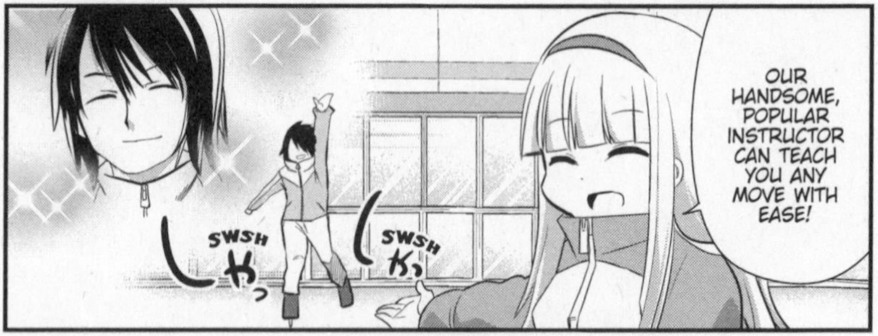
OUR HANDSOME, POPULAR INSTRUCTOR CAN TEACH YOU ANY MOVE WITH EASE!
SWSH
SWSH

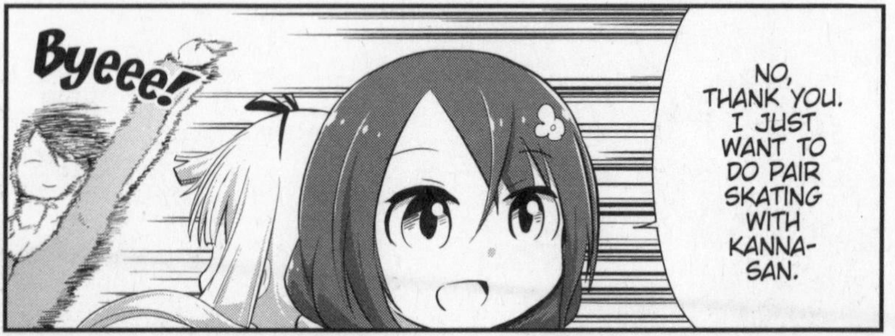
NO, THANK YOU. I JUST WANT TO DO PAIR SKATING WITH KANNA-SAN.
Byeee!

ONLOOKER'S PERSPECTIVE

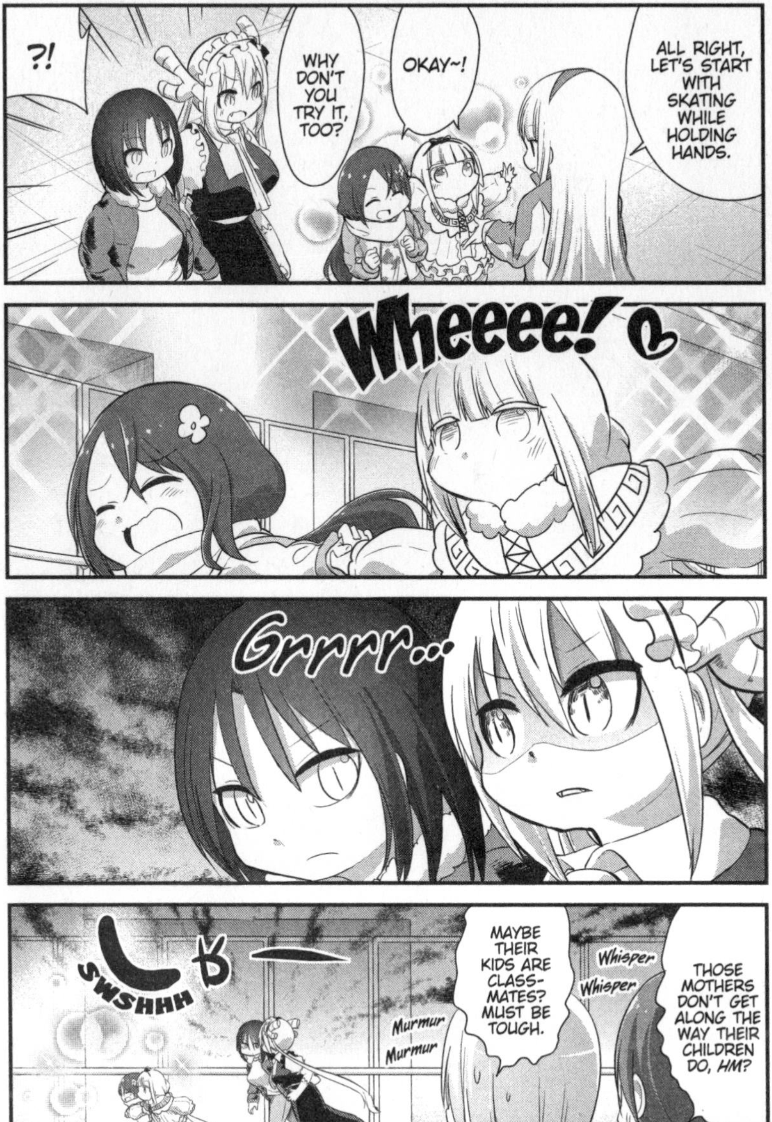
ALL RIGHT, LET'S START WITH SKATING WHILE HOLDING HANDS.
OKAY~!
WHY DON'T YOU TRY IT, TOO?
?!
Wheeee! ♡
Grrrr...
THOSE MOTHERS DON'T GET ALONG THE WAY THEIR CHILDREN DO, HM?
Whisper
Whisper
MAYBE THEIR KIDS ARE CLASSMATES? MUST BE TOUGH.
Murmur
Murmur
SWSHHH

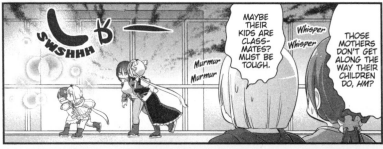

BLIND SPOT

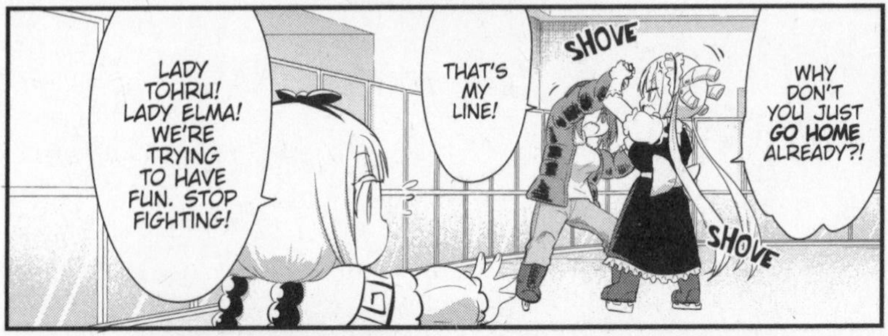
WHY DON'T YOU JUST GO HOME ALREADY?!
SHOVE
THAT'S MY LINE!
SHOVE
LADY TOHRU! LADY ELMA! WE'RE TRYING TO HAVE FUN. STOP FIGHTING!

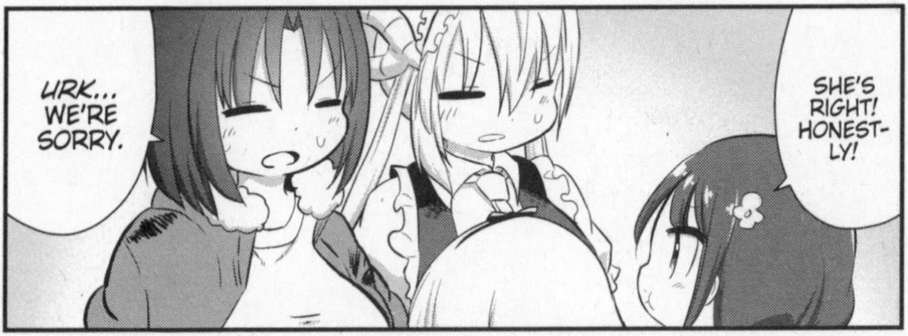
SHE'S RIGHT! HONEST-LY!
URK... WE'RE SORRY.

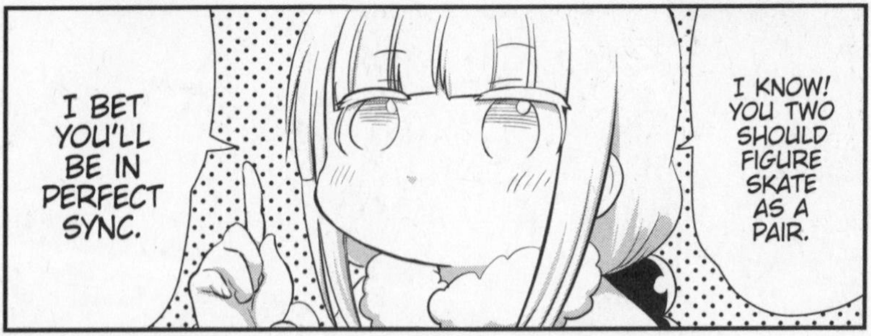
I KNOW! YOU TWO SHOULD FIGURE SKATE AS A PAIR.
I BET YOU'LL BE IN PERFECT SYNC.

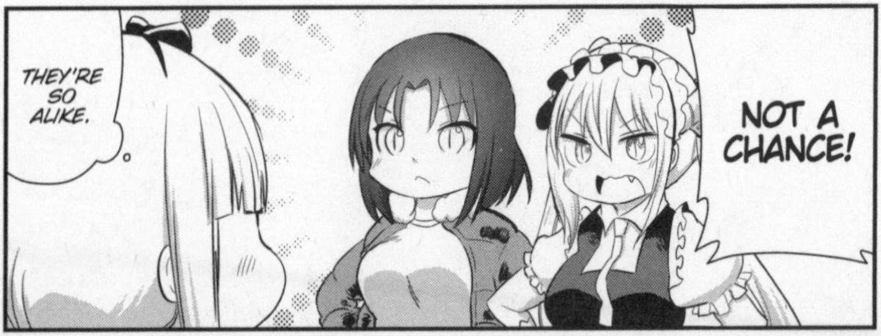
NOT A CHANCE!
THEY'RE SO ALIKE.

I NEED MANA...OR CAKE...

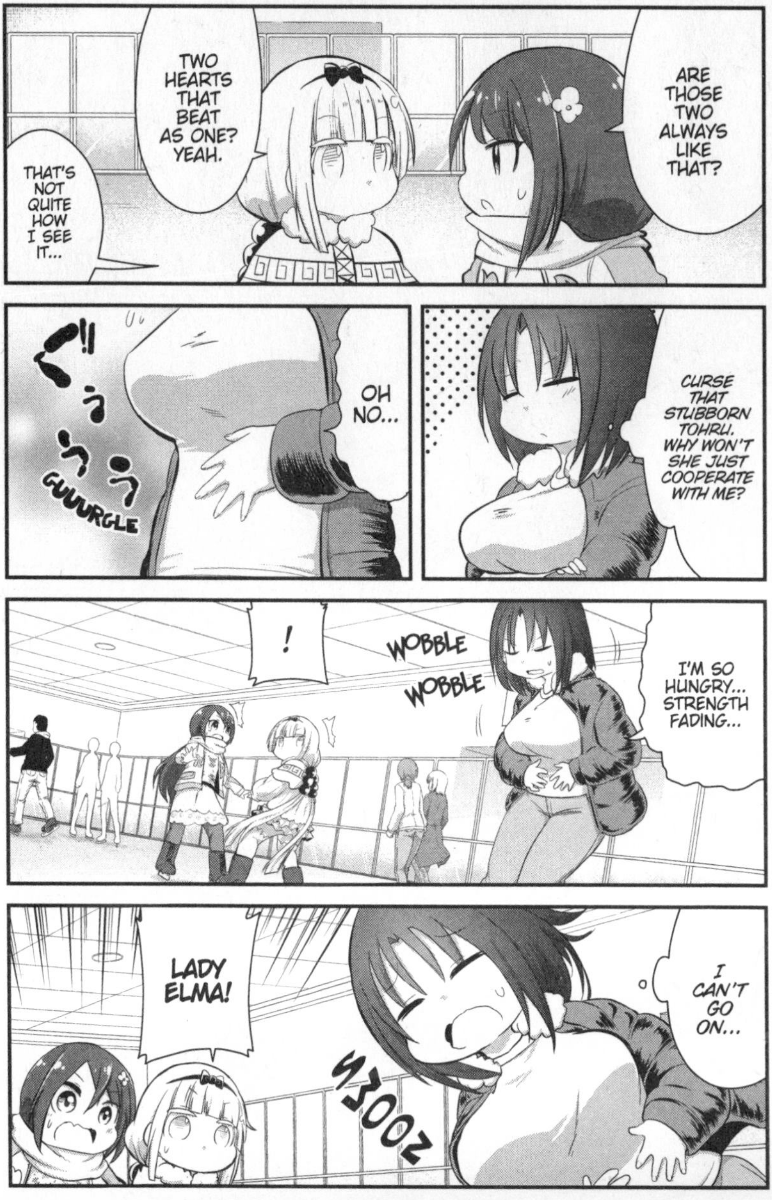
ARE THOSE TWO ALWAYS LIKE THAT?
TWO HEARTS THAT BEAT AS ONE? YEAH.
THAT'S NOT QUITE HOW I SEE IT...
CURSE THAT STUBBORN TOHRU. WHY WON'T SHE JUST COOPERATE WITH ME?
OH NO...
GUUURGLE
I'M SO HUNGRY... STRENGTH FADING...
WOBBLE
WOBBLE
!
I CAN'T GO ON...
LADY ELMA!

COMMON ENEMY

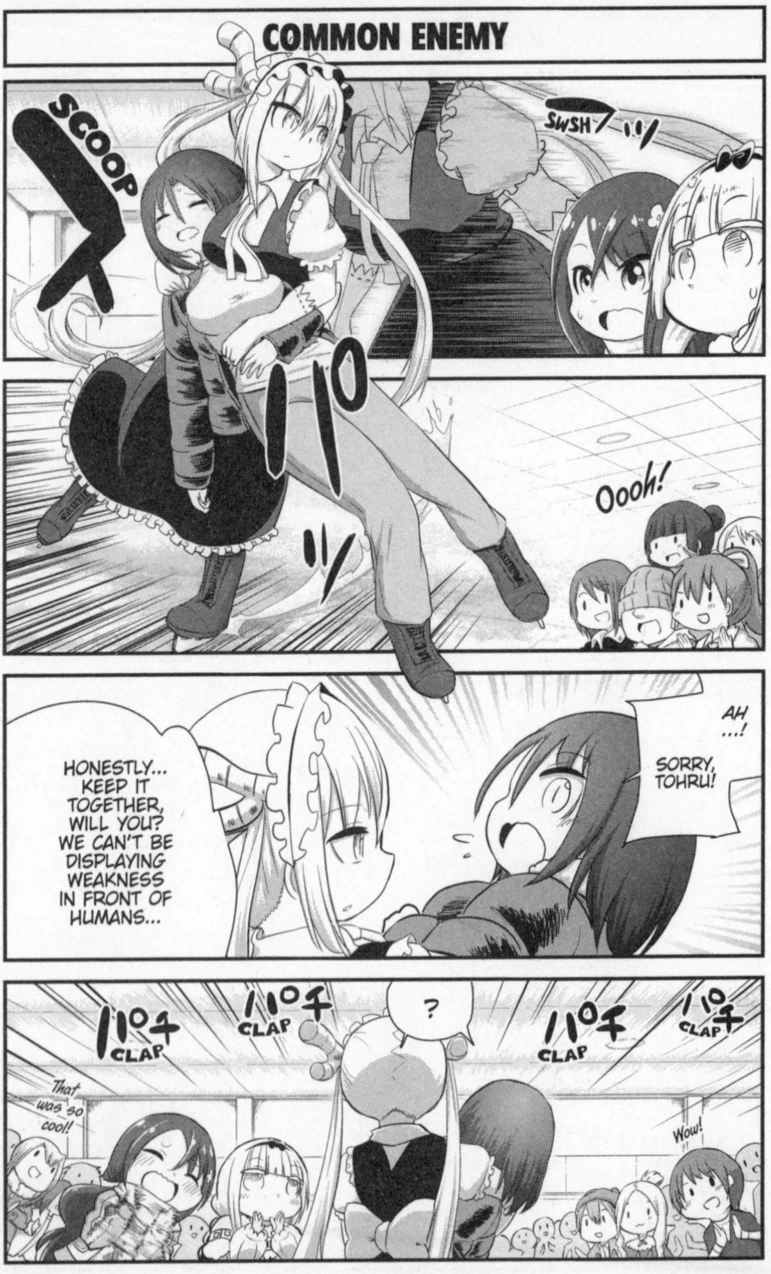
SWSH
SCOOP
Oooh!
AH...!
SORRY, TOHRU!
HONESTLY... KEEP IT TOGETHER, WILL YOU? WE CAN'T BE DISPLAYING WEAKNESS IN FRONT OF HUMANS...
CLAP
CLAP
?
CLAP
CLAP
Wow!
That was so cool!!

KANNA-CHAN SEES ALL

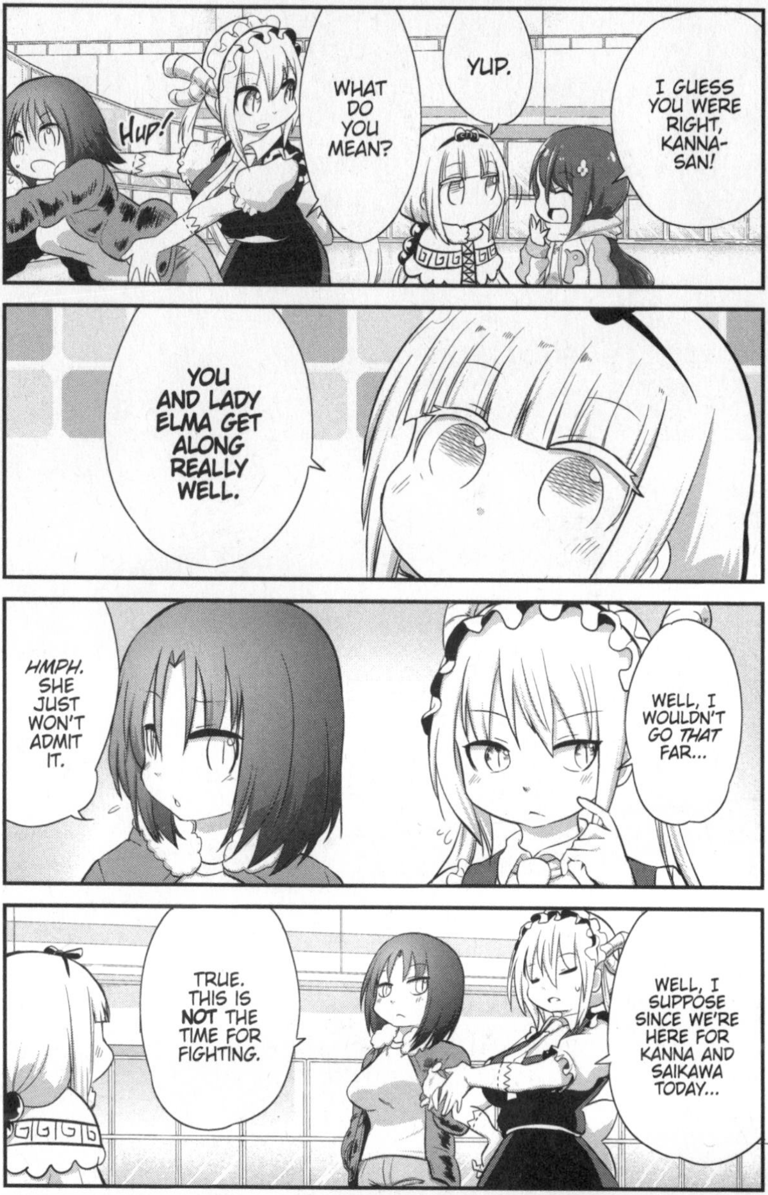
I GUESS YOU WERE RIGHT, KANNA-SAN!
YUP.
WHAT DO YOU MEAN?
Hup!
YOU AND LADY ELMA GET ALONG REALLY WELL.
WELL, I WOULDN'T GO *THAT* FAR...
HMPH. SHE JUST WON'T ADMIT IT.
WELL, I SUPPOSE SINCE WE'RE HERE FOR KANNA AND SAIKAWA TODAY...
TRUE. THIS IS **NOT** THE TIME FOR FIGHTING.

LEADING QUESTIONS

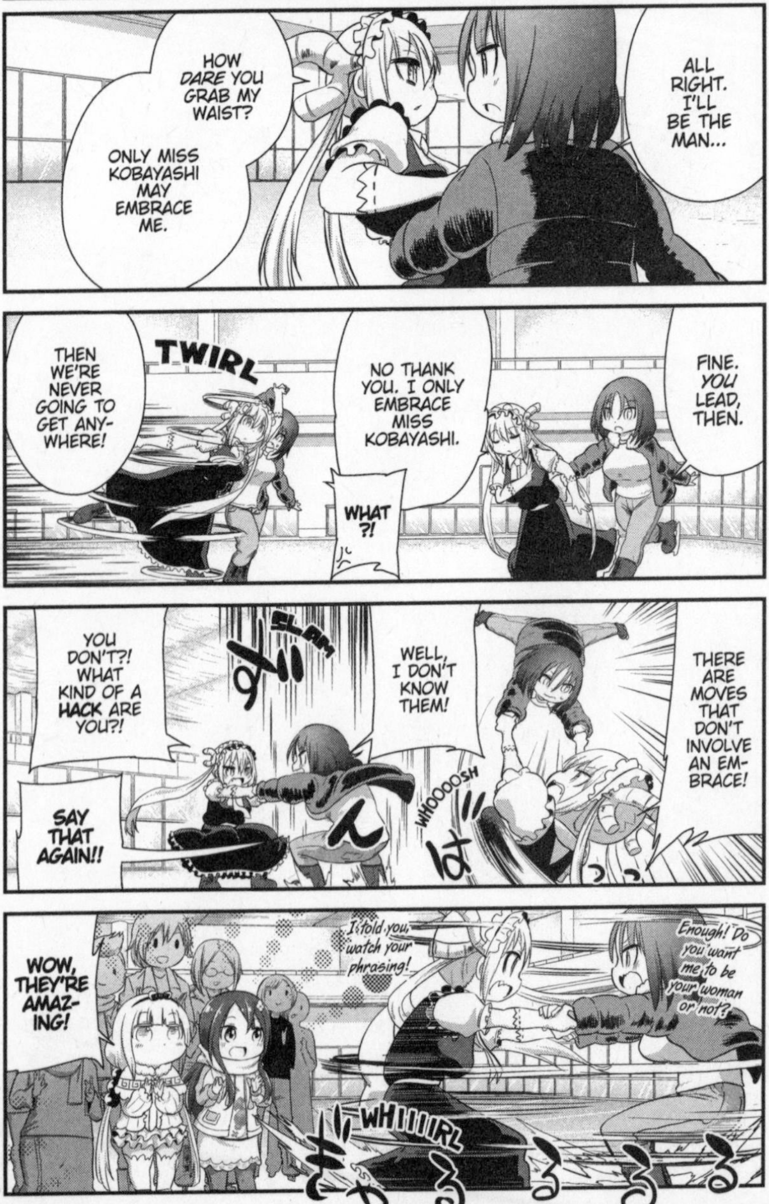
ALL RIGHT. I'LL BE THE MAN...
HOW *DARE* YOU GRAB MY WAIST?
ONLY MISS KOBAYASHI MAY EMBRACE ME.
FINE. *YOU* LEAD, THEN.
NO THANK YOU. I ONLY EMBRACE MISS KOBAYASHI.
WHAT?!
TWIRL
THEN WE'RE NEVER GOING TO GET ANY-WHERE!
THERE ARE MOVES THAT DON'T INVOLVE AN EM-BRACE!
WHOOOOSH
WELL, I DON'T KNOW THEM!
SLAM
YOU DON'T?! WHAT KIND OF A HACK ARE YOU?!
SAY THAT AGAIN!!
Enough! Do you want me to be your woman or not?!
I told you, watch your phrasing!
WOW, THEY'RE AMAZ-ING!
WHIIIIRL

PICTURE PERFECT

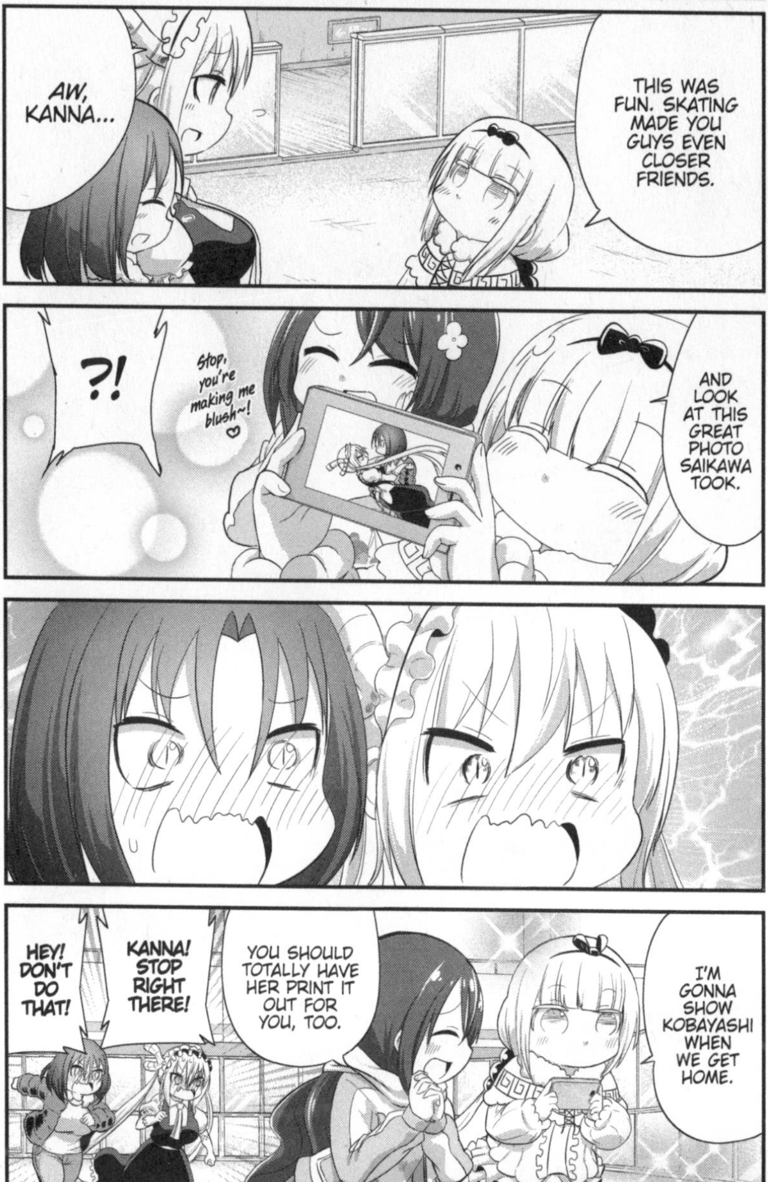
THIS WAS FUN. SKATING MADE YOU GUYS EVEN CLOSER FRIENDS.
AW, KANNA...
AND LOOK AT THIS GREAT PHOTO SAIKAWA TOOK.
Stop, you're making me blush~! ♡
?!
I'M GONNA SHOW KOBAYASHI WHEN WE GET HOME.
YOU SHOULD TOTALLY HAVE HER PRINT IT OUT FOR YOU, TOO.
KANNA! STOP RIGHT THERE!
HEY! DON'T DO THAT!

TIME FOR SKATING/END

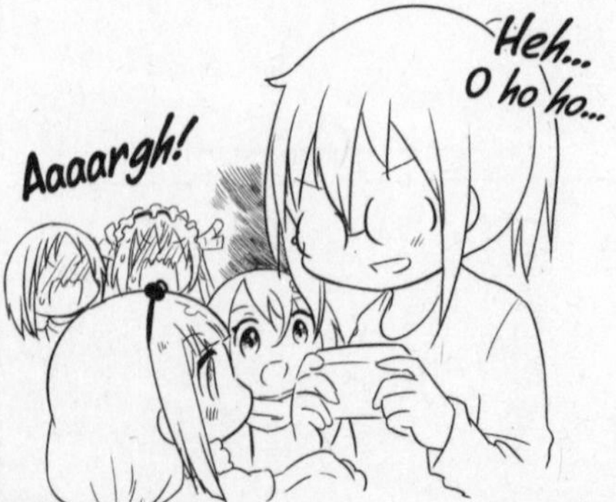
Heh... O ho ho...
Aaaargh!

Miss Kobayashi's Dragon Maid
Kanna's Daily Life

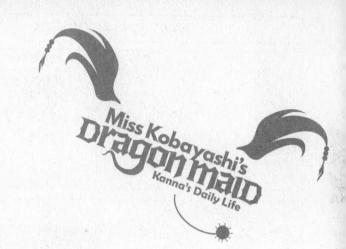

WHAT SPRING BRINGS

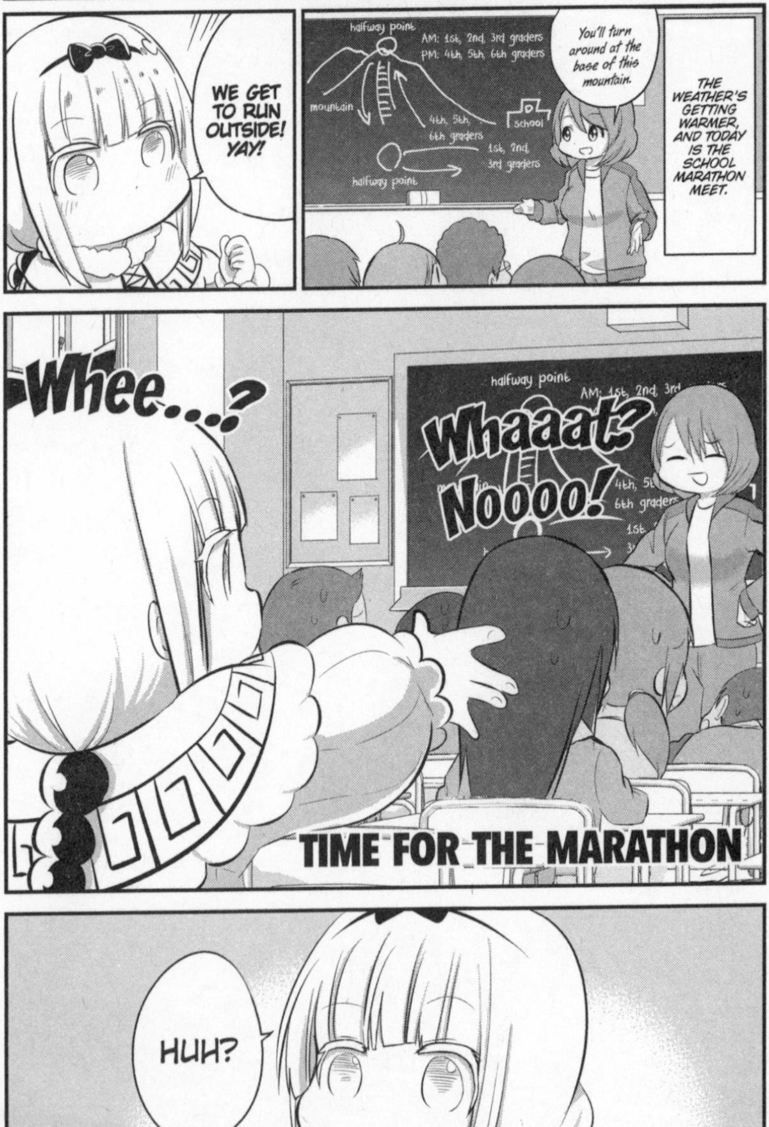
THE WEATHER'S GETTING WARMER, AND TODAY IS THE SCHOOL MARATHON MEET.
You'll turn around at the base of this mountain.
halfway point
AM: 1st, 2nd, 3rd graders
PM: 4th, 5th, 6th graders
mountain
4th, 5th, 6th graders
school
1st, 2nd, 3rd graders
halfway point
WE GET TO RUN OUTSIDE! YAY!
Whaaat? Noooo!
Whee...?
TIME FOR THE MARATHON
HUH?

THE RIGHT MOTIVATION

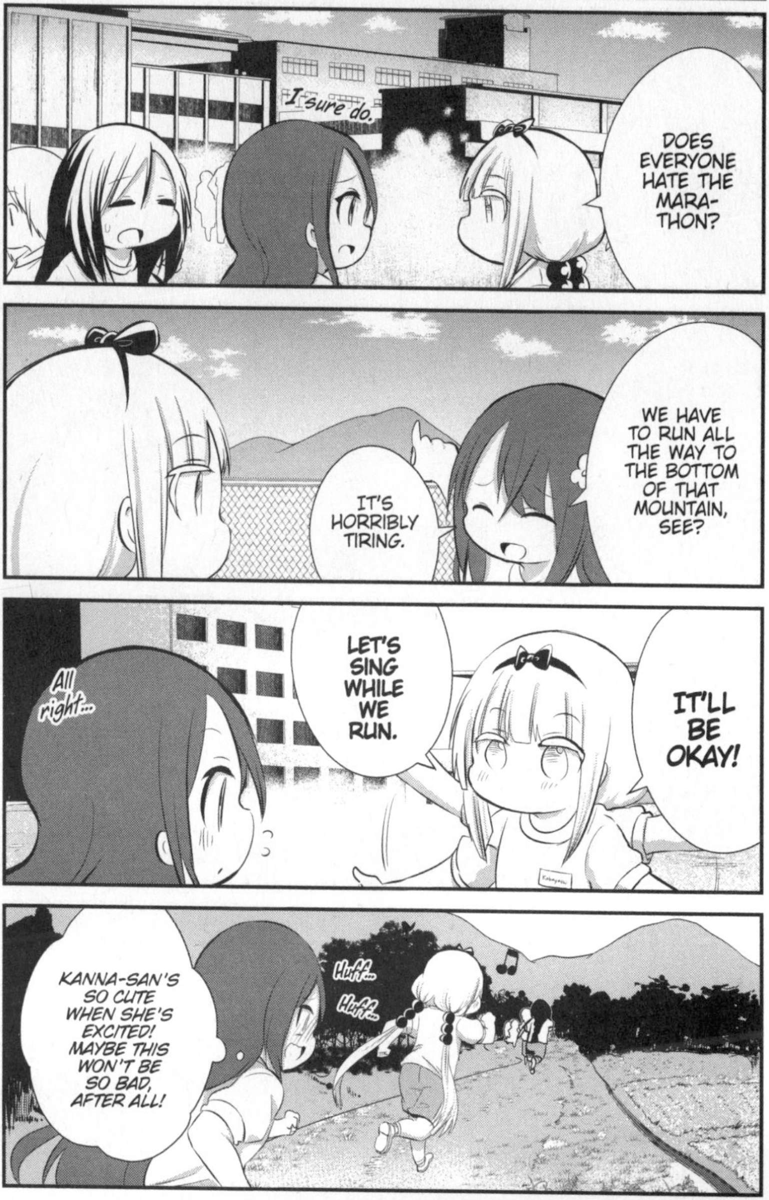
DOES EVERYONE HATE THE MARA-THON?
I sure do.
WE HAVE TO RUN ALL THE WAY TO THE BOTTOM OF THAT MOUNTAIN, SEE?
IT'S HORRIBLY TIRING.
IT'LL BE OKAY!
LET'S SING WHILE WE RUN.
All right...
Huff...
Huff...
KANNA-SAN'S SO CUTE WHEN SHE'S EXCITED! MAYBE THIS WON'T BE SO BAD, AFTER ALL!

A SPRING DISCOVERY?

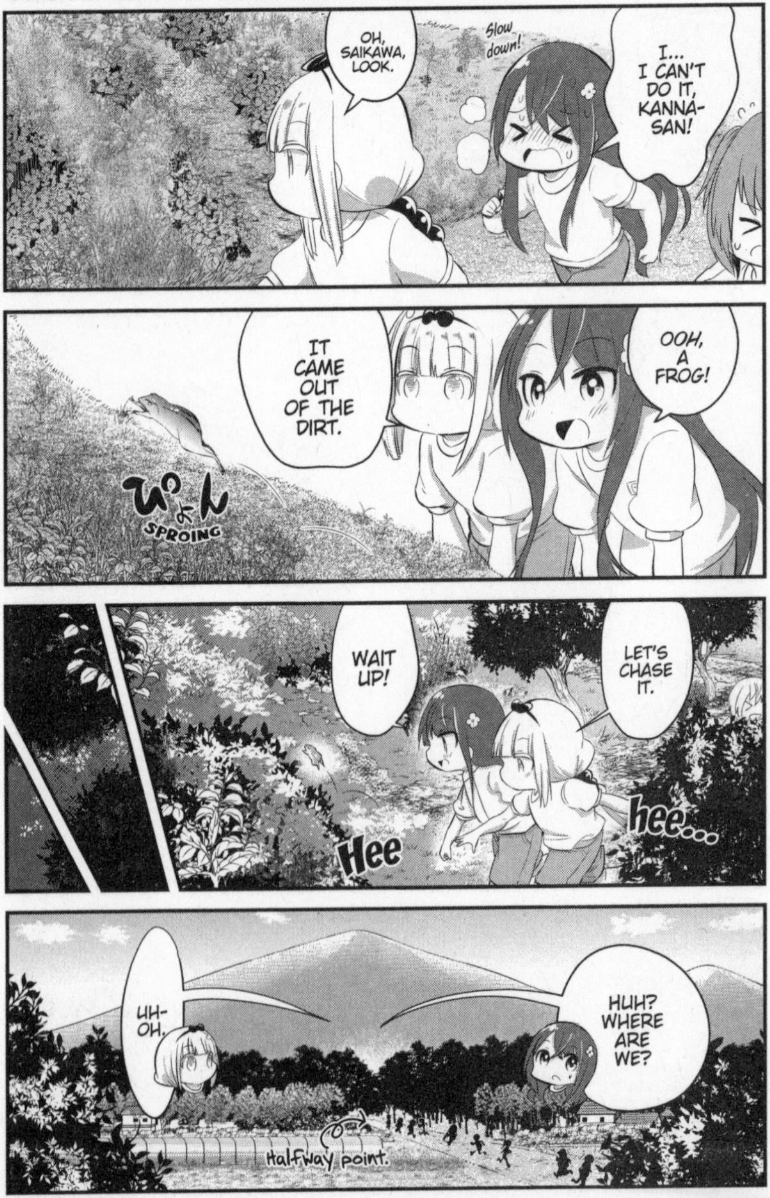
I... I CAN'T DO IT, KANNA-SAN!
Slow down!
OH, SAIKAWA, LOOK.
OOH, A FROG!
IT CAME OUT OF THE DIRT.
ぴょん
SPROING
LET'S CHASE IT.
WAIT UP!
hee...
Hee
HUH? WHERE ARE WE?
UH-OH.
Halfway point.

THE TOP OF THE FOOD CHAIN

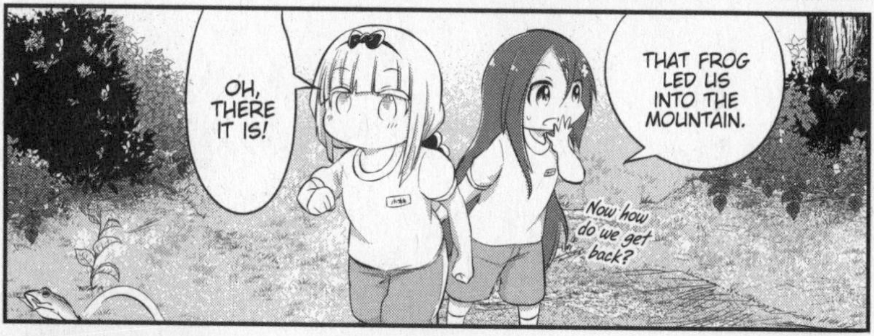
THAT FROG LED US INTO THE MOUNTAIN.
OH, THERE IT IS!
Now how do we get back?

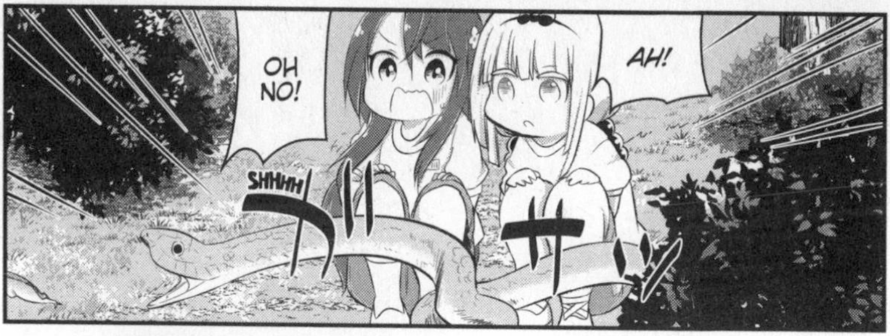
AH!
OH NO!
SHHHH

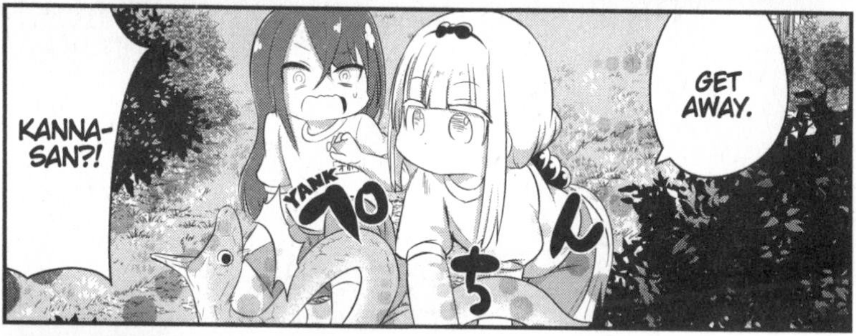
GET AWAY.
YANK
KANNA-SAN?!

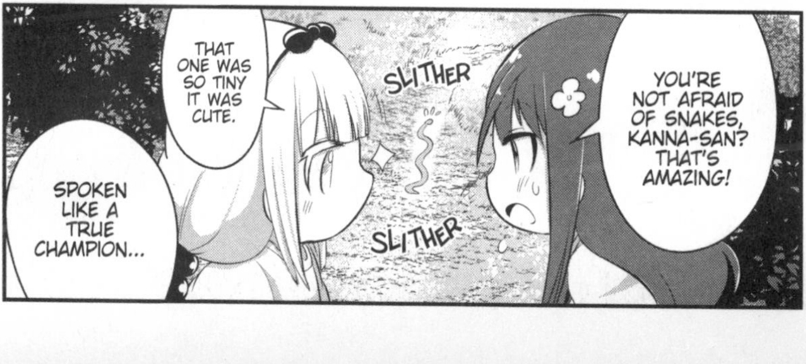
YOU'RE NOT AFRAID OF SNAKES, KANNA-SAN? THAT'S AMAZING!
SLITHER
THAT ONE WAS SO TINY IT WAS CUTE.
SLITHER
SPOKEN LIKE A TRUE CHAMPION...

UNEXPECTED DISCOVERY!!

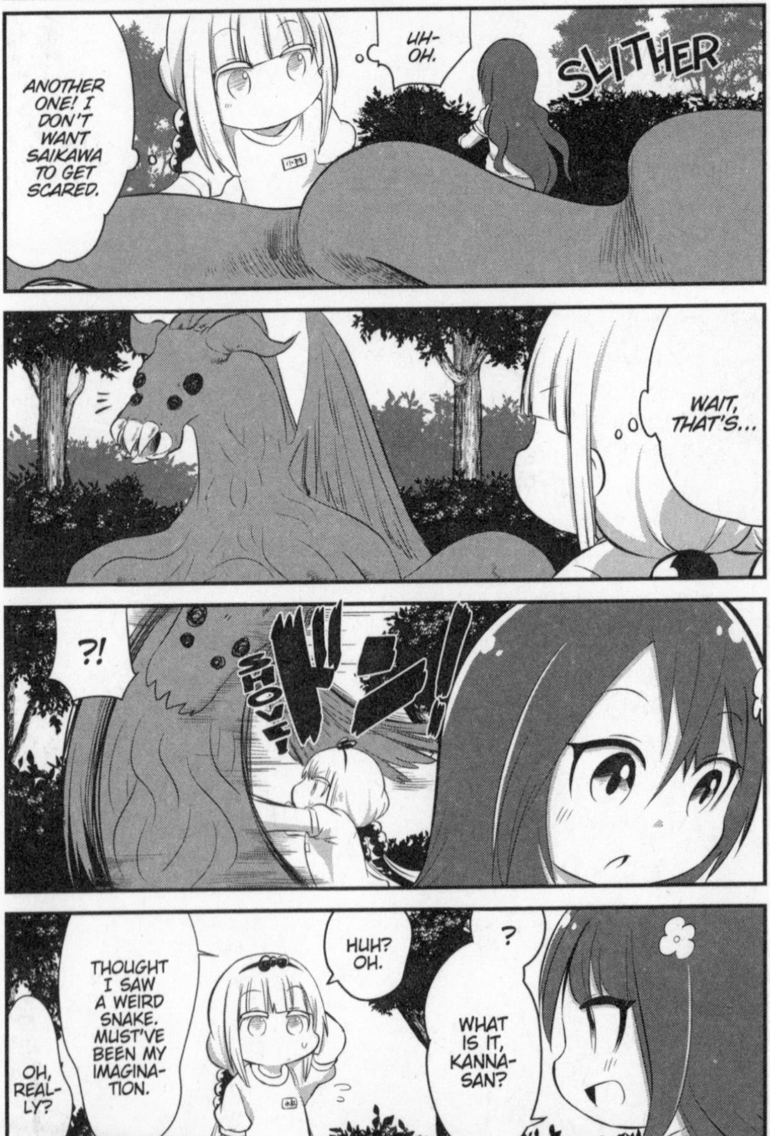
SLITHER
UH-OH.
ANOTHER ONE! I DON'T WANT SAIKAWA TO GET SCARED.
WAIT, THAT'S...
SHOVE!
?!
?
WHAT IS IT, KANNA-SAN?
HUH? OH.
THOUGHT I SAW A WEIRD SNAKE. MUST'VE BEEN MY IMAGINATION.
OH, REALLY?

I HEARD ABOUT IT ON TV

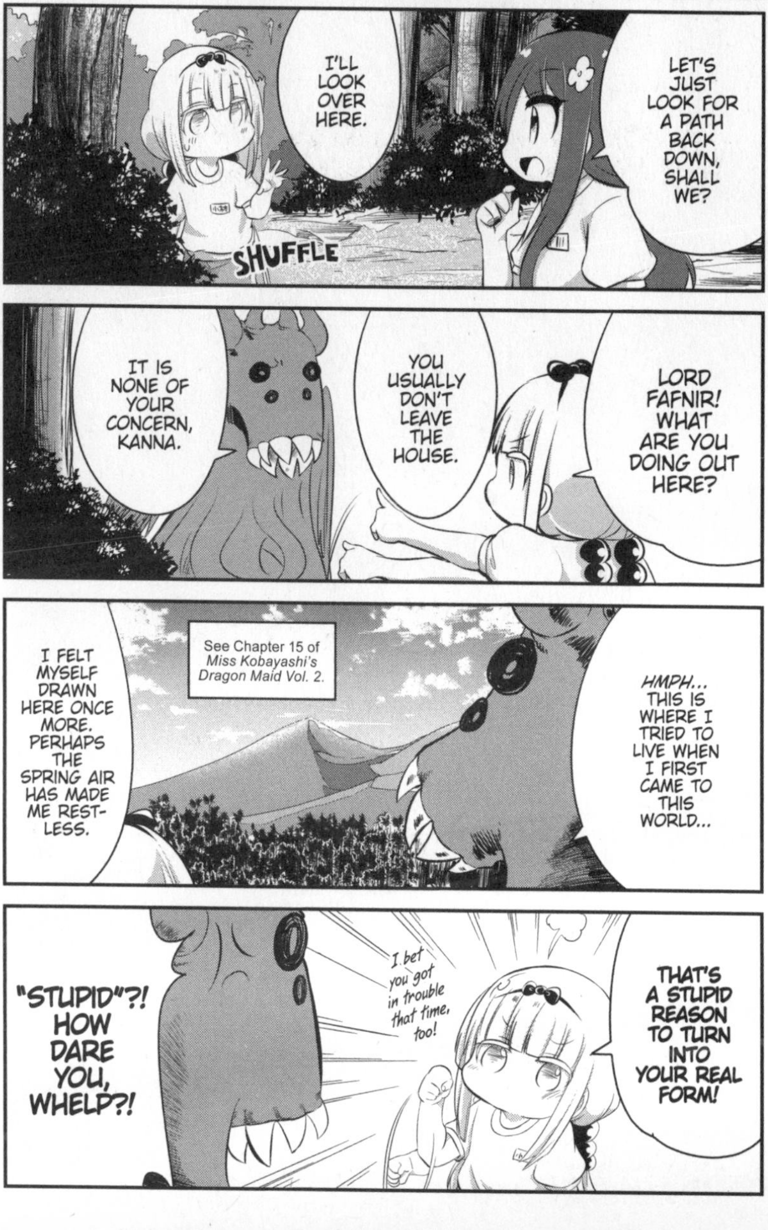
LET'S JUST LOOK FOR A PATH BACK DOWN, SHALL WE?
I'LL LOOK OVER HERE.
SHUFFLE
LORD FAFNIR! WHAT ARE YOU DOING OUT HERE?
YOU USUALLY DON'T LEAVE THE HOUSE.
IT IS NONE OF YOUR CONCERN, KANNA.
HMPH... THIS IS WHERE I TRIED TO LIVE WHEN I FIRST CAME TO THIS WORLD...
See Chapter 15 of *Miss Kobayashi's Dragon Maid Vol. 2.*
I FELT MYSELF DRAWN HERE ONCE MORE. PERHAPS THE SPRING AIR HAS MADE ME REST-LESS.
THAT'S A STUPID REASON TO TURN INTO YOUR REAL FORM!
I bet you got in trouble that time, too!
"STUPID"?! HOW DARE YOU, WHELP?!

DOUBLE TROUBLE!

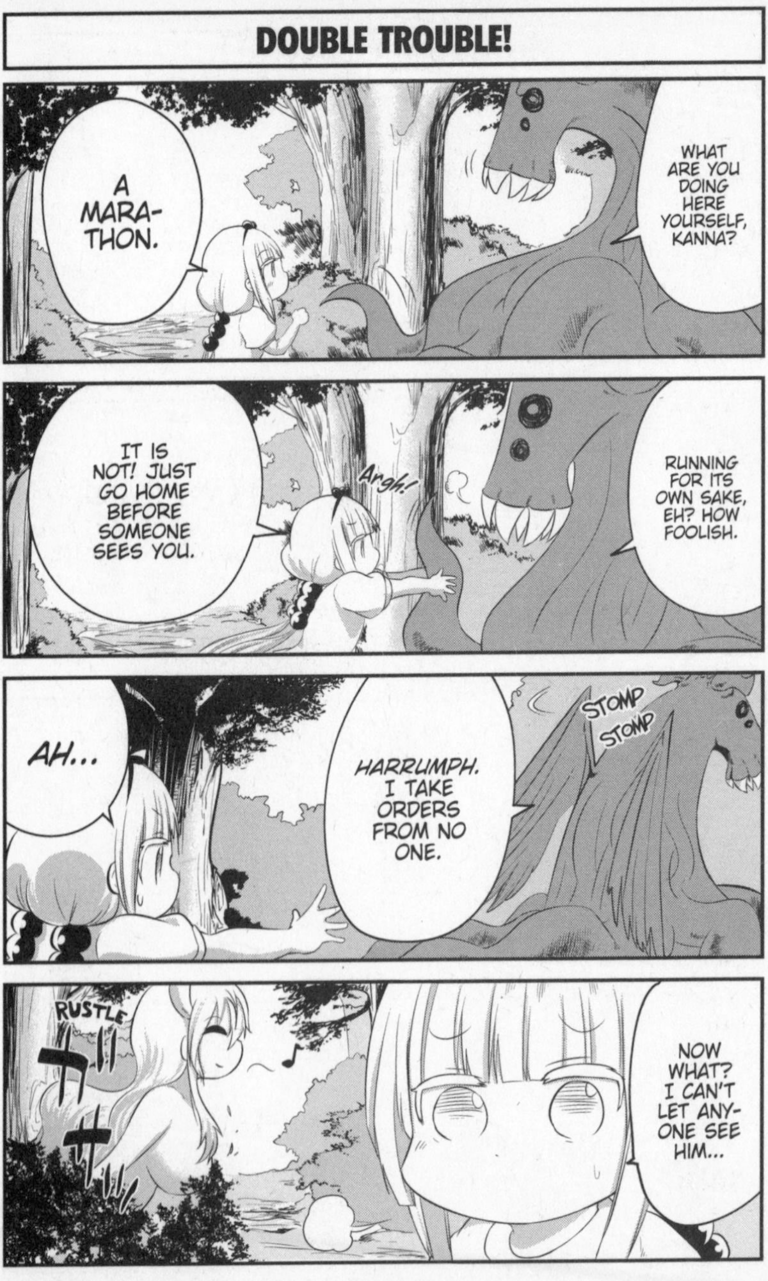
WHAT ARE YOU DOING HERE YOURSELF, KANNA?
A MARA-THON.
RUNNING FOR ITS OWN SAKE, EH? HOW FOOLISH.
Argh!
IT IS NOT! JUST GO HOME BEFORE SOMEONE SEES YOU.
STOMP STOMP
HARRUMPH. I TAKE ORDERS FROM NO ONE.
AH...
NOW WHAT? I CAN'T LET ANY-ONE SEE HIM...
RUSTLE

MISPLACED GENEROSITY

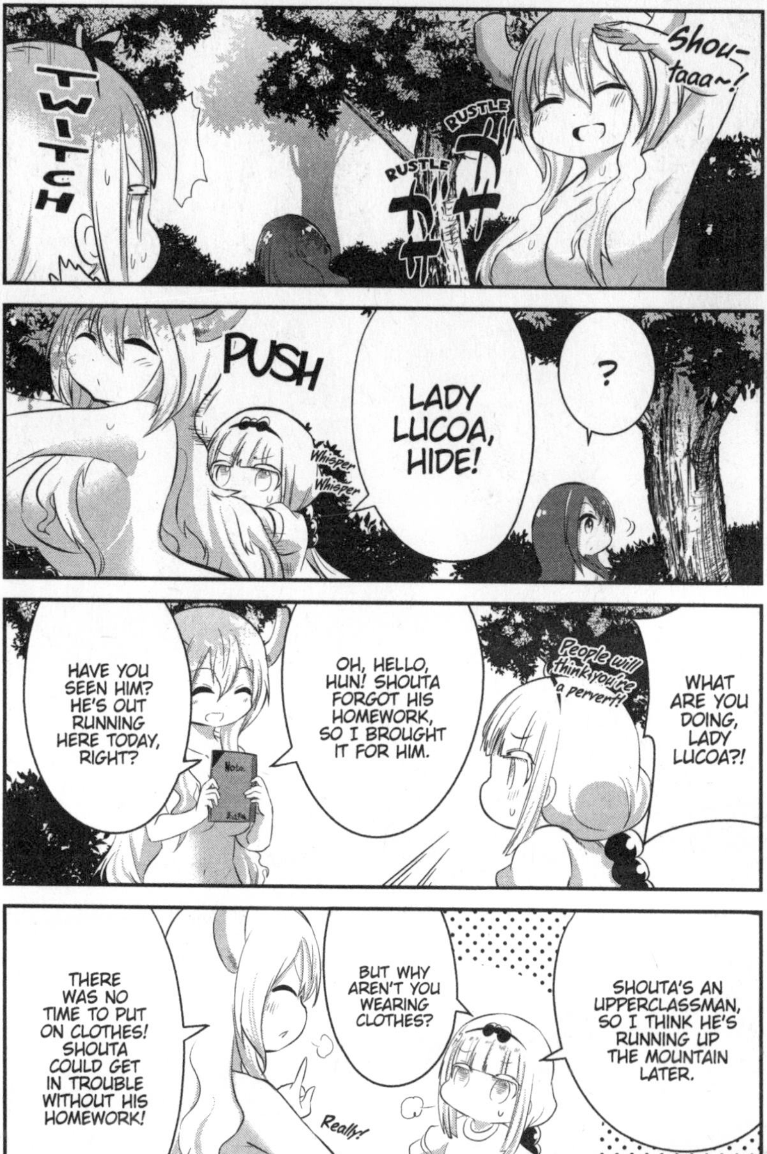
Shou-taaa~!
RUSTLE
RUSTLE
TWITCH
?
LADY LUCOA, HIDE!
Whisper
Whisper
PUSH
WHAT ARE YOU DOING, LADY LUCOA?!
People will think you're a pervert!
OH, HELLO, HUN! SHOUTA FORGOT HIS HOMEWORK, SO I BROUGHT IT FOR HIM.
HAVE YOU SEEN HIM? HE'S OUT RUNNING HERE TODAY, RIGHT?
SHOUTA'S AN UPPERCLASSMAN, SO I THINK HE'S RUNNING UP THE MOUNTAIN LATER.
BUT WHY AREN'T YOU WEARING CLOTHES?
Really!
THERE WAS NO TIME TO PUT ON CLOTHES! SHOUTA COULD GET IN TROUBLE WITHOUT HIS HOMEWORK!

MAKING A MOLEHILL OUT OF A MOUNTAIN

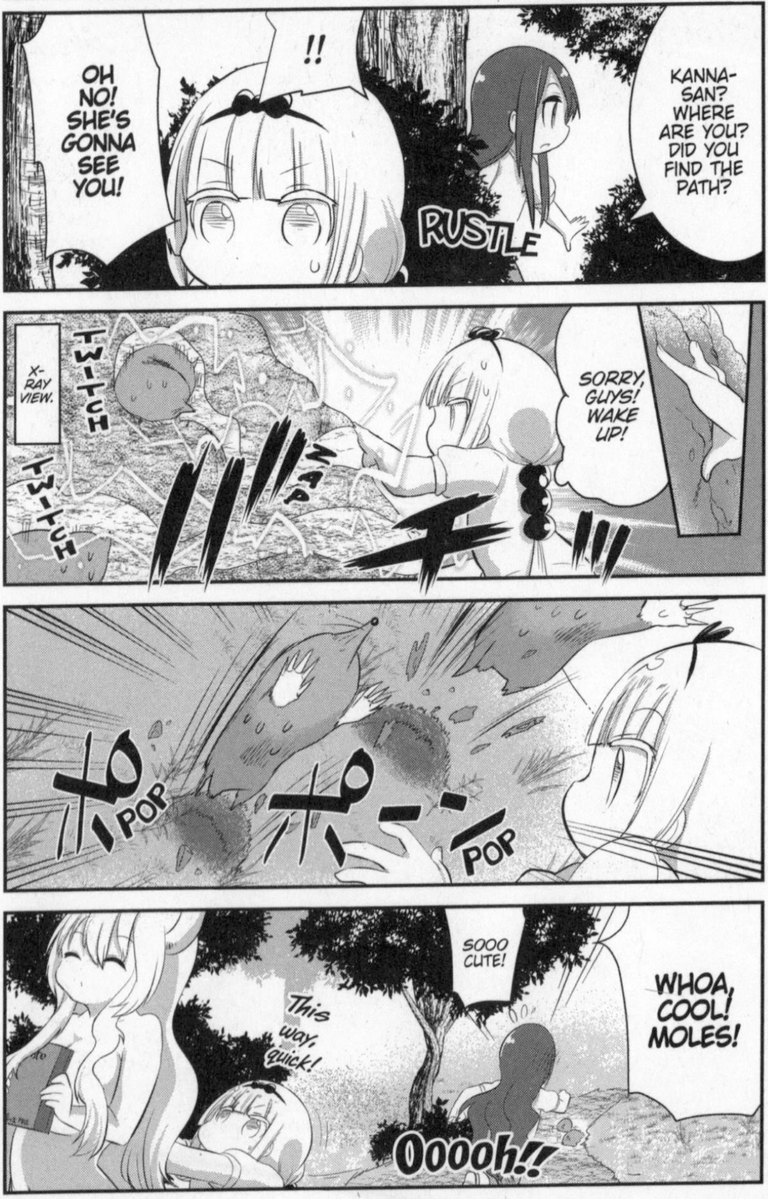
KANNA-SAN? WHERE ARE YOU? DID YOU FIND THE PATH?
!!
RUSTLE
OH NO! SHE'S GONNA SEE YOU!
SORRY, GUYS! WAKE UP!
ZAP
TWITCH
TWITCH
X-RAY VIEW.
POP
POP
WHOA, COOL! MOLES!
SOOO CUTE!
This way, quick!
Oooh!!

FAFNIR THE FRUSTRATING

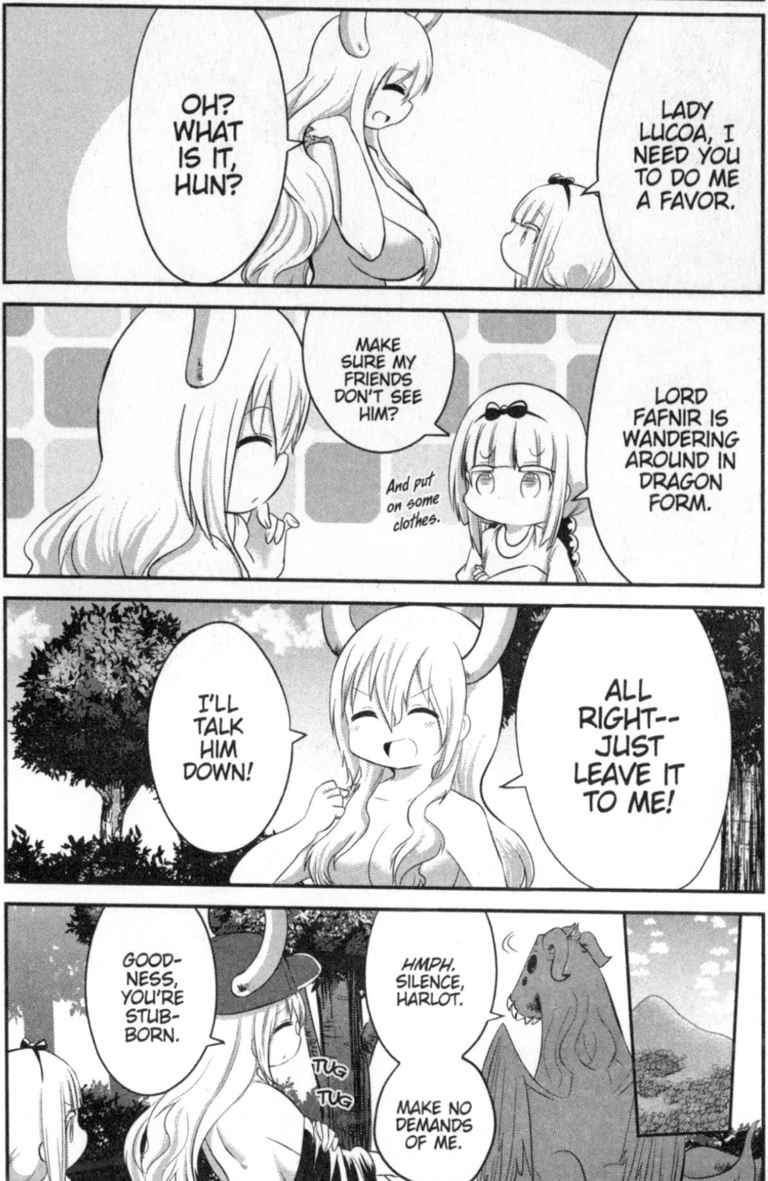
LADY LUCOA, I NEED YOU TO DO ME A FAVOR.
OH? WHAT IS IT, HUN?
LORD FAFNIR IS WANDERING AROUND IN DRAGON FORM.
MAKE SURE MY FRIENDS DON'T SEE HIM?
And put on some clothes.
ALL RIGHT--JUST LEAVE IT TO ME!
I'LL TALK HIM DOWN!
HMPH. SILENCE, HARLOT.
MAKE NO DEMANDS OF ME.
TUG
TUG
GOOD-NESS, YOU'RE STUB-BORN.

I SHAN'T BE COMPARED TO HER

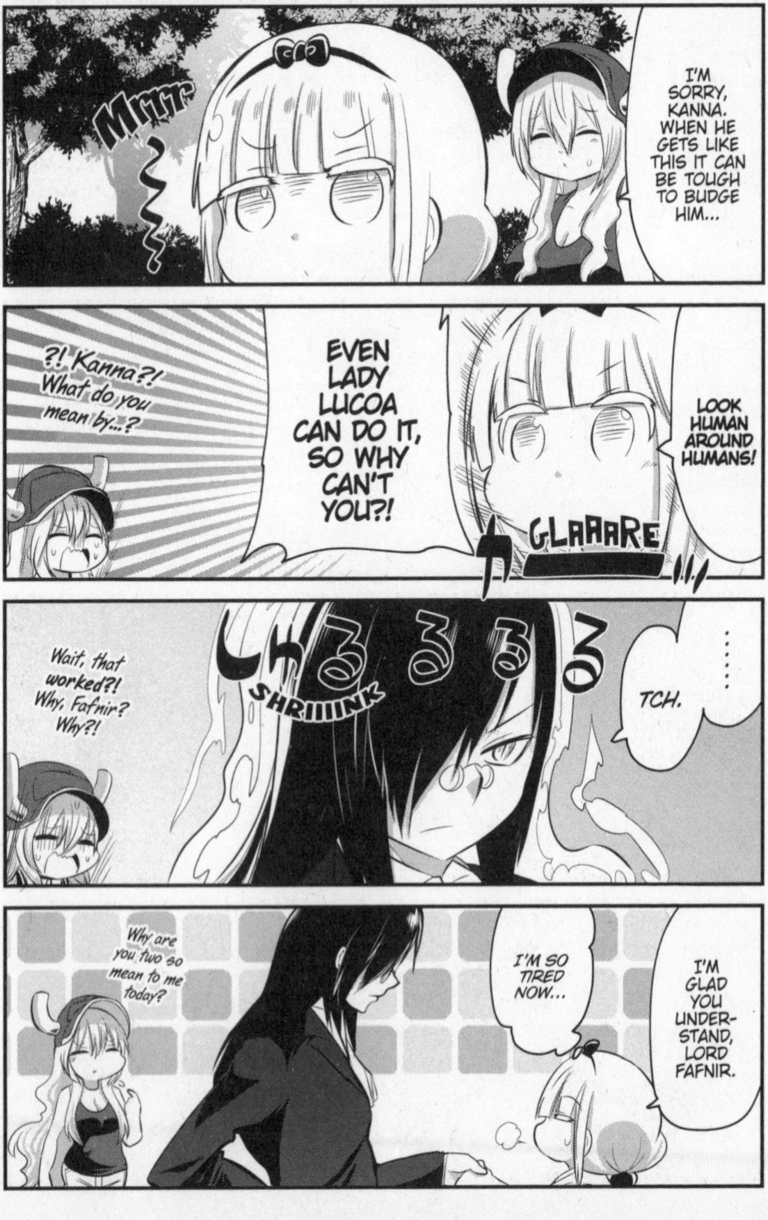
I'M SORRY, KANNA. WHEN HE GETS LIKE THIS IT CAN BE TOUGH TO BUDGE HIM...
Mrrrr
LOOK HUMAN AROUND HUMANS!
EVEN LADY LUCOA CAN DO IT, SO WHY CAN'T YOU?!
GLAAARE
?! Kanna?! What do you mean by...?
......
TCH.
しゅるるるる
SHRIIIINK
Wait, that worked?! Why, Fafnir? Why?!
I'M GLAD YOU UNDERSTAND, LORD FAFNIR.
I'M SO TIRED NOW...
Why are you two so mean to me today?

DEAD-WEIGHT DRAGONS

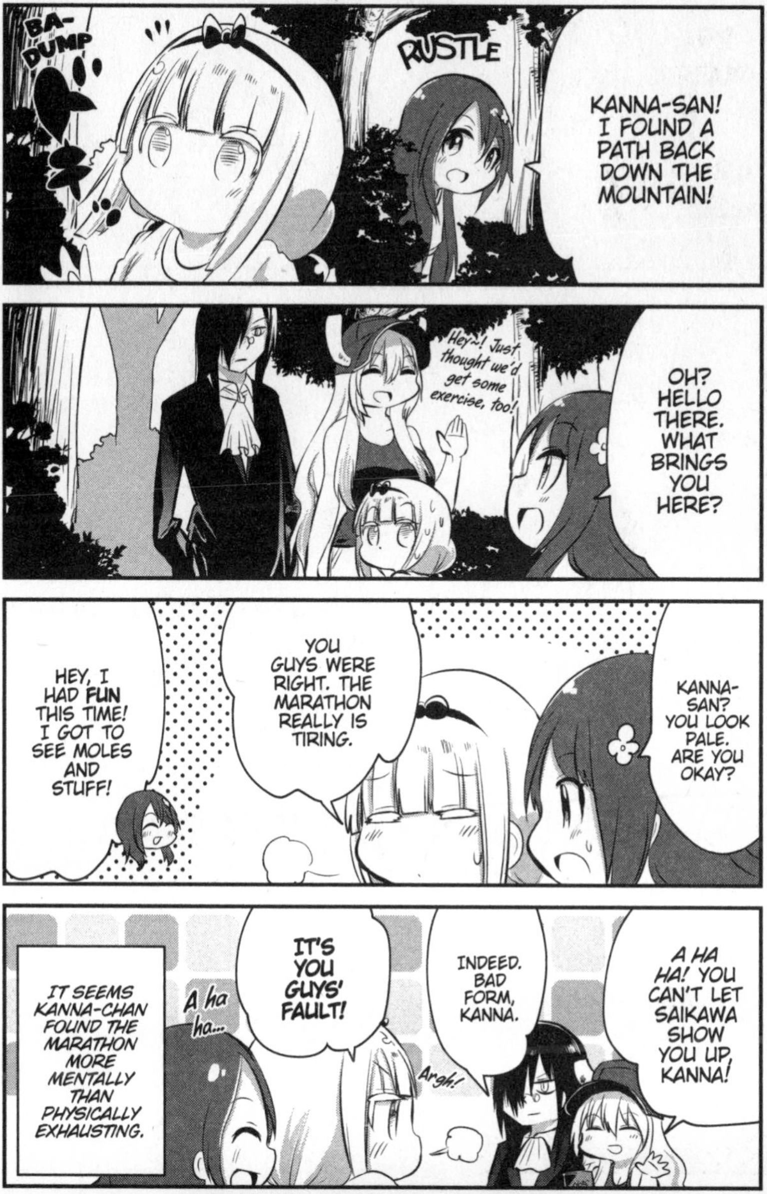
KANNA-SAN! I FOUND A PATH BACK DOWN THE MOUNTAIN!
RUSTLE
BA-DUMP
OH? HELLO THERE. WHAT BRINGS YOU HERE?
Hey~! Just thought we'd get some exercise, too!
KANNA-SAN? YOU LOOK PALE. ARE YOU OKAY?
YOU GUYS WERE RIGHT. THE MARATHON REALLY IS TIRING.
HEY, I HAD **FUN** THIS TIME! I GOT TO SEE MOLES AND STUFF!
A HA HA! YOU CAN'T LET SAIKAWA SHOW YOU UP, KANNA!
INDEED. BAD FORM, KANNA.
Argh!
IT'S YOU GUYS' FAULT!
A ha ha...
IT SEEMS KANNA-CHAN FOUND THE MARATHON MORE MENTALLY THAN PHYSICALLY EXHAUSTING.

TIME FOR THE MARATHON/END

CANDY PRIZE

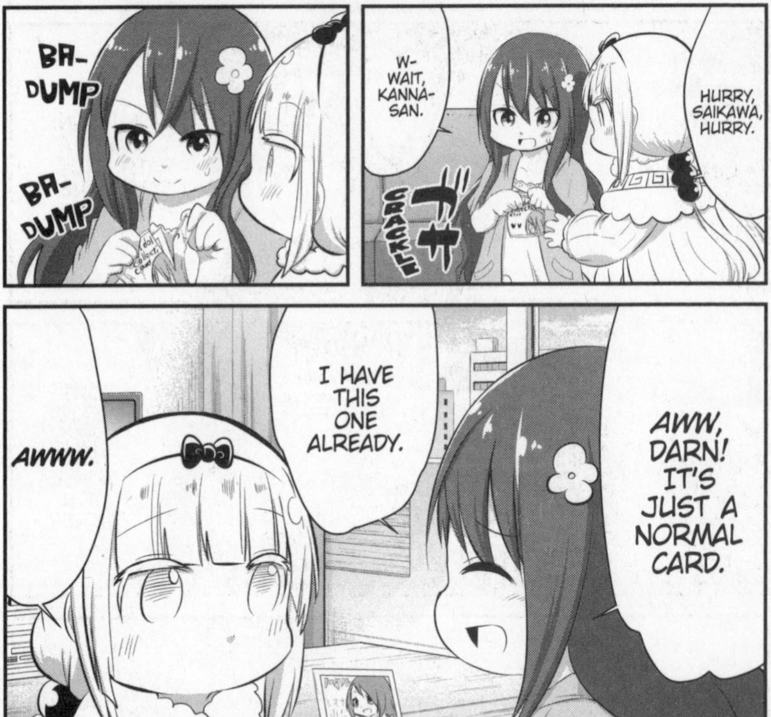
HURRY, SAIKAWA, HURRY.
W-WAIT, KANNA-SAN.
CRACKLE
BA-DUMP
BA-DUMP
AWW, DARN! IT'S JUST A NORMAL CARD.
I HAVE THIS ONE ALREADY.
AWWW.
TIME FOR THE CANDY STORE

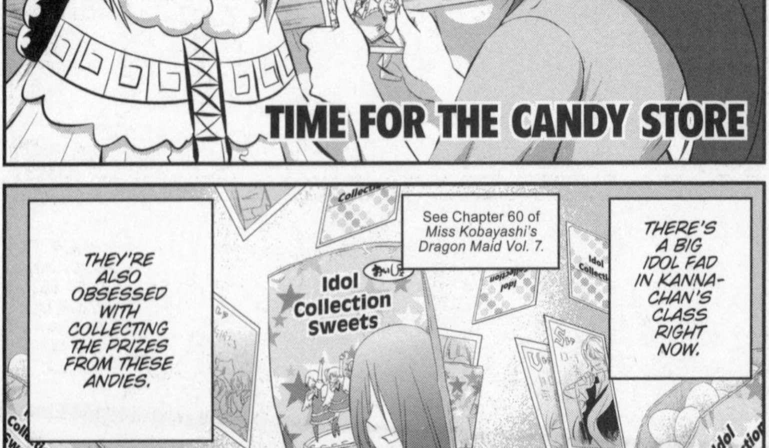
THERE'S A BIG IDOL FAD IN KANNA-CHAN'S CLASS RIGHT NOW.
See Chapter 60 of *Miss Kobayashi's Dragon Maid Vol. 7.*
Idol Collection Sweets
THEY'RE ALSO OBSESSED WITH COLLECTING THE PRIZES FROM THESE ANDIES.

IN TOO DEEP!

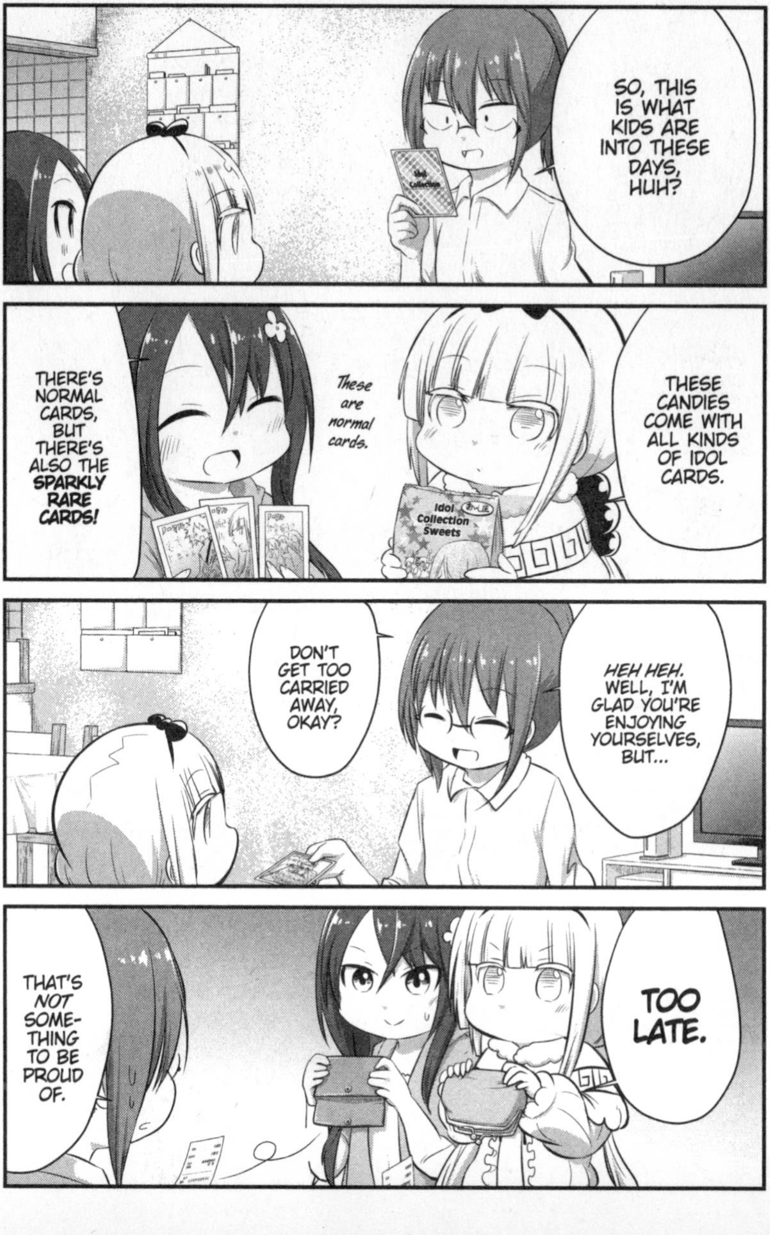
SO, THIS IS WHAT KIDS ARE INTO THESE DAYS, HUH?
THESE CANDIES COME WITH ALL KINDS OF IDOL CARDS.
Idol Collection Sweets
These are normal cards.
THERE'S NORMAL CARDS, BUT THERE'S ALSO THE SPARKLY RARE CARDS!
HEH HEH. WELL, I'M GLAD YOU'RE ENJOYING YOURSELVES, BUT...
DON'T GET TOO CARRIED AWAY, OKAY?
TOO LATE.
THAT'S NOT SOME-THING TO BE PROUD OF.

A STROKE OF GENIUS

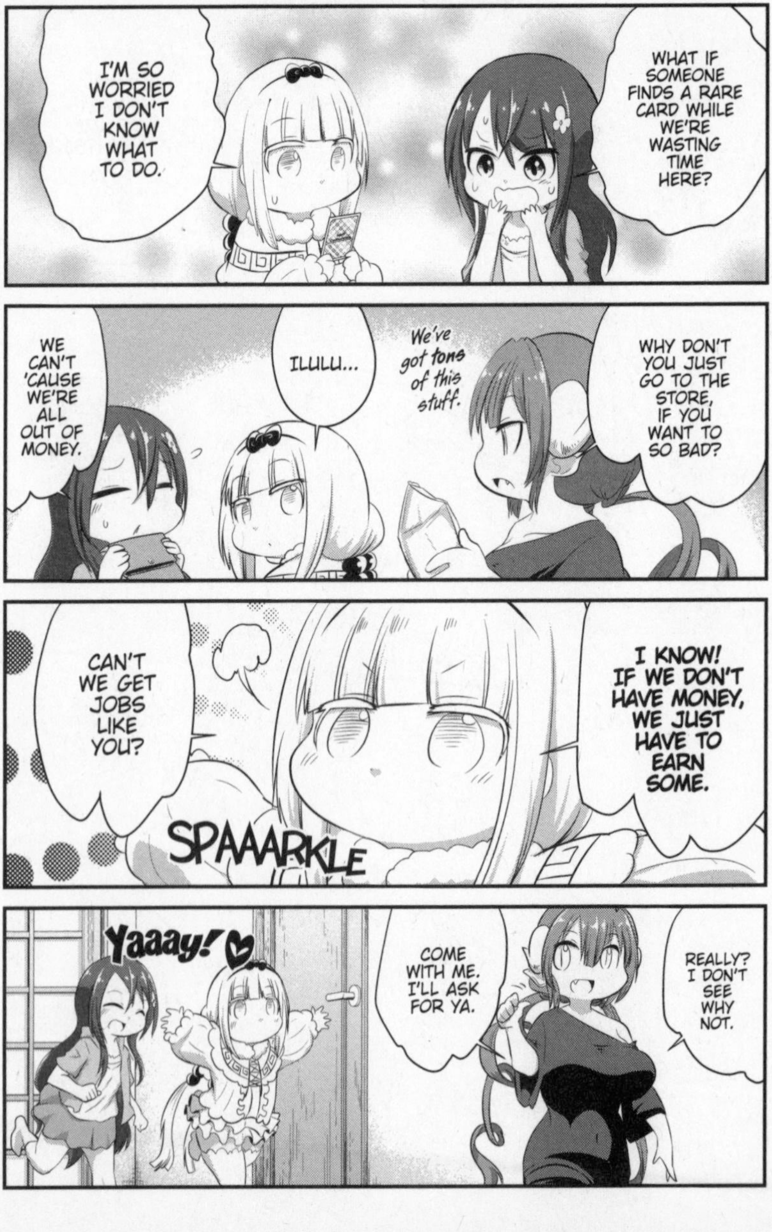
WHAT IF SOMEONE FINDS A RARE CARD WHILE WE'RE WASTING TIME HERE?
I'M SO WORRIED I DON'T KNOW WHAT TO DO.
WHY DON'T YOU JUST GO TO THE STORE, IF YOU WANT TO SO BAD?
We've got tons of this stuff.
ILULU...
WE CAN'T 'CAUSE WE'RE ALL OUT OF MONEY.
I KNOW! IF WE DON'T HAVE MONEY, WE JUST HAVE TO EARN SOME.
SPAAARKLE
CAN'T WE GET JOBS LIKE YOU?
REALLY? I DON'T SEE WHY NOT.
COME WITH ME. I'LL ASK FOR YA.
Yaaay!♥

APPLYING AT OBORO SHOP!

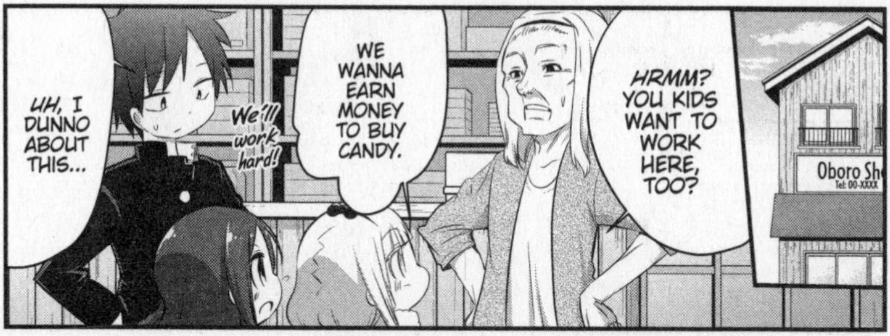
Oboro Sh
Tel: 00-XXXX
HRMM? YOU KIDS WANT TO WORK HERE, TOO?
WE WANNA EARN MONEY TO BUY CANDY.
We'll work hard!
UH, I DUNNO ABOUT THIS...

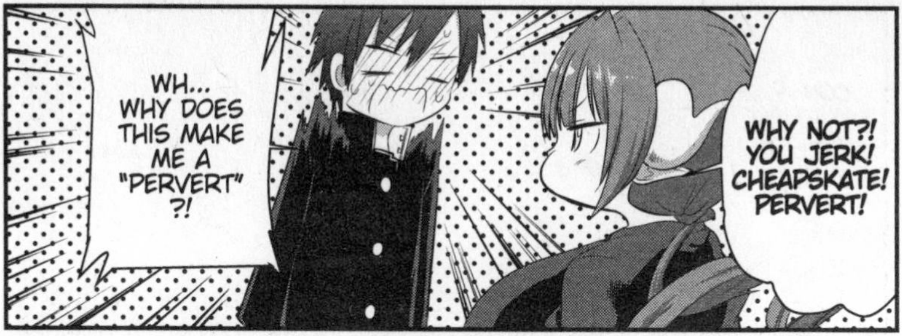
WHY NOT?! YOU JERK! CHEAPSKATE! PERVERT!
WH... WHY DOES THIS MAKE ME A "PERVERT" ?!

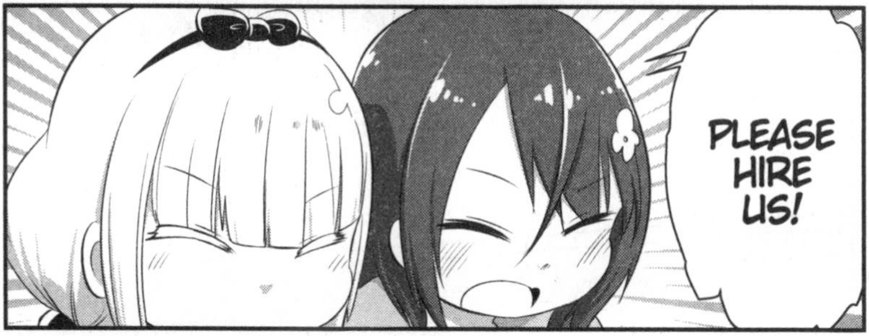
PLEASE HIRE US!

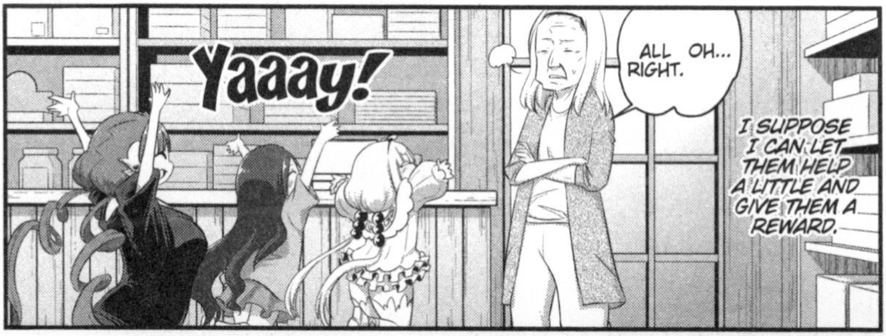
I SUPPOSE I CAN LET THEM HELP A LITTLE AND GIVE THEM A REWARD.
OH... ALL RIGHT.
Yaaay!

PROUD OF HER FRIENDS

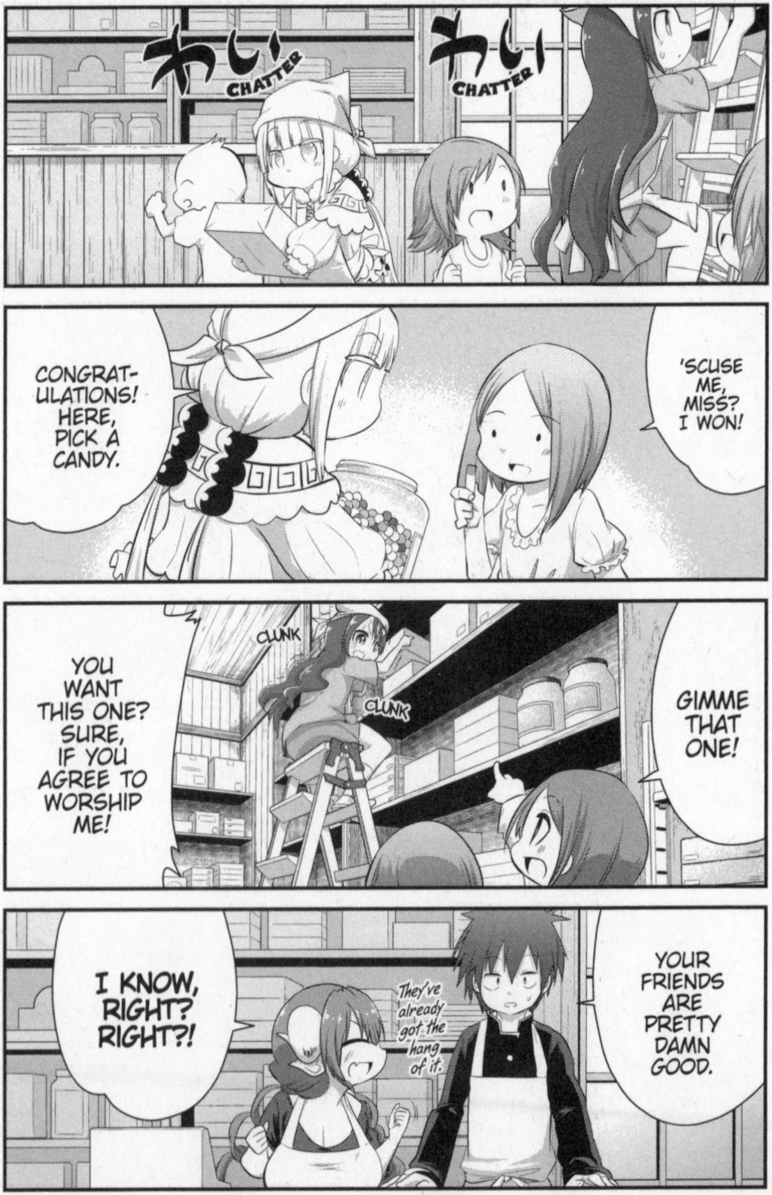
わい
CHATTER
わい
CHATTER
'SCUSE ME, MISS? I WON!
CONGRAT-ULATIONS! HERE, PICK A CANDY.
CLUNK
CLUNK
GIMME THAT ONE!
YOU WANT THIS ONE? SURE, IF YOU AGREE TO WORSHIP ME!
YOUR FRIENDS ARE PRETTY DAMN GOOD.
They've already got the hang of it.
I KNOW, RIGHT? RIGHT?!

HEAVEN AND HELL

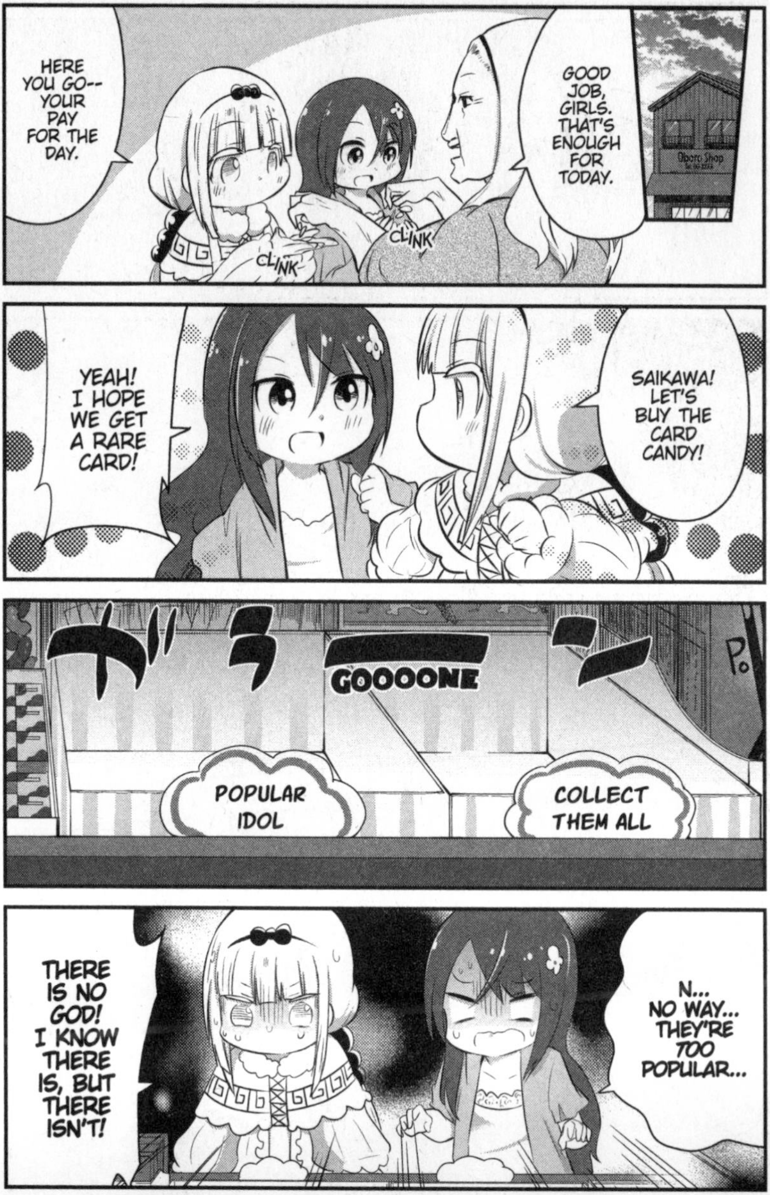
GOOD JOB, GIRLS. THAT'S ENOUGH FOR TODAY.
HERE YOU GO-- YOUR PAY FOR THE DAY.
CLINK
CLINK
SAIKAWA! LET'S BUY THE CARD CANDY!
YEAH! I HOPE WE GET A RARE CARD!
GOOOONE
COLLECT THEM ALL
POPULAR IDOL
N... NO WAY... THEY'RE *TOO* POPULAR...
THERE IS NO GOD! I KNOW THERE IS, BUT THERE ISN'T!

THE DODGEBALL GUYS RETURN!

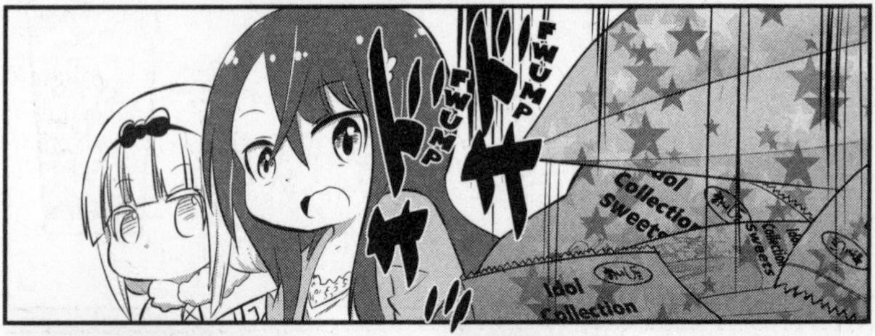
FWUMP
FWUMP
FWUMP
Idol Collection Sweets
Idol Collection

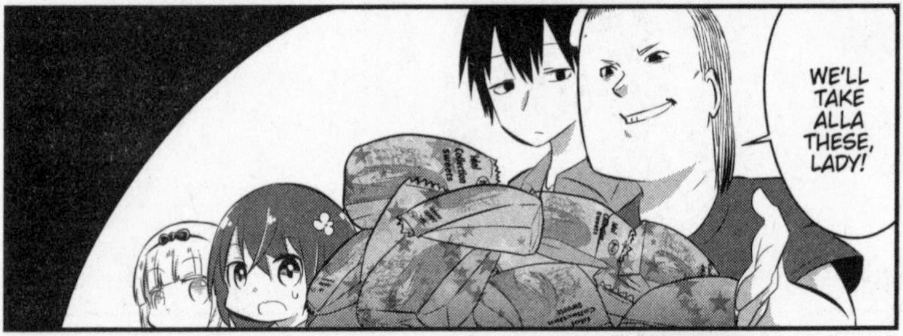
WE'LL TAKE ALLA THESE, LADY!

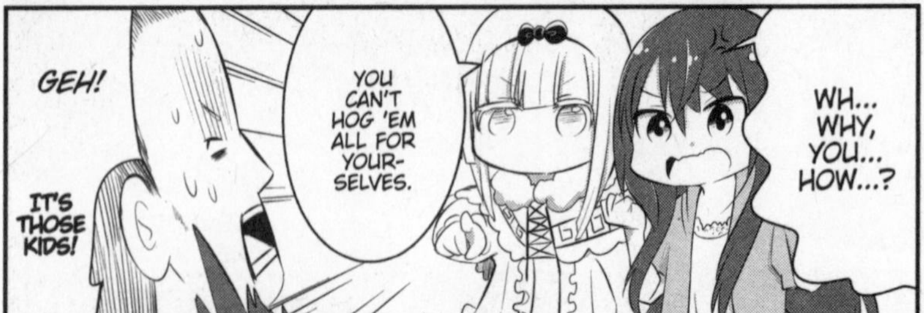
WH... WHY, YOU... HOW...?
YOU CAN'T HOG 'EM ALL FOR YOUR-SELVES.
GEH!
IT'S THOSE KIDS!

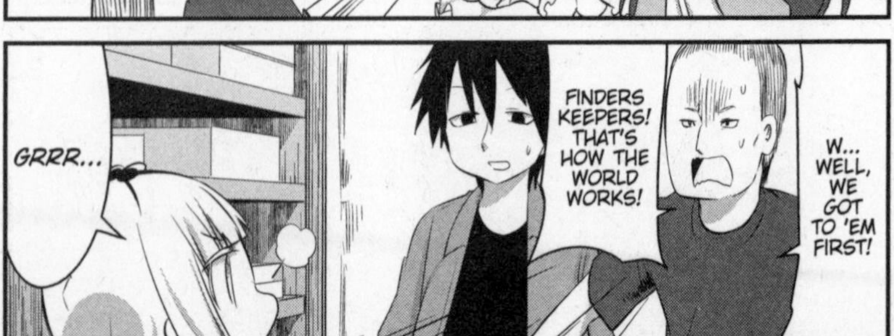
W... WELL, WE GOT TO 'EM FIRST!
FINDERS KEEPERS! THAT'S HOW THE WORLD WORKS!
GRRR...

LESS WHINING, MORE WINNING

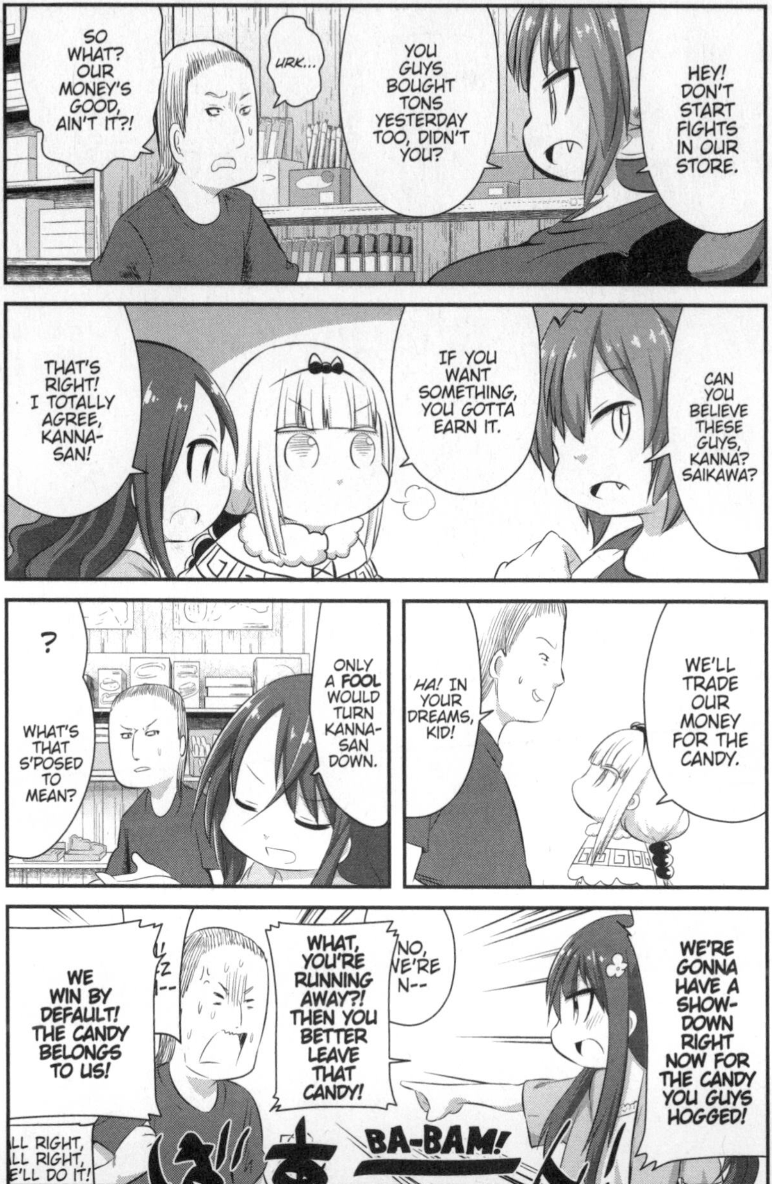
HEY! DON'T START FIGHTS IN OUR STORE.
YOU GUYS BOUGHT TONS YESTERDAY TOO, DIDN'T YOU?
URK...
SO WHAT? OUR MONEY'S GOOD, AIN'T IT?!
CAN YOU BELIEVE THESE GUYS, KANNA? SAIKAWA?
IF YOU WANT SOMETHING, YOU GOTTA EARN IT.
THAT'S RIGHT! I TOTALLY AGREE, KANNA-SAN!
WE'LL TRADE OUR MONEY FOR THE CANDY.
HA! IN YOUR DREAMS, KID!
ONLY A FOOL WOULD TURN KANNA-SAN DOWN.
?
WHAT'S THAT S'POSED TO MEAN?
WE'RE GONNA HAVE A SHOWDOWN RIGHT NOW FOR THE CANDY YOU GUYS HOGGED!
BA-BAM!
NO, WE'RE N--
WHAT, YOU'RE RUNNING AWAY?! THEN YOU BETTER LEAVE THAT CANDY!
WE WIN BY DEFAULT! THE CANDY BELONGS TO US!
LL RIGHT, LL RIGHT, E'LL DO IT!

ILULU'S IDEA

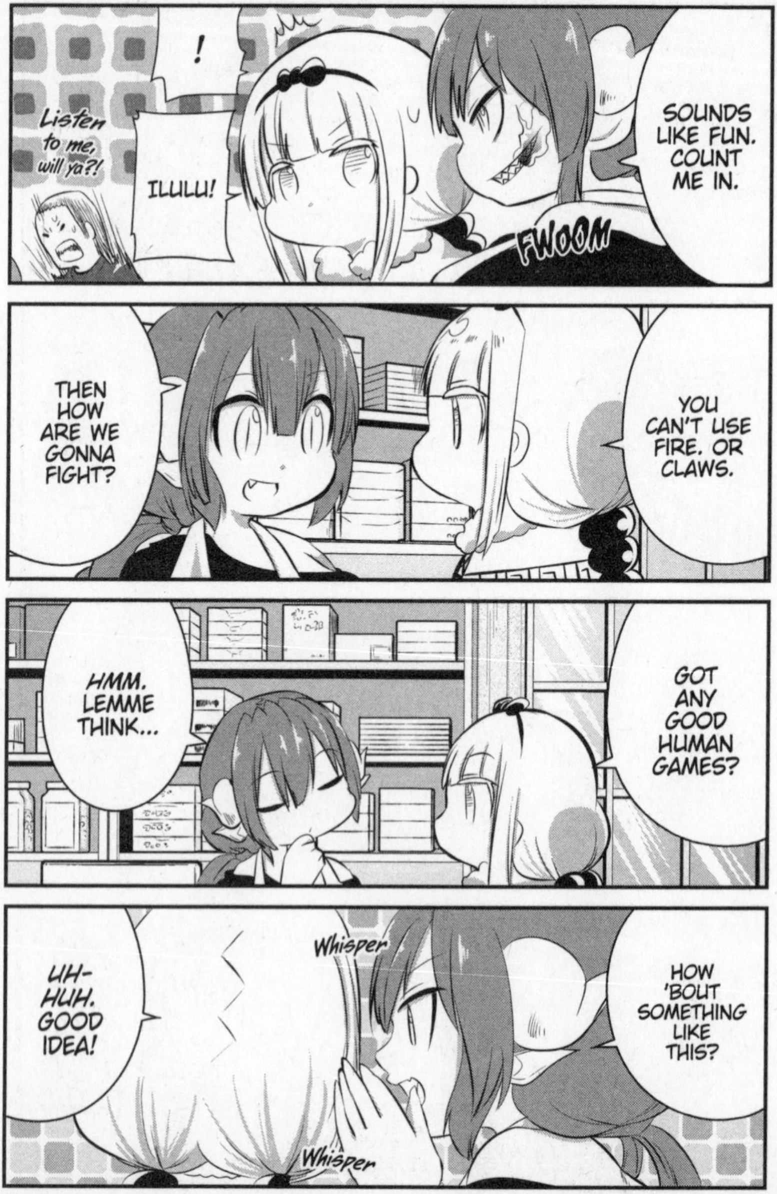
SOUNDS LIKE FUN. COUNT ME IN.
FWOOM
!
ILULU!
Listen to me, will ya?!
YOU CAN'T USE FIRE. OR CLAWS.
THEN HOW ARE WE GONNA FIGHT?
GOT ANY GOOD HUMAN GAMES?
HMM. LEMME THINK...
HOW 'BOUT SOMETHING LIKE THIS?
Whisper
Whisper
UH-HUH. GOOD IDEA!

FLIPPIN' COOL

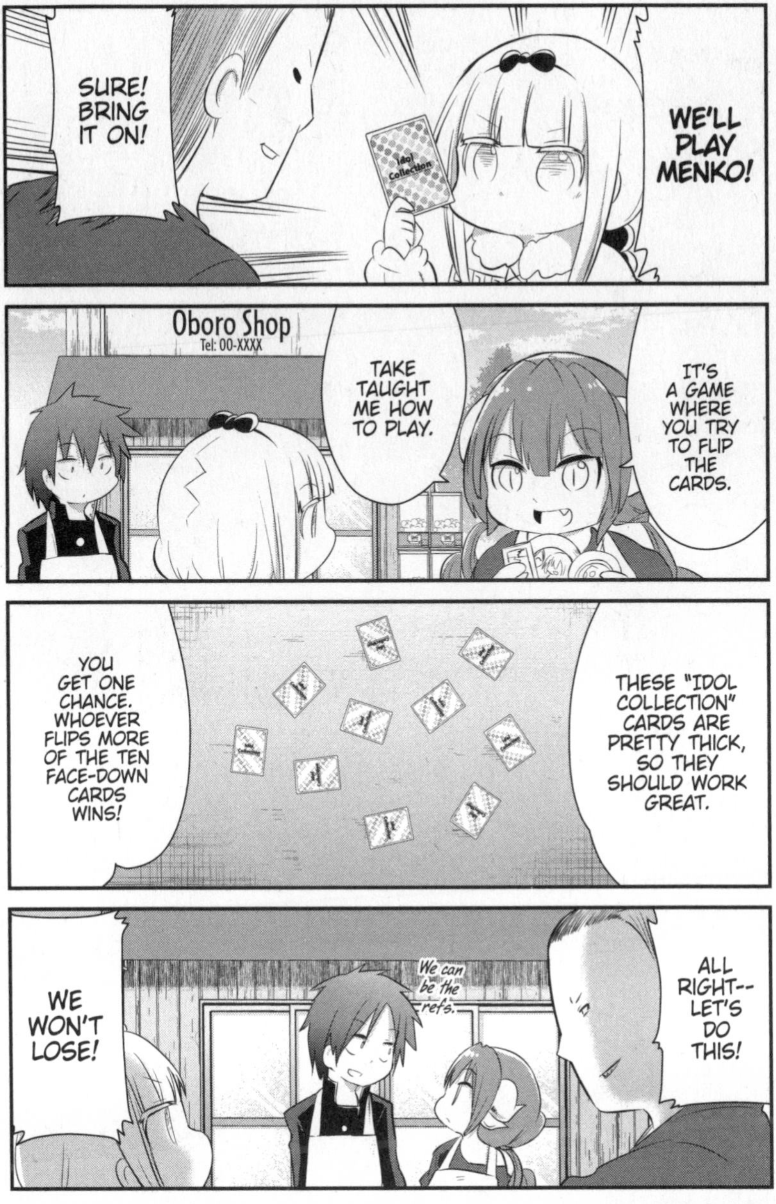
WE'LL PLAY MENKO!
Idol Collection
SURE! BRING IT ON!
IT'S A GAME WHERE YOU TRY TO FLIP THE CARDS.
TAKE TAUGHT ME HOW TO PLAY.
Oboro Shop
Tel: 00-XXXX
THESE "IDOL COLLECTION" CARDS ARE PRETTY THICK, SO THEY SHOULD WORK GREAT.
YOU GET ONE CHANCE. WHOEVER FLIPS MORE OF THE TEN FACE-DOWN CARDS WINS!
ALL RIGHT--LET'S DO THIS!
We can be the refs.
WE WON'T LOSE!

TOTAL VICTORY!!

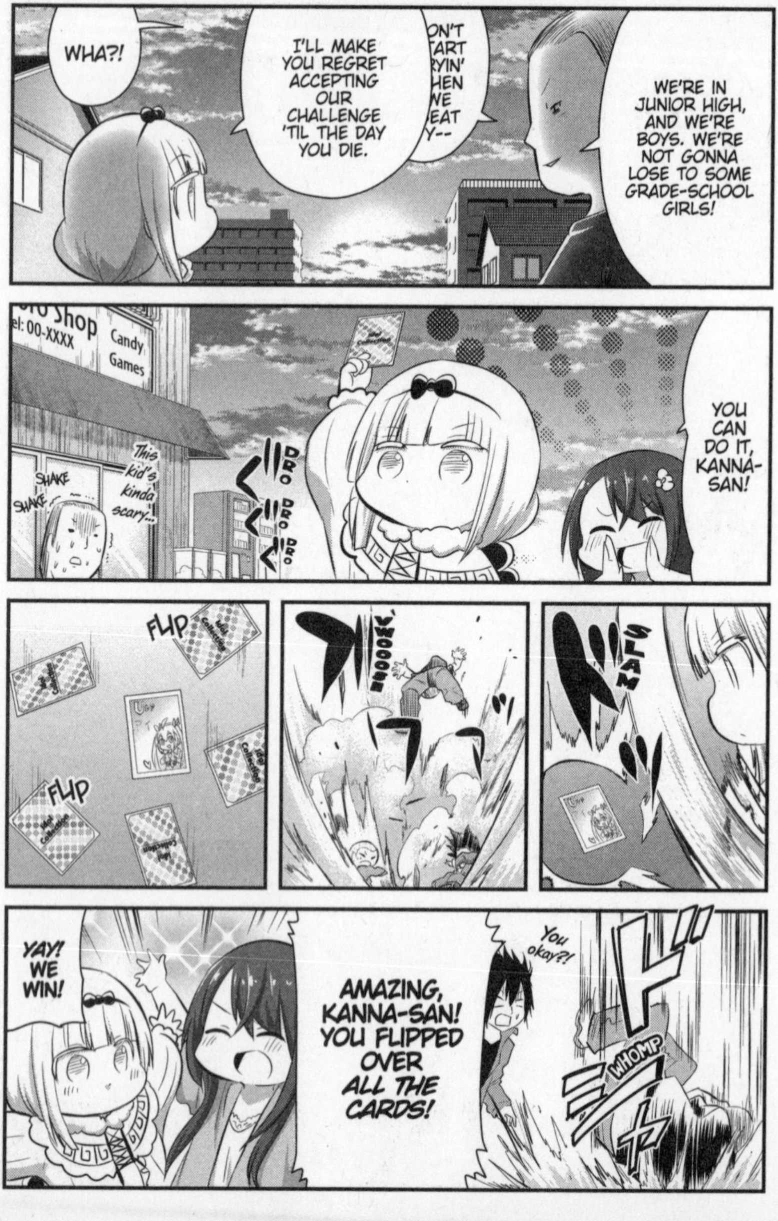

WE'RE IN JUNIOR HIGH, AND WE'RE BOYS. WE'RE NOT GONNA LOSE TO SOME GRADE-SCHOOL GIRLS!
ON'T TART RYIN' HEN WE EAT Y--
I'LL MAKE YOU REGRET ACCEPTING OUR CHALLENGE 'TIL THE DAY YOU DIE.
WHA?!
YOU CAN DO IT, KANNA-SAN!
DRO DRO DRO
Shop
el: 00-XXXX
Candy
Games
This kid's kinda scary...
SHAKE SHAKE
SLAM
VWOOOSH
FLIP
FLIP
WHOMP
You okay?!
AMAZING, KANNA-SAN! YOU FLIPPED OVER ALL THE CARDS!
YAY! WE WIN!

THE MORE THE MERRIER

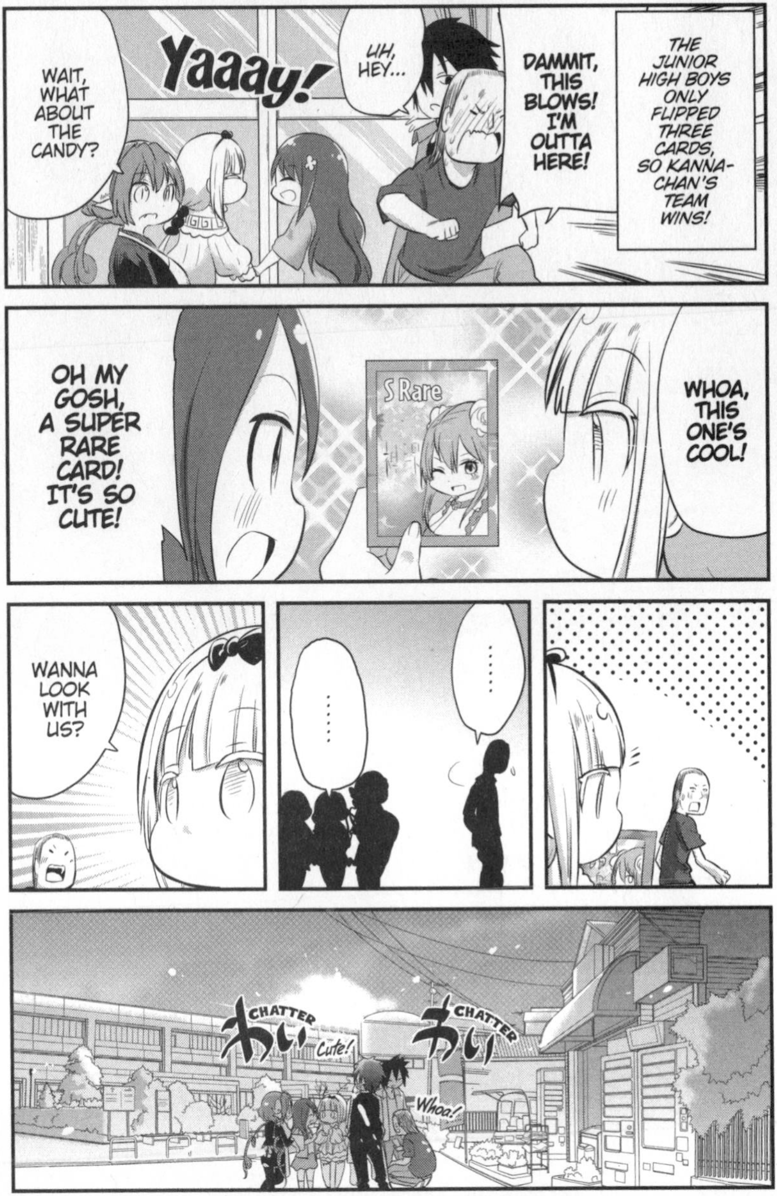
THE JUNIOR HIGH BOYS ONLY FLIPPED THREE CARDS, SO KANNA-CHAN'S TEAM WINS!
DAMMIT, THIS BLOWS! I'M OUTTA HERE!
UH, HEY...
Yaaay!
WAIT, WHAT ABOUT THE CANDY?
WHOA, THIS ONE'S COOL!
S Rare
OH MY GOSH, A SUPER RARE CARD! IT'S SO CUTE!
......
......
WANNA LOOK WITH US?
CHATTER
Whoa!
Cute!
CHATTER

TIME FOR THE CANDY STORE/END

Miss Kobayashi's Dragon Maid
Kanna's Daily Life

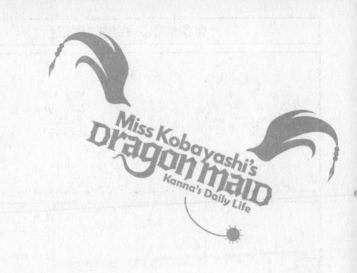

A ONCE-A-YEAR MEAL!

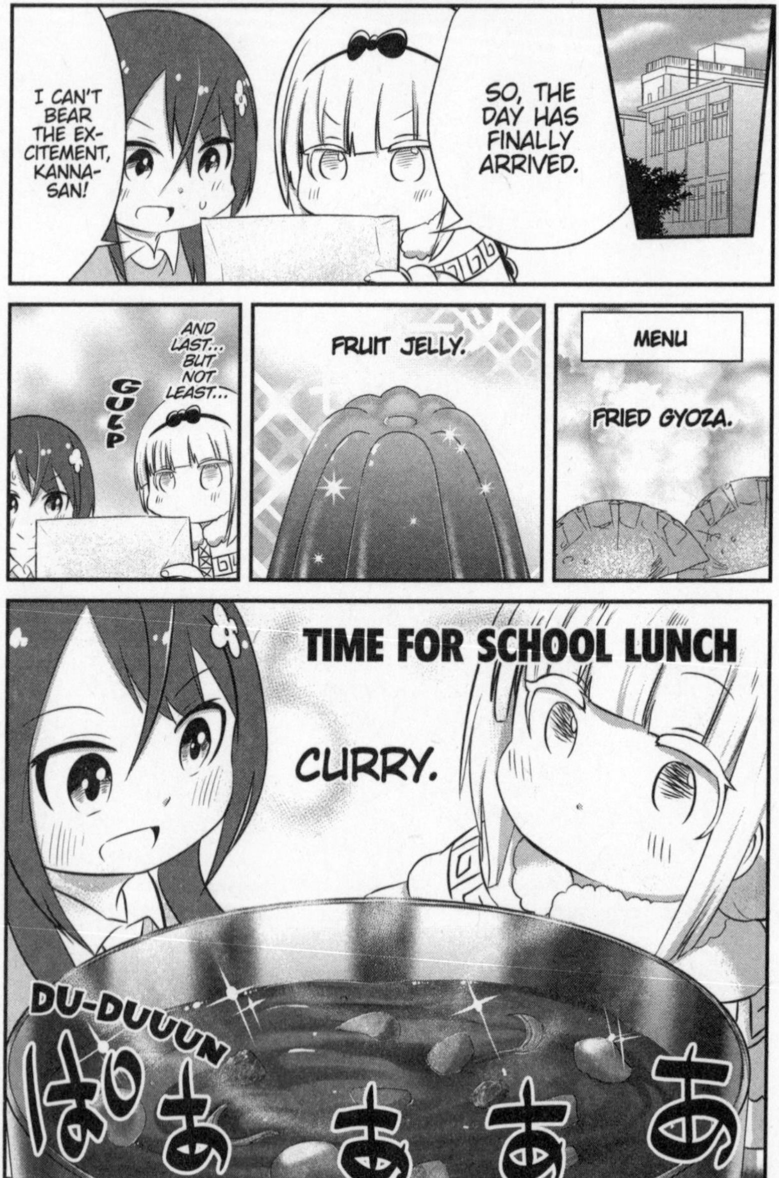
SO, THE DAY HAS FINALLY ARRIVED.
I CAN'T BEAR THE EX-CITEMENT, KANNA-SAN!
MENU
FRIED GYOZA.
FRUIT JELLY.
AND LAST... BUT NOT LEAST...
GULP
TIME FOR SCHOOL LUNCH
CURRY.
DU-DUUUN
ぱあああ

SOMETHING IN THE AIR

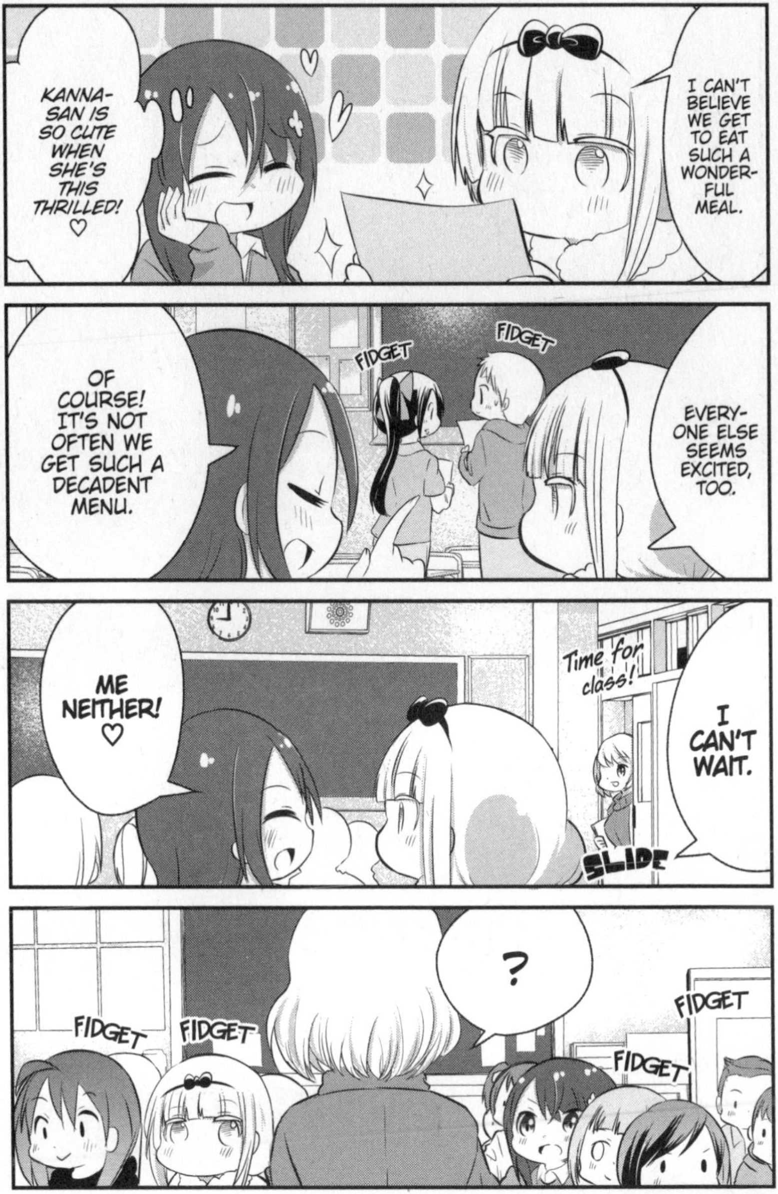
I CAN'T BELIEVE WE GET TO EAT SUCH A WONDERFUL MEAL.
KANNA-SAN IS SO CUTE WHEN SHE'S THIS THRILLED! ♡
EVERYONE ELSE SEEMS EXCITED, TOO.
FIDGET
FIDGET
OF COURSE! IT'S NOT OFTEN WE GET SUCH A DECADENT MENU.
I CAN'T WAIT.
SLIDE
Time for class!
ME NEITHER! ♡
?
FIDGET
FIDGET
FIDGET
FIDGET

A SURGE OF EMOTION

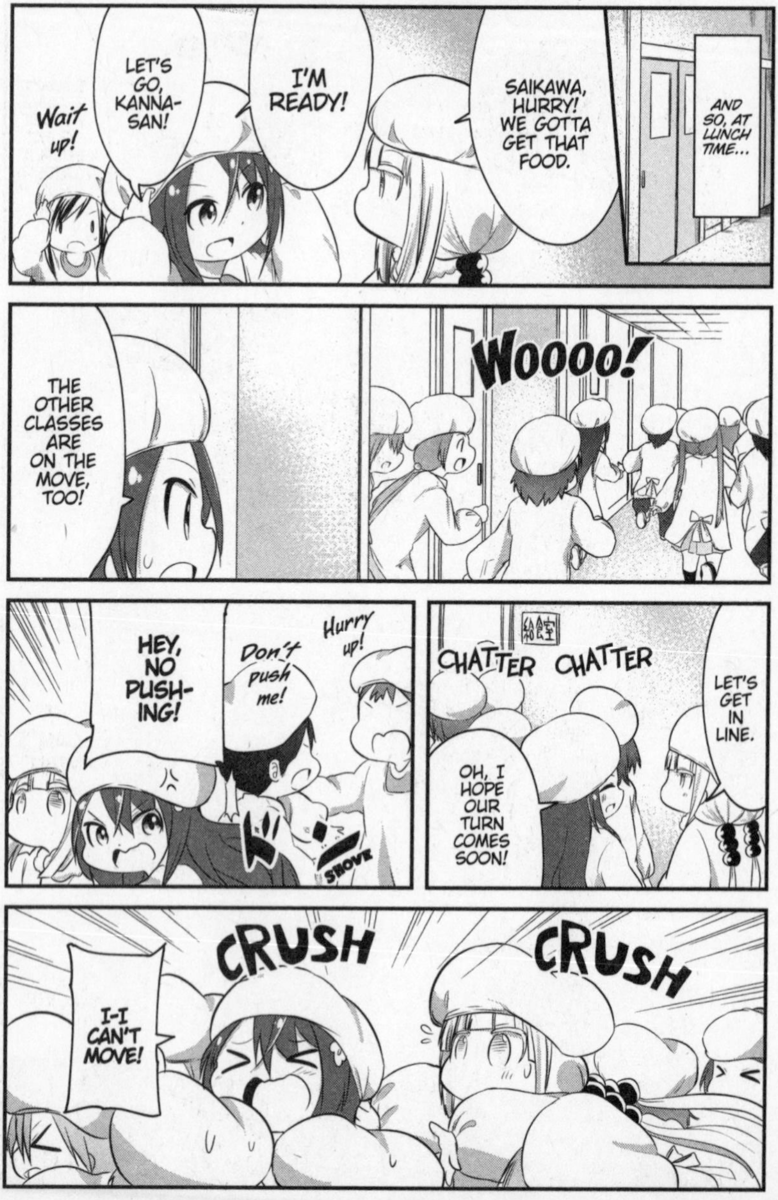
AND SO, AT LUNCH TIME...
SAIKAWA, HURRY! WE GOTTA GET THAT FOOD.
I'M READY!
LET'S GO, KANNA-SAN!
Wait up!
WOOOO!
THE OTHER CLASSES ARE ON THE MOVE, TOO!
LET'S GET IN LINE.
給食室
CHATTER CHATTER
OH, I HOPE OUR TURN COMES SOON!
Hurry up!
Don't push me!
HEY, NO PUSHING!
SHOVE
CRUSH CRUSH
I-I CAN'T MOVE!

DISASTER!

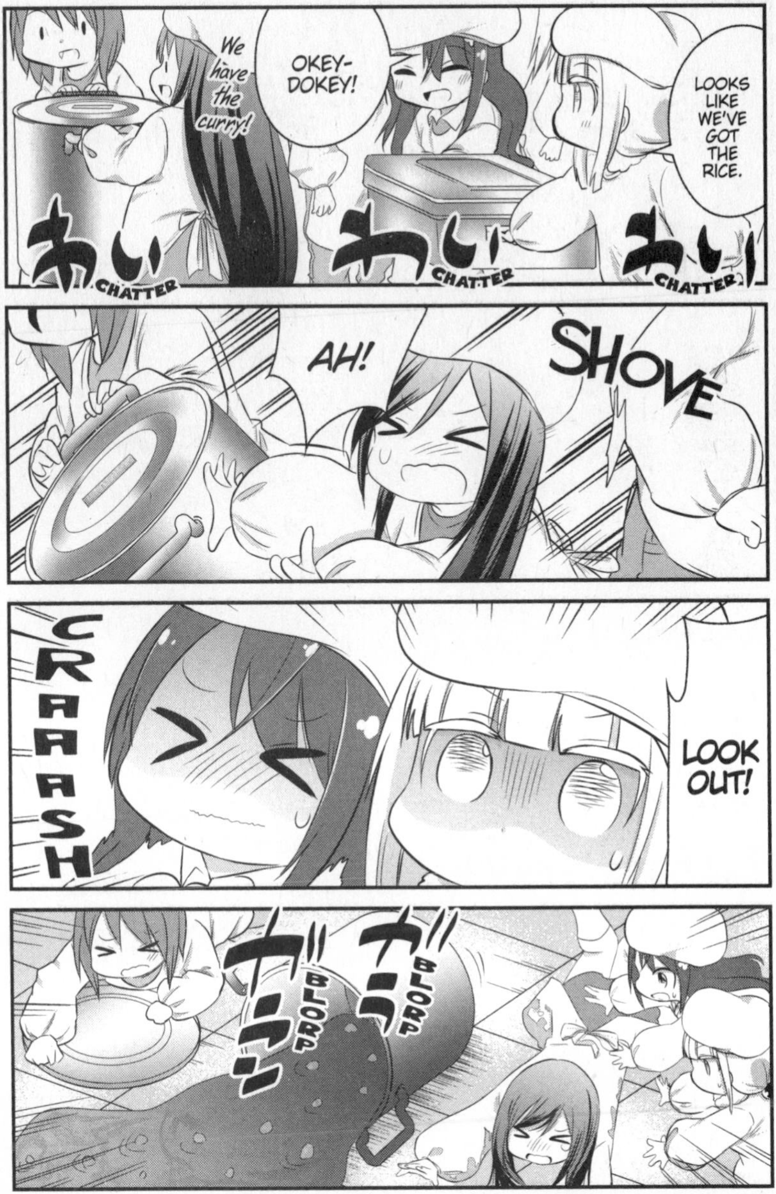
LOOKS LIKE WE'VE GOT THE RICE.
OKEY-DOKEY!
We have the curry!
わい CHATTER
わい CHATTER
わい CHATTER
SHOVE
AH!
LOOK OUT!
CRAAASH
BLORP
BLORP

BRING BACK THE CURRY

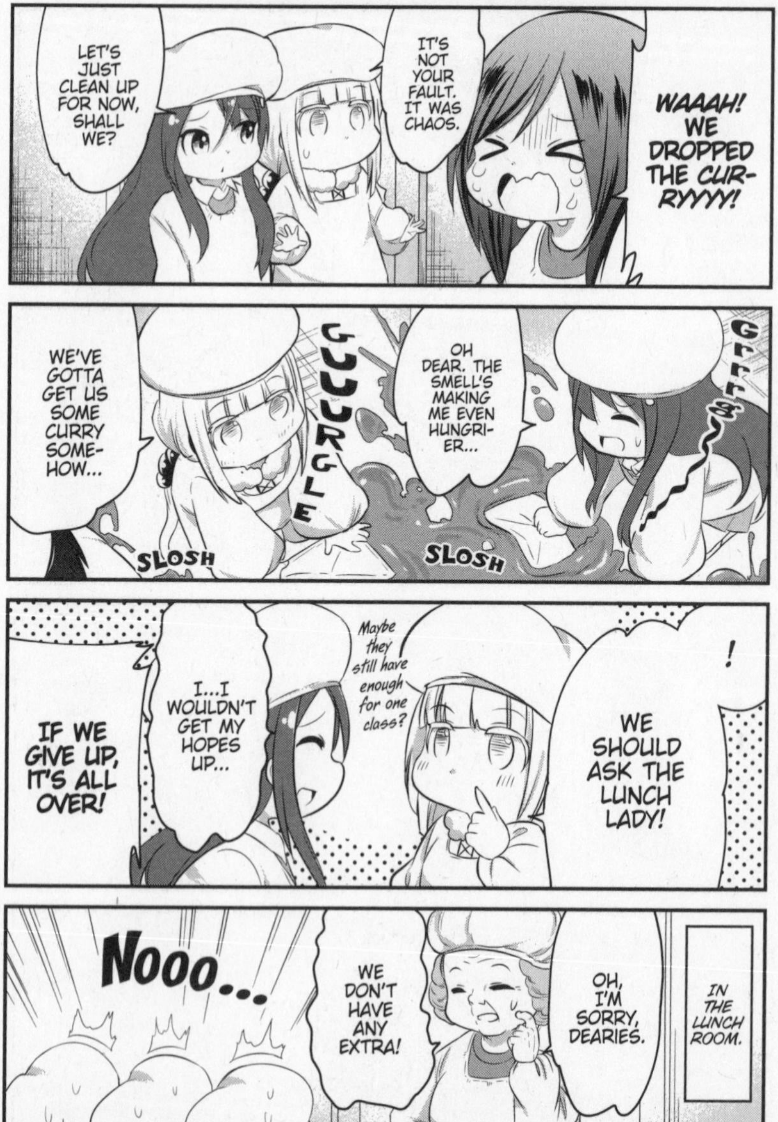

WAAAH! WE DROPPED THE CURRYYYY!
IT'S NOT YOUR FAULT. IT WAS CHAOS.
LET'S JUST CLEAN UP FOR NOW, SHALL WE?
OH DEAR. THE SMELL'S MAKING ME EVEN HUNGRIER...
GUUURGLE
WE'VE GOTTA GET US SOME CURRY SOMEHOW...
SLOSH
SLOSH
!
WE SHOULD ASK THE LUNCH LADY!
Maybe they still have enough for one class?
I...I WOULDN'T GET MY HOPES UP...
IF WE GIVE UP, IT'S ALL OVER!
IN THE LUNCH ROOM.
OH, I'M SORRY, DEARIES.
WE DON'T HAVE ANY EXTRA!
Nooo...

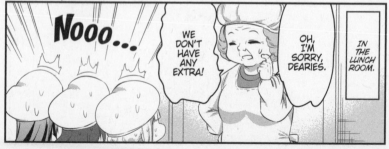

LIGHT BULB!

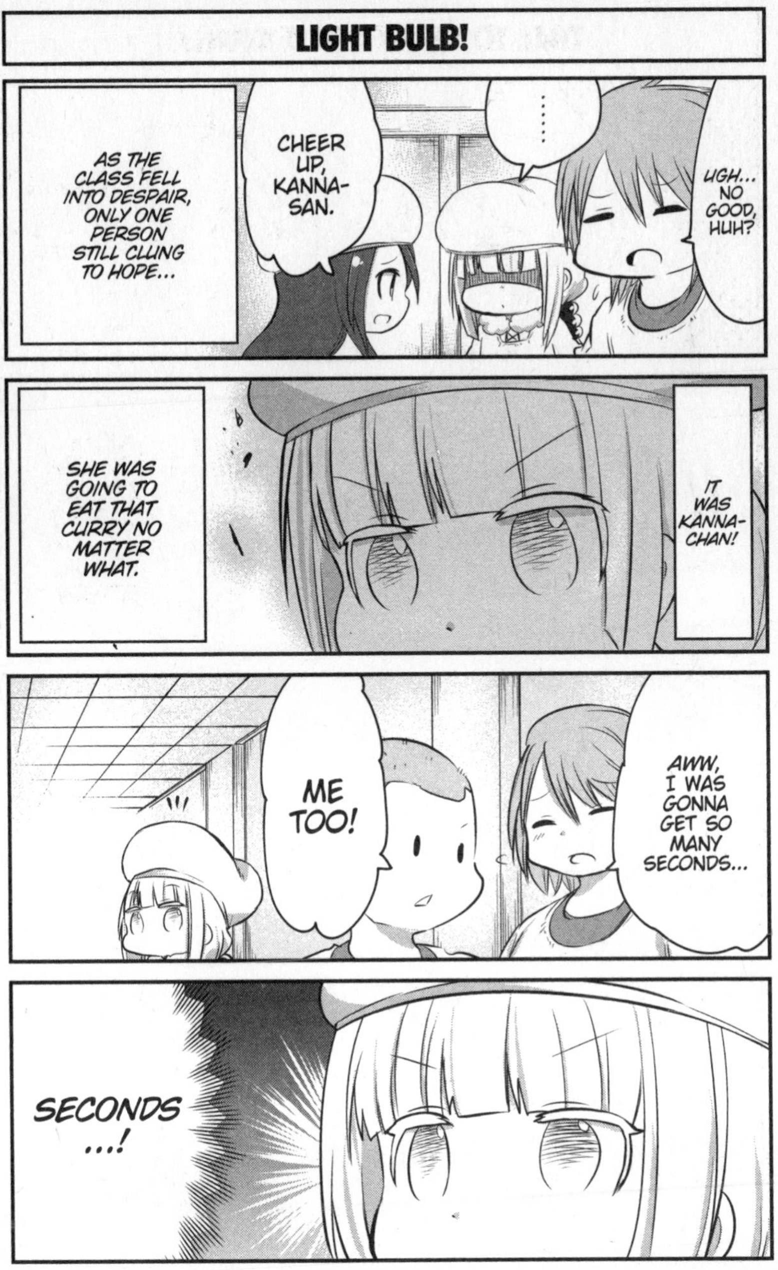
UGH... NO GOOD, HUH?
......
CHEER UP, KANNA-SAN.
AS THE CLASS FELL INTO DESPAIR, ONLY ONE PERSON STILL CLUNG TO HOPE...
IT WAS KANNA-CHAN!
SHE WAS GOING TO EAT THAT CURRY NO MATTER WHAT.
AWW, I WAS GONNA GET SO MANY SECONDS...
ME TOO!
SECONDS ...!

TIME TO SHARE SOME CURRY!

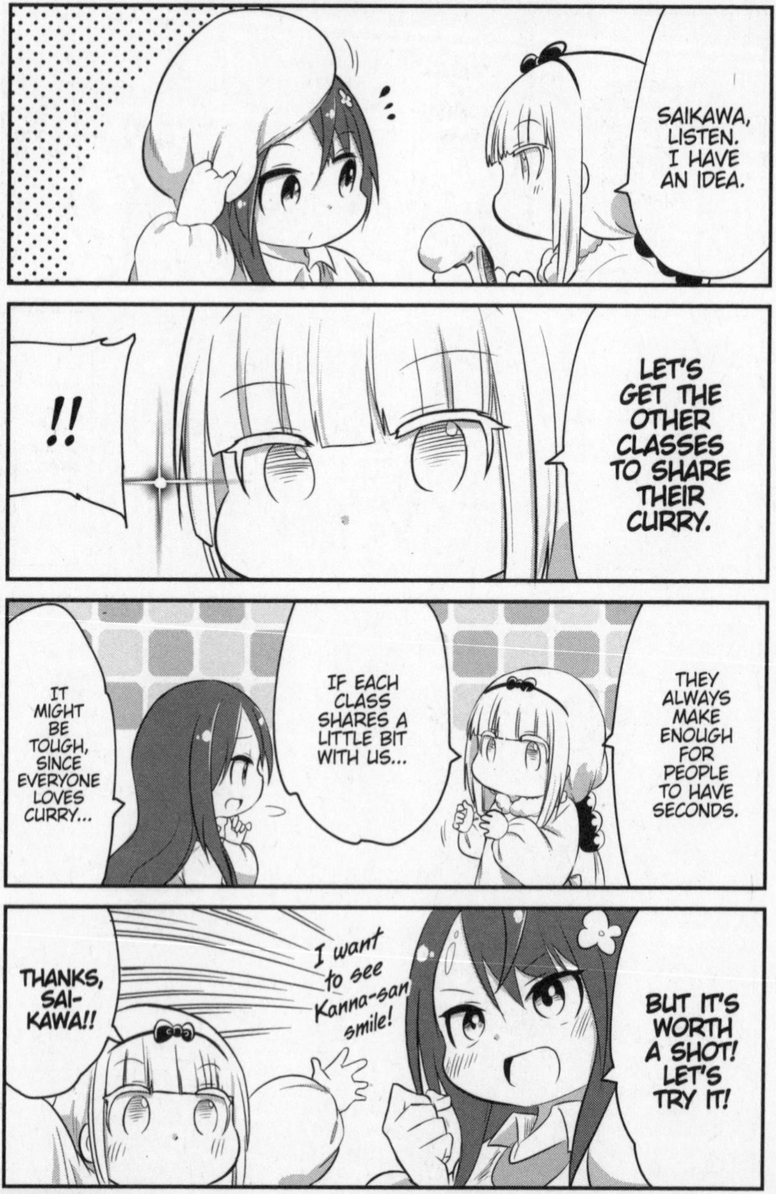
SAIKAWA, LISTEN. I HAVE AN IDEA.
LET'S GET THE OTHER CLASSES TO SHARE THEIR CURRY.
!!
THEY ALWAYS MAKE ENOUGH FOR PEOPLE TO HAVE SECONDS.
IF EACH CLASS SHARES A LITTLE BIT WITH US...
IT MIGHT BE TOUGH, SINCE EVERYONE LOVES CURRY...
BUT IT'S WORTH A SHOT! LET'S TRY IT!
I want to see Kanna-san smile!
THANKS, SAI-KAWA!!

A SAFE BET

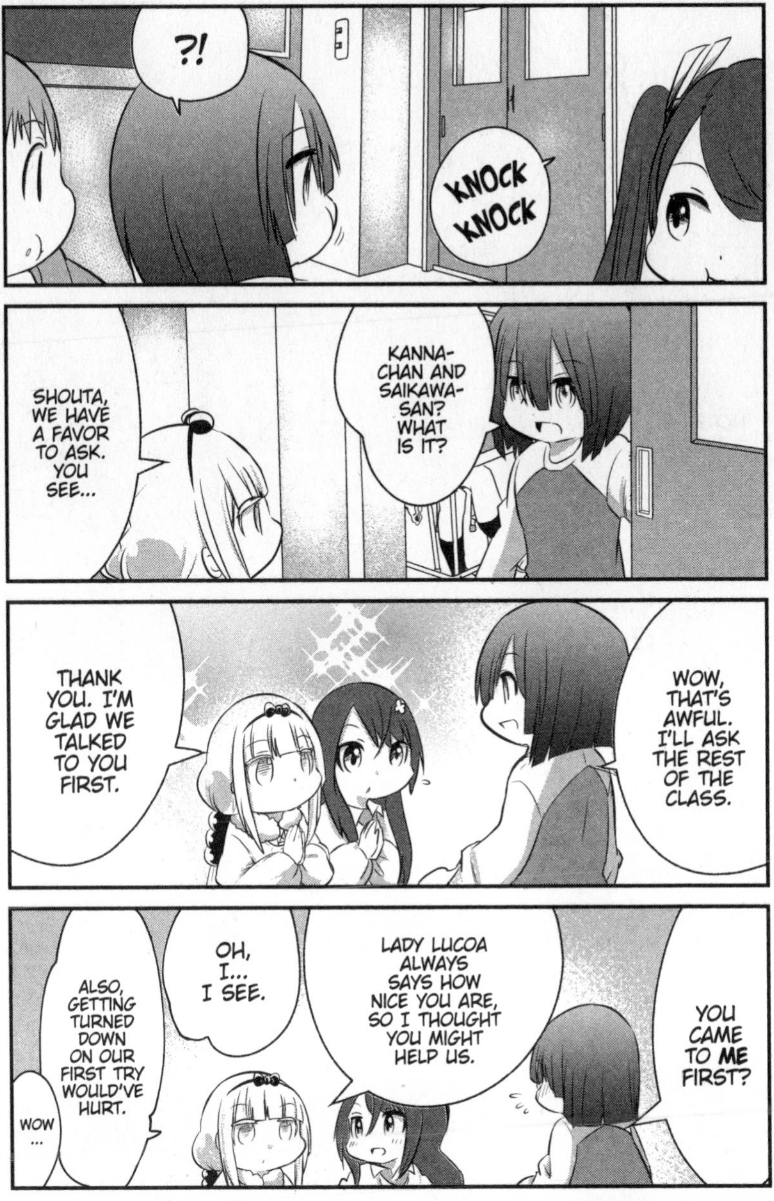
KNOCK KNOCK
?!
KANNA-CHAN AND SAIKAWA-SAN? WHAT IS IT?
SHOUTA, WE HAVE A FAVOR TO ASK. YOU SEE...
WOW, THAT'S AWFUL. I'LL ASK THE REST OF THE CLASS.
THANK YOU. I'M GLAD WE TALKED TO YOU FIRST.
YOU CAME TO **ME** FIRST?
LADY LUCOA ALWAYS SAYS HOW NICE YOU ARE, SO I THOUGHT YOU MIGHT HELP US.
OH, I... I SEE.
ALSO, GETTING TURNED DOWN ON OUR FIRST TRY WOULD'VE HURT.
WOW...

THE FRUITS OF EVERYONE'S KINDNESS...!

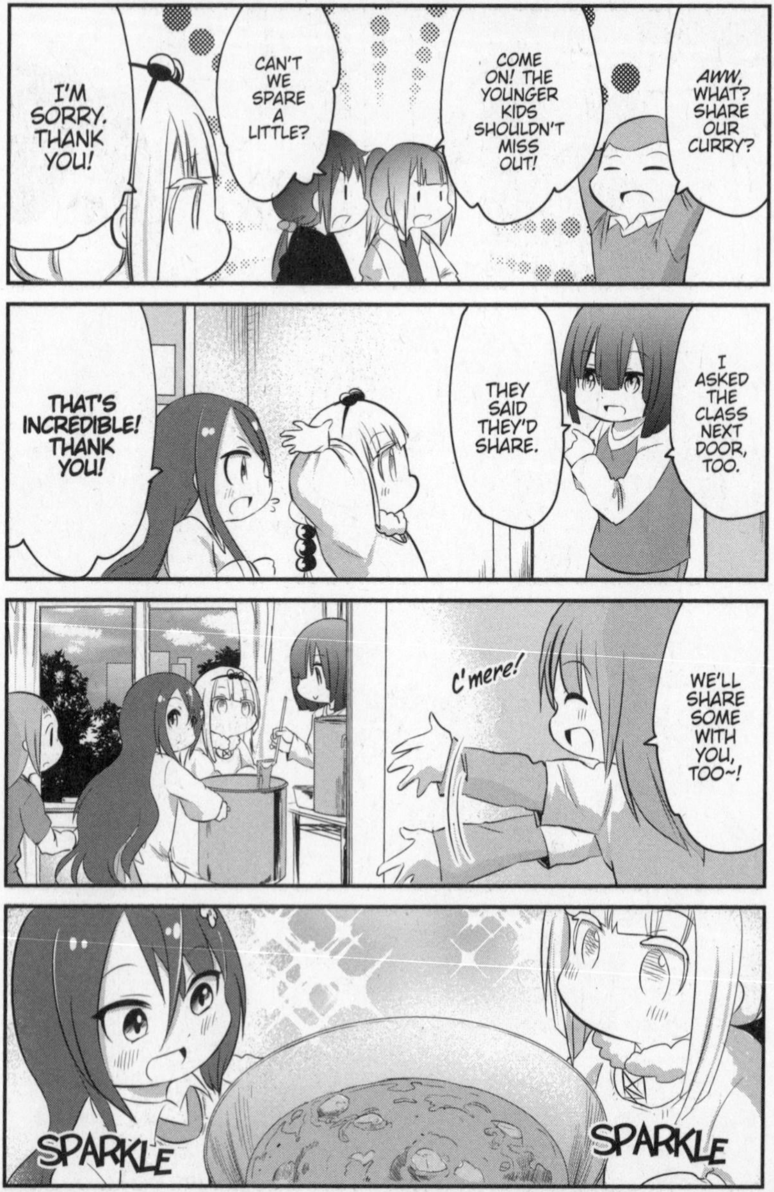
AWW, WHAT? SHARE OUR CURRY?
COME ON! THE YOUNGER KIDS SHOULDN'T MISS OUT!
CAN'T WE SPARE A LITTLE?
I'M SORRY. THANK YOU!
I ASKED THE CLASS NEXT DOOR, TOO.
THEY SAID THEY'D SHARE.
THAT'S INCREDIBLE! THANK YOU!
WE'LL SHARE SOME WITH YOU, TOO~!
C'mere!
SPARKLE
SPARKLE

QUIT WHILE YOU'RE AHEAD

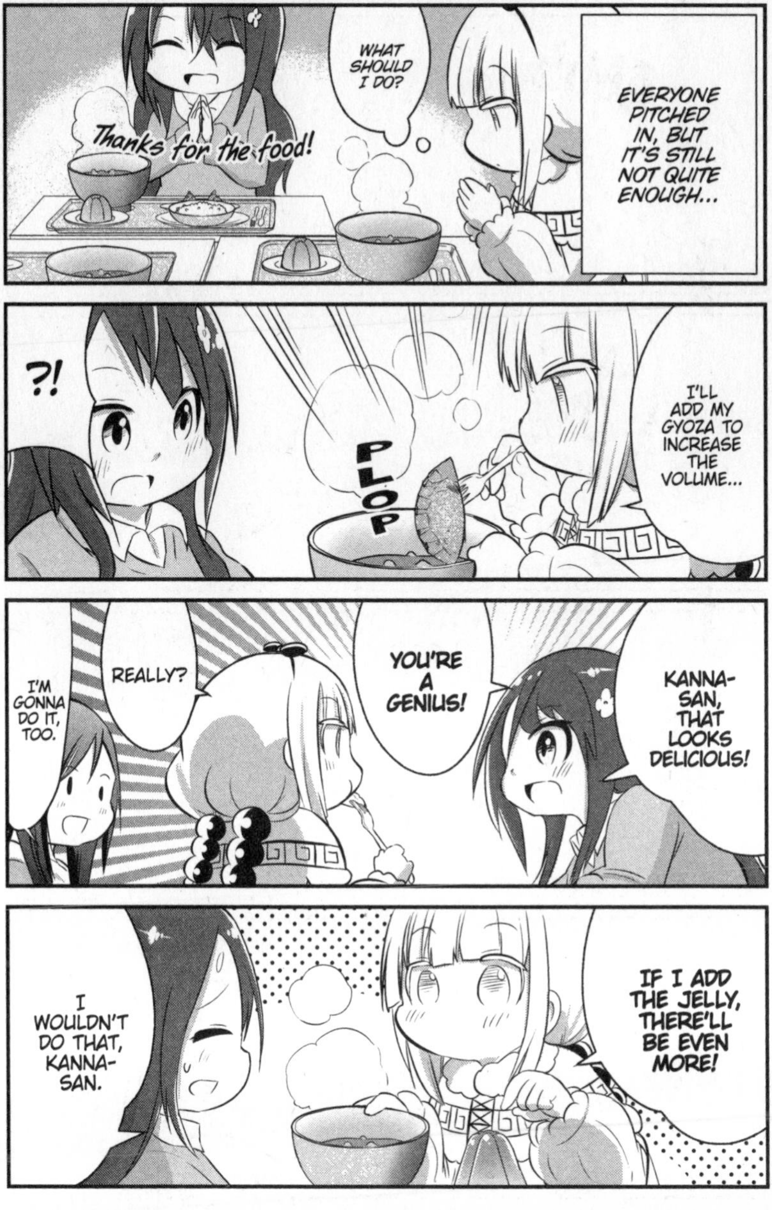
EVERYONE PITCHED IN, BUT IT'S STILL NOT QUITE ENOUGH...
WHAT SHOULD I DO?
Thanks for the food!
I'LL ADD MY GYOZA TO INCREASE THE VOLUME...
PLOP
?!
KANNA-SAN, THAT LOOKS DELICIOUS!
YOU'RE A GENIUS!
REALLY?
I'M GONNA DO IT, TOO.
IF I ADD THE JELLY, THERE'LL BE EVEN MORE!
I WOULDN'T DO THAT, KANNA-SAN.

FULL OF HAPPINESS

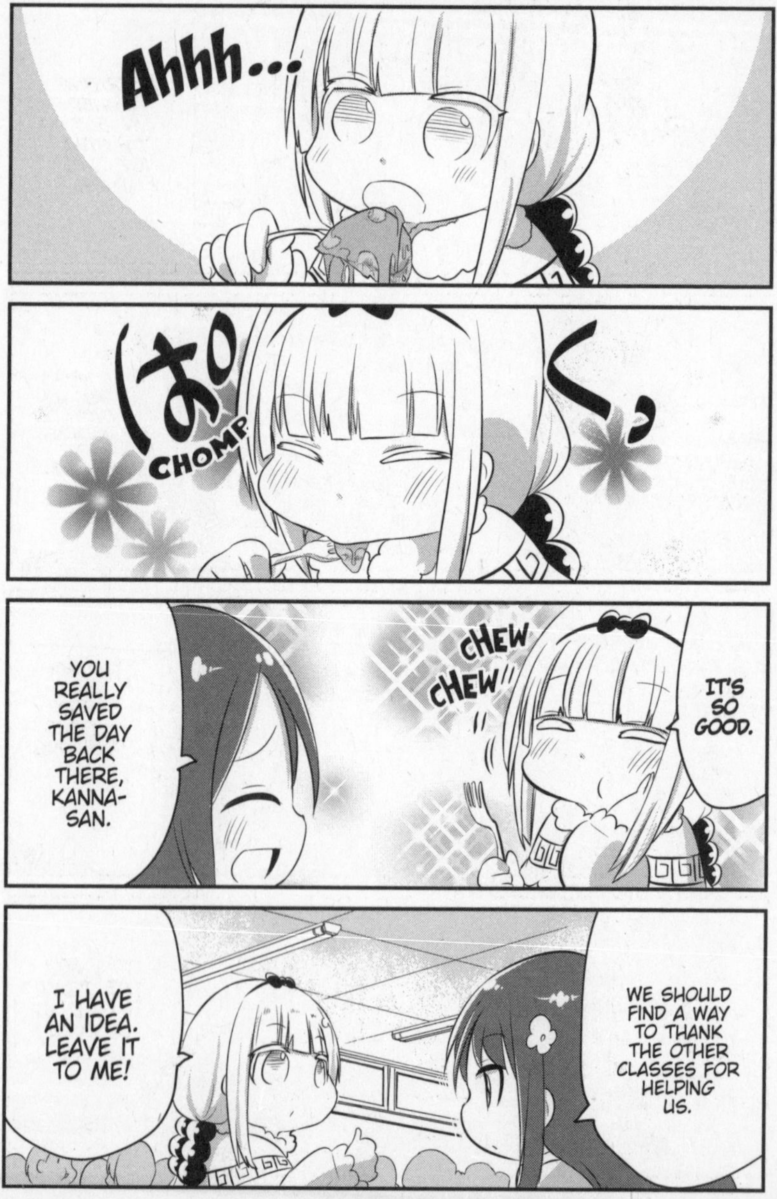
Ahhh...
CHOMP
IT'S SO GOOD.
CHEW CHEW
YOU REALLY SAVED THE DAY BACK THERE, KANNA-SAN.
WE SHOULD FIND A WAY TO THANK THE OTHER CLASSES FOR HELPING US.
I HAVE AN IDEA. LEAVE IT TO ME!

PLEASE ACCEPT OUR THANKS

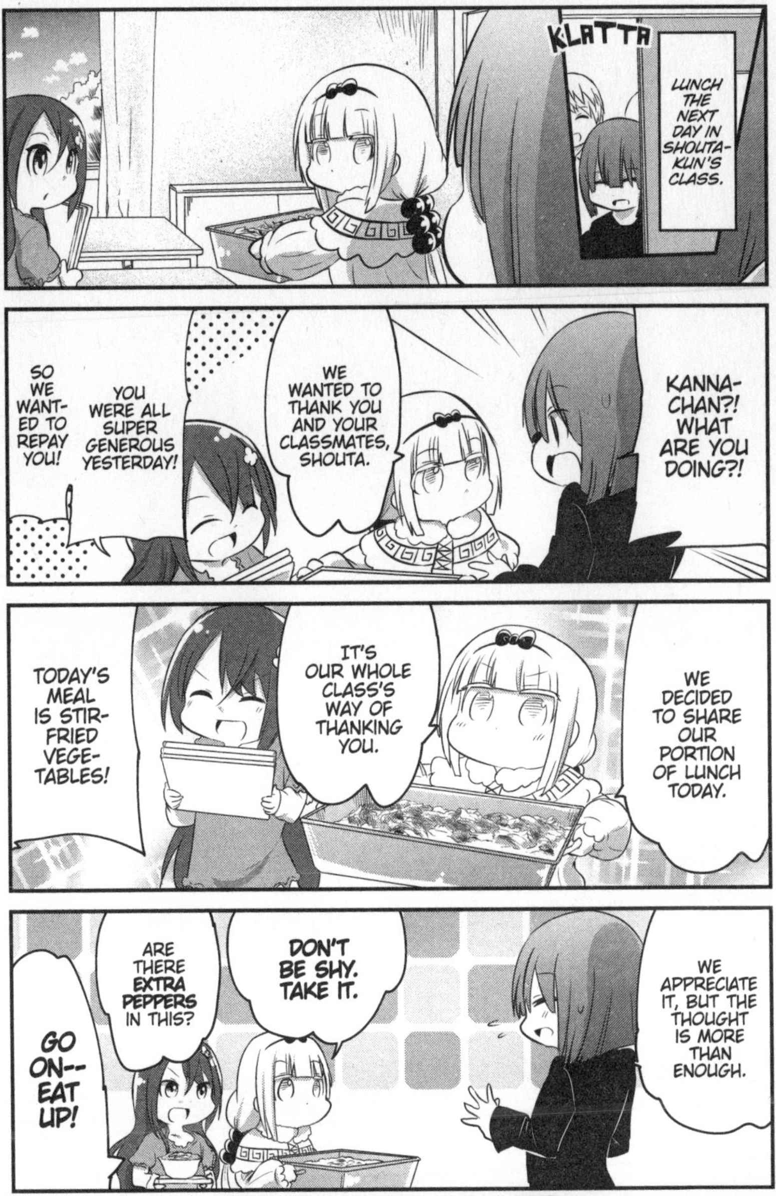
KLATTA
LUNCH THE NEXT DAY IN SHOUTA-KUN'S CLASS.
KANNA-CHAN?! WHAT ARE YOU DOING?!
WE WANTED TO THANK YOU AND YOUR CLASSMATES, SHOUTA.
YOU WERE ALL SUPER GENEROUS YESTERDAY!
SO WE WANTED TO REPAY YOU!
WE DECIDED TO SHARE OUR PORTION OF LUNCH TODAY.
IT'S OUR WHOLE CLASS'S WAY OF THANKING YOU.
TODAY'S MEAL IS STIR-FRIED VEGETABLES!
WE APPRECIATE IT, BUT THE THOUGHT IS MORE THAN ENOUGH.
DON'T BE SHY. TAKE IT.
ARE THERE EXTRA PEPPERS IN THIS?
GO ON--EAT UP!

TIME FOR SCHOOL LUNCH/END

Miss Kobayashi's Dragon Maid
Kanna's Daily Life

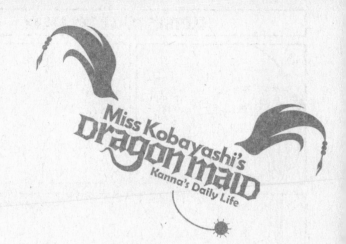

CLOTHES MAKE THE MAID!

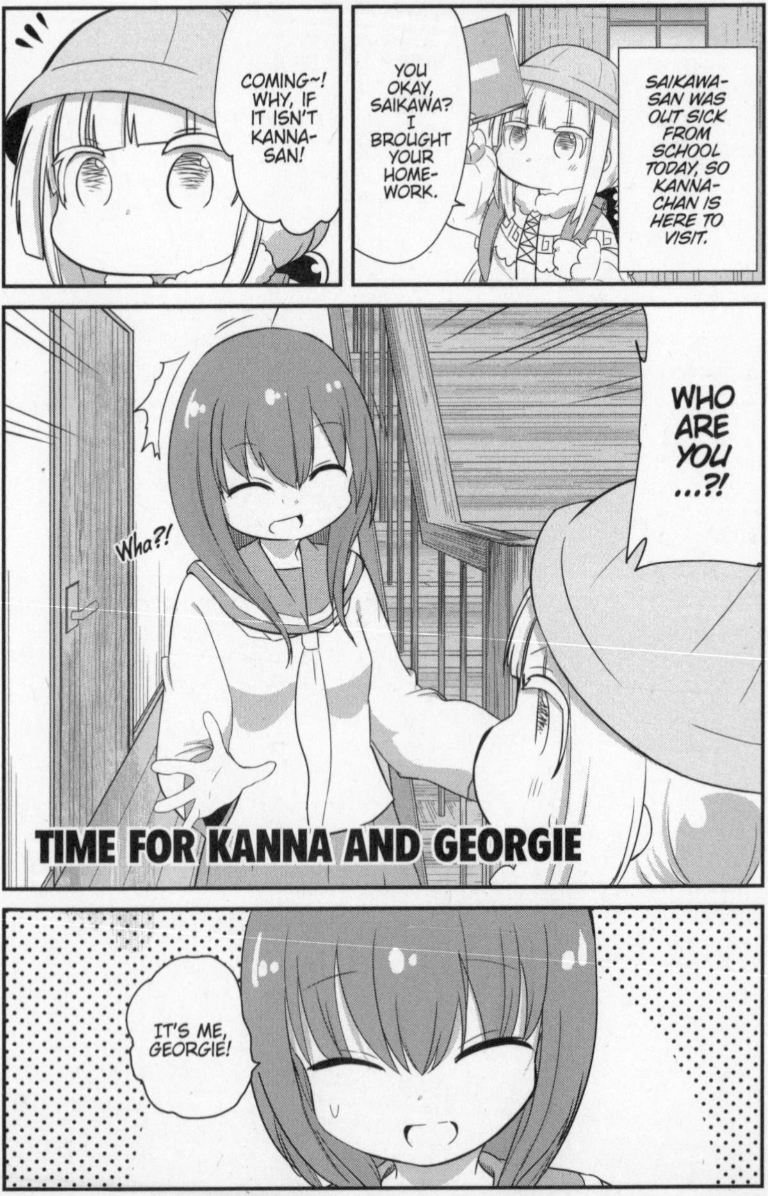
SAIKAWA-SAN WAS OUT SICK FROM SCHOOL TODAY, SO KANNA-CHAN IS HERE TO VISIT.
YOU OKAY, SAIKAWA? I BROUGHT YOUR HOMEWORK.
COMING~! WHY, IF IT ISN'T KANNA-SAN!
WHO ARE YOU ...?!
Wha?!
TIME FOR KANNA AND GEORGIE
IT'S ME, GEORGIE!

NOT USED TO IT

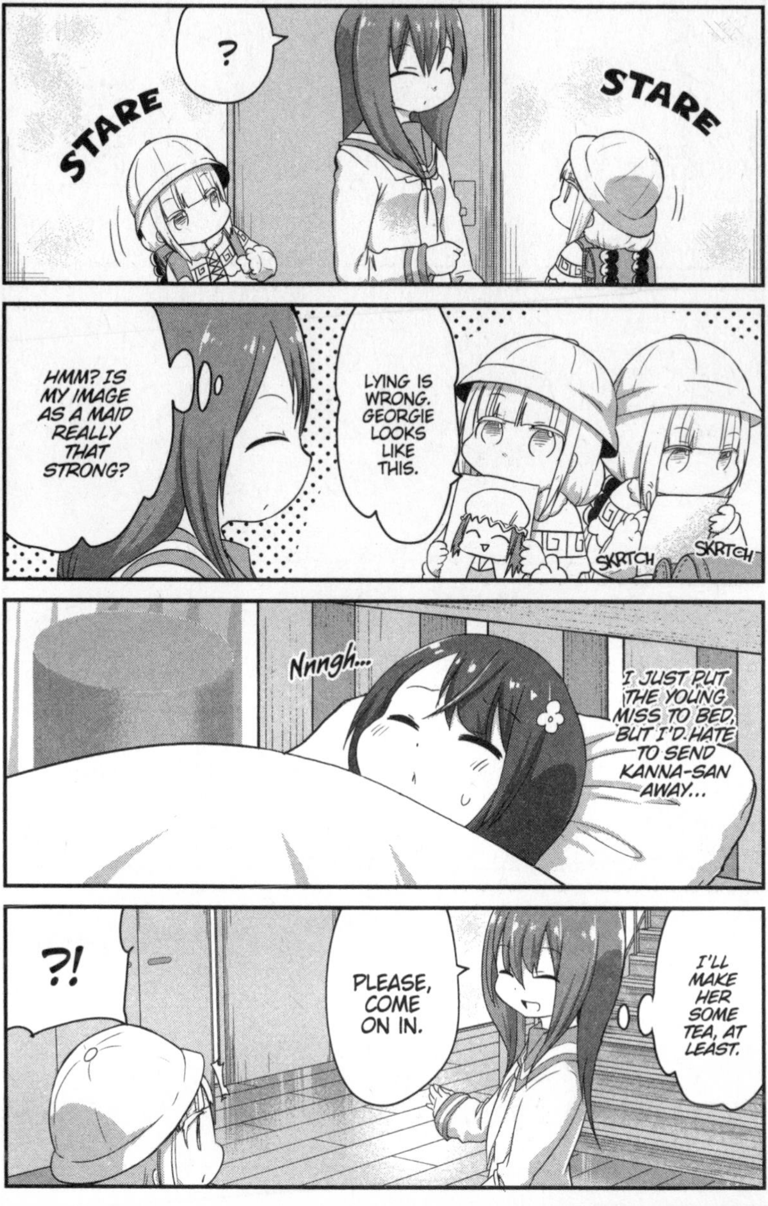
STARE
?
STARE
SKRTCH
SKRTCH
LYING IS WRONG. GEORGIE LOOKS LIKE THIS.
HMM? IS MY IMAGE AS A MAID REALLY THAT STRONG?
I JUST PUT THE YOUNG MISS TO BED, BUT I'D HATE TO SEND KANNA-SAN AWAY...
Nnngh...
I'LL MAKE HER SOME TEA, AT LEAST.
PLEASE, COME ON IN.
?!

INTRUDER!

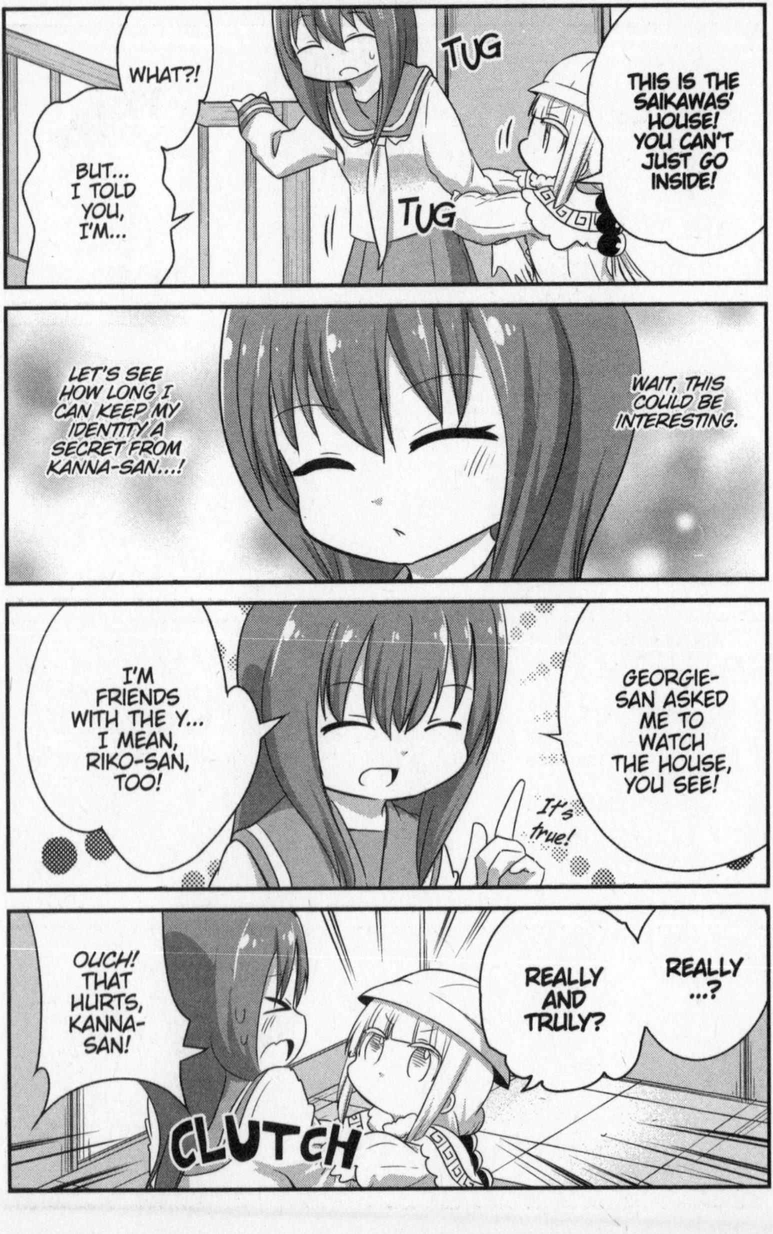
THIS IS THE SAIKAWAS' HOUSE! YOU CAN'T JUST GO INSIDE!
TUG
TUG
WHAT?!
BUT... I TOLD YOU, I'M...
WAIT, THIS COULD BE INTERESTING.
LET'S SEE HOW LONG I CAN KEEP MY IDENTITY A SECRET FROM KANNA-SAN...!
GEORGIE-SAN ASKED ME TO WATCH THE HOUSE, YOU SEE!
It's true!
I'M FRIENDS WITH THE Y... I MEAN, RIKO-SAN, TOO!
REALLY ...?
REALLY AND TRULY?
OUCH! THAT HURTS, KANNA-SAN!
CLUTCH

THE NOSE KNOWS

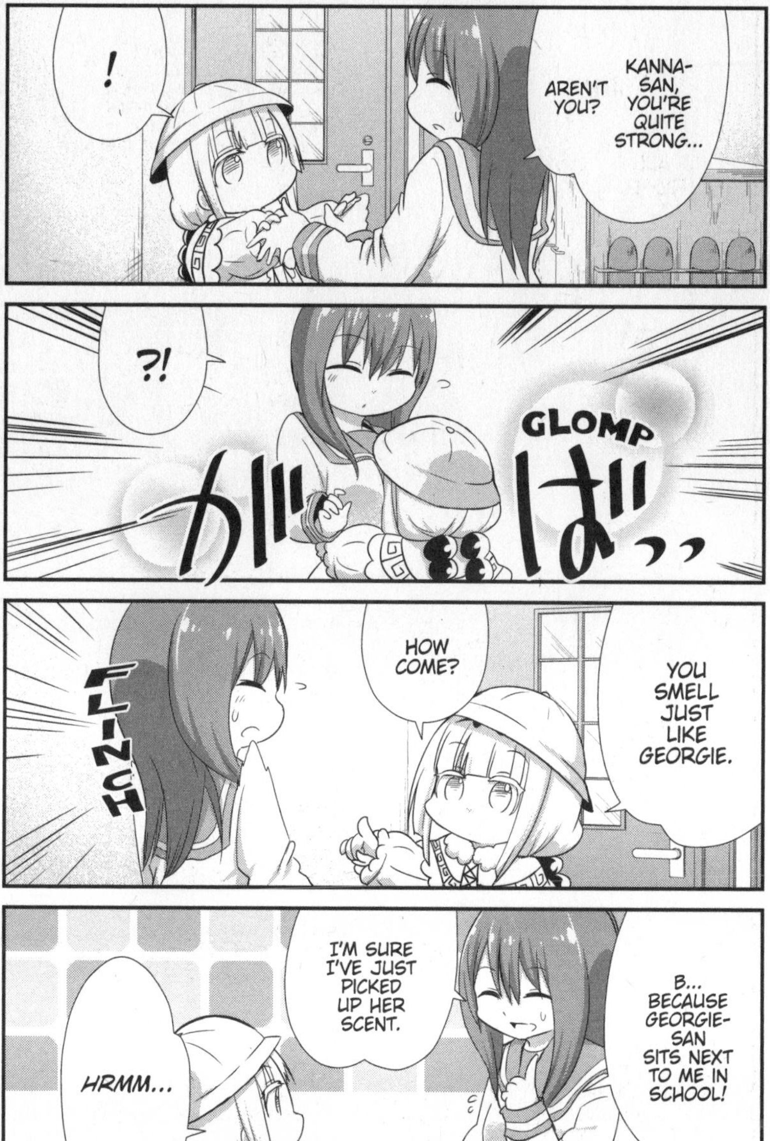

KANNA-SAN, YOU'RE QUITE STRONG...
AREN'T YOU?
!
GLOMP
がばっ
?!
YOU SMELL JUST LIKE GEORGIE.
HOW COME?
FLINCH
B... BECAUSE GEORGIE-SAN SITS NEXT TO ME IN SCHOOL!
I'M SURE I'VE JUST PICKED UP HER SCENT.
HRMM...

FRIEND OF THE FAMILY

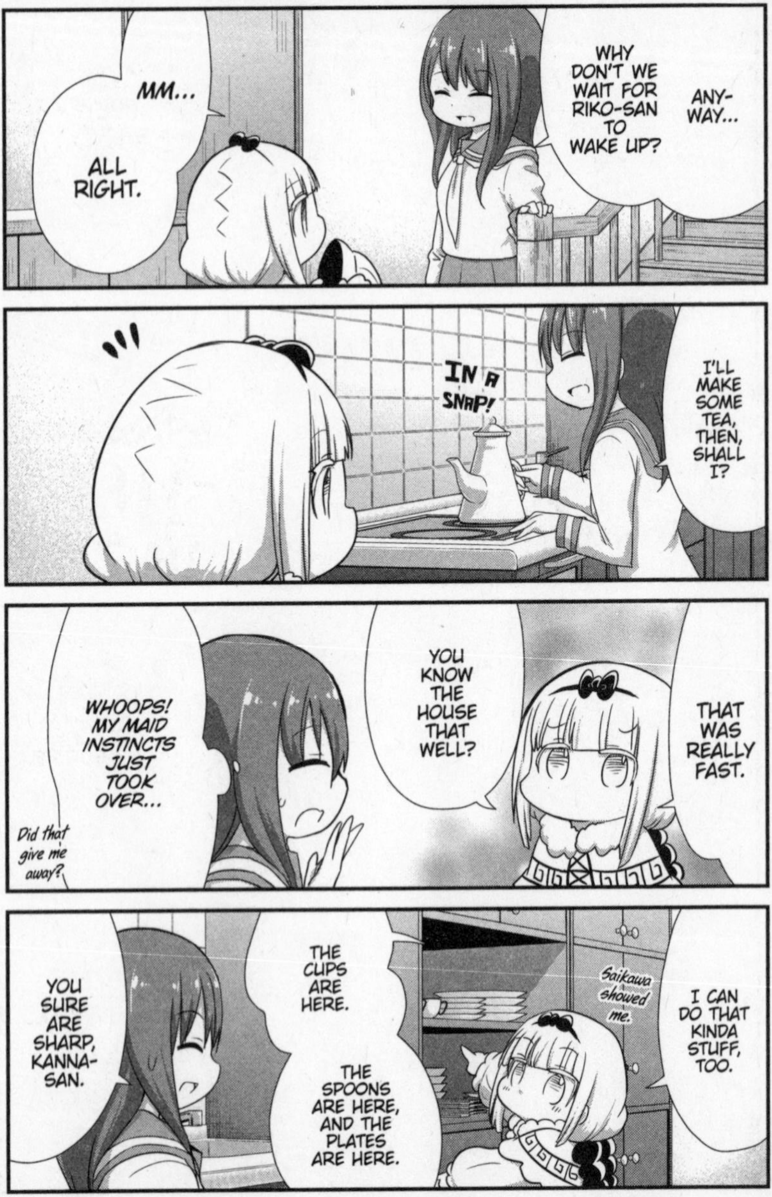
ANY-WAY...
WHY DON'T WE WAIT FOR RIKO-SAN TO WAKE UP?
MM... ALL RIGHT.
I'LL MAKE SOME TEA, THEN, SHALL I?
IN A SNAP!
THAT WAS REALLY FAST.
YOU KNOW THE HOUSE THAT WELL?
WHOOPS! MY MAID INSTINCTS JUST TOOK OVER...
Did that give me away?
I CAN DO THAT KINDA STUFF, TOO.
Saikawa showed me.
THE CUPS ARE HERE.
THE SPOONS ARE HERE, AND THE PLATES ARE HERE.
YOU SURE ARE SHARP, KANNA-SAN.

CURIOUS BIG SISTER

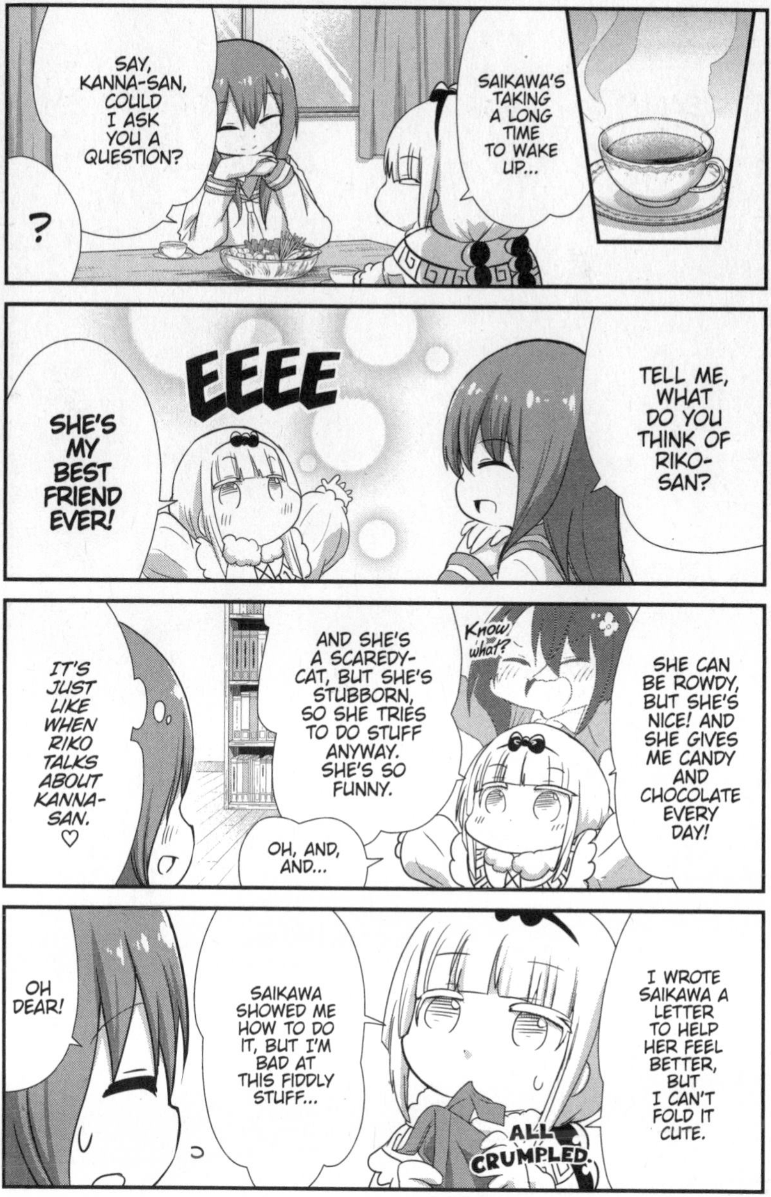
SAIKAWA'S TAKING A LONG TIME TO WAKE UP...
SAY, KANNA-SAN, COULD I ASK YOU A QUESTION?
?
TELL ME, WHAT DO YOU THINK OF RIKO-SAN?
EEEE
SHE'S MY BEST FRIEND EVER!
SHE CAN BE ROWDY, BUT SHE'S NICE! AND SHE GIVES ME CANDY AND CHOCOLATE EVERY DAY!
Know what?
AND SHE'S A SCAREDY-CAT, BUT SHE'S STUBBORN, SO SHE TRIES TO DO STUFF ANYWAY. SHE'S SO FUNNY.
OH, AND, AND...
IT'S JUST LIKE WHEN RIKO TALKS ABOUT KANNA-SAN. ♡
I WROTE SAIKAWA A LETTER TO HELP HER FEEL BETTER, BUT I CAN'T FOLD IT CUTE.
ALL CRUMPLED.
SAIKAWA SHOWED ME HOW TO DO IT, BUT I'M BAD AT THIS FIDDLY STUFF...
OH DEAR!

A NATURAL CHARMER!

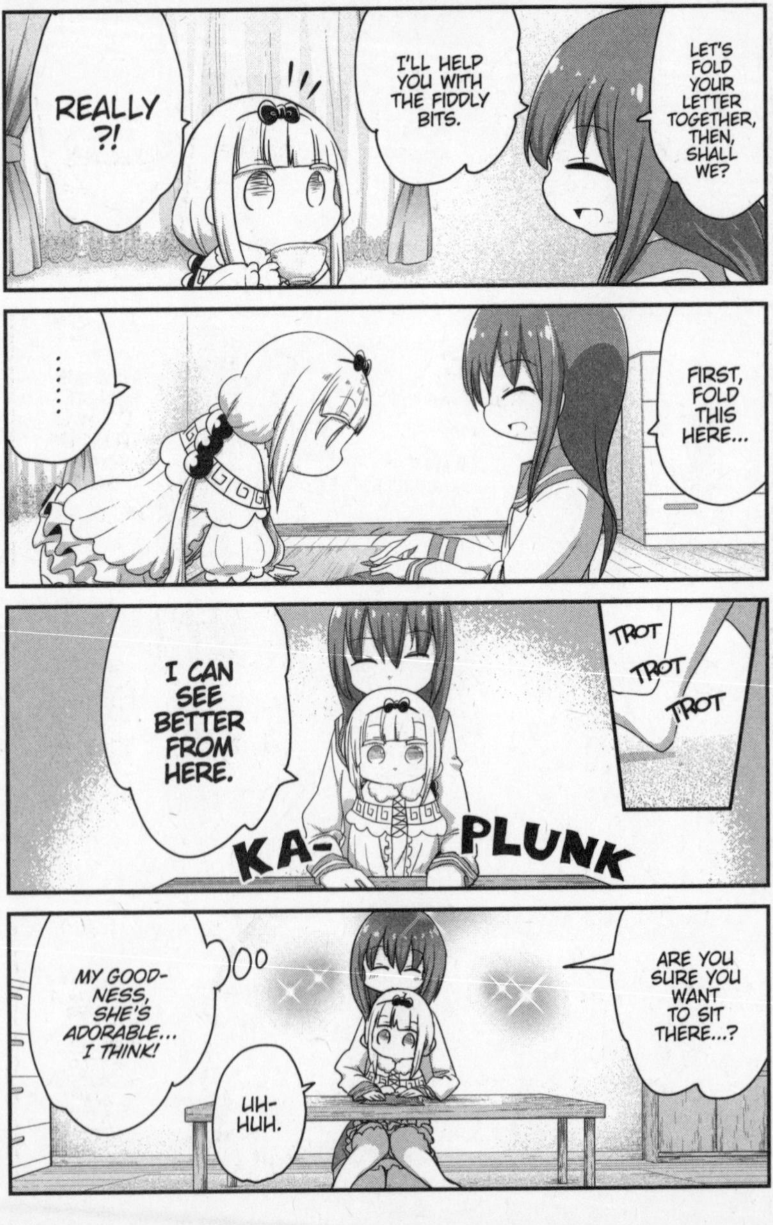
LET'S FOLD YOUR LETTER TOGETHER, THEN, SHALL WE?
I'LL HELP YOU WITH THE FIDDLY BITS.
REALLY ?!
FIRST, FOLD THIS HERE...
......
TROT TROT TROT
I CAN SEE BETTER FROM HERE.
KA-PLUNK
ARE YOU SURE YOU WANT TO SIT THERE...?
UH-HUH.
MY GOODNESS, SHE'S ADORABLE... I THINK!

WHO'S THE REAL DRAGON?

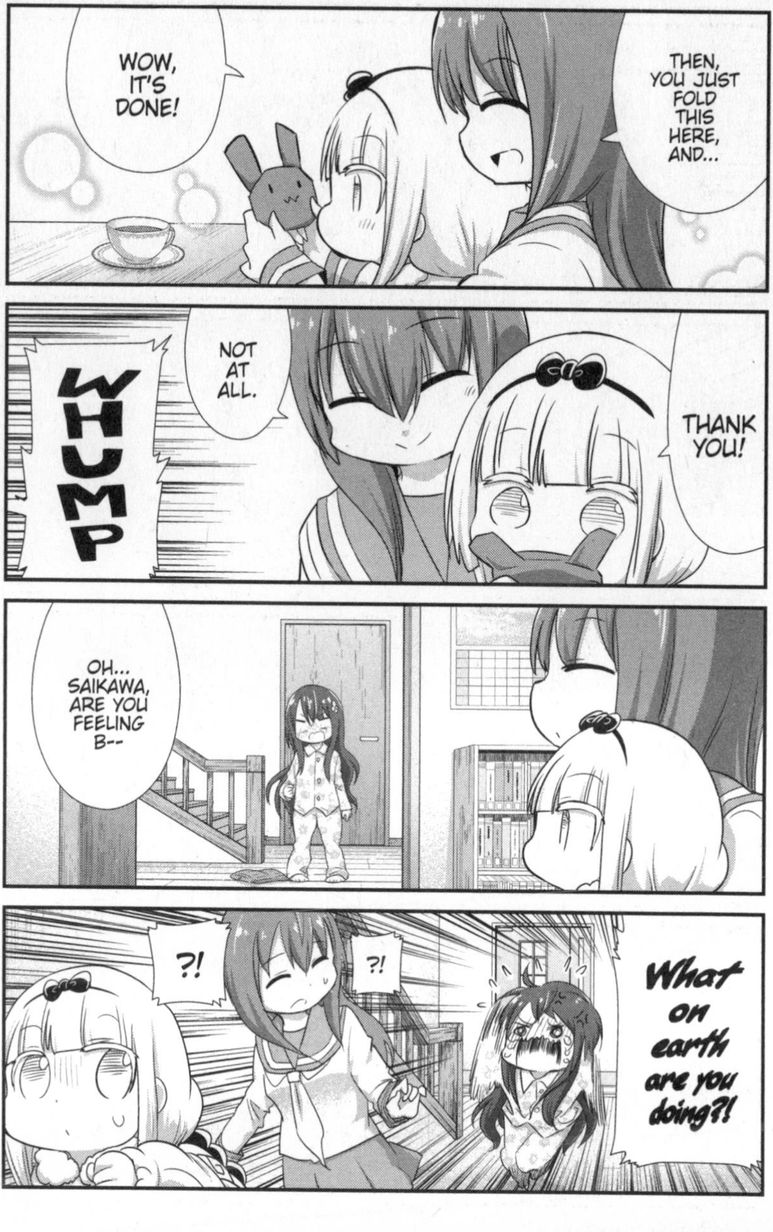
THEN, YOU JUST FOLD THIS HERE, AND...
WOW, IT'S DONE!
THANK YOU!
NOT AT ALL.
WHUMP
OH... SAIKAWA, ARE YOU FEELING B--
What on earth are you doing?!
?!
?!

SAIKAWA-SAN ON A RAMPAGE

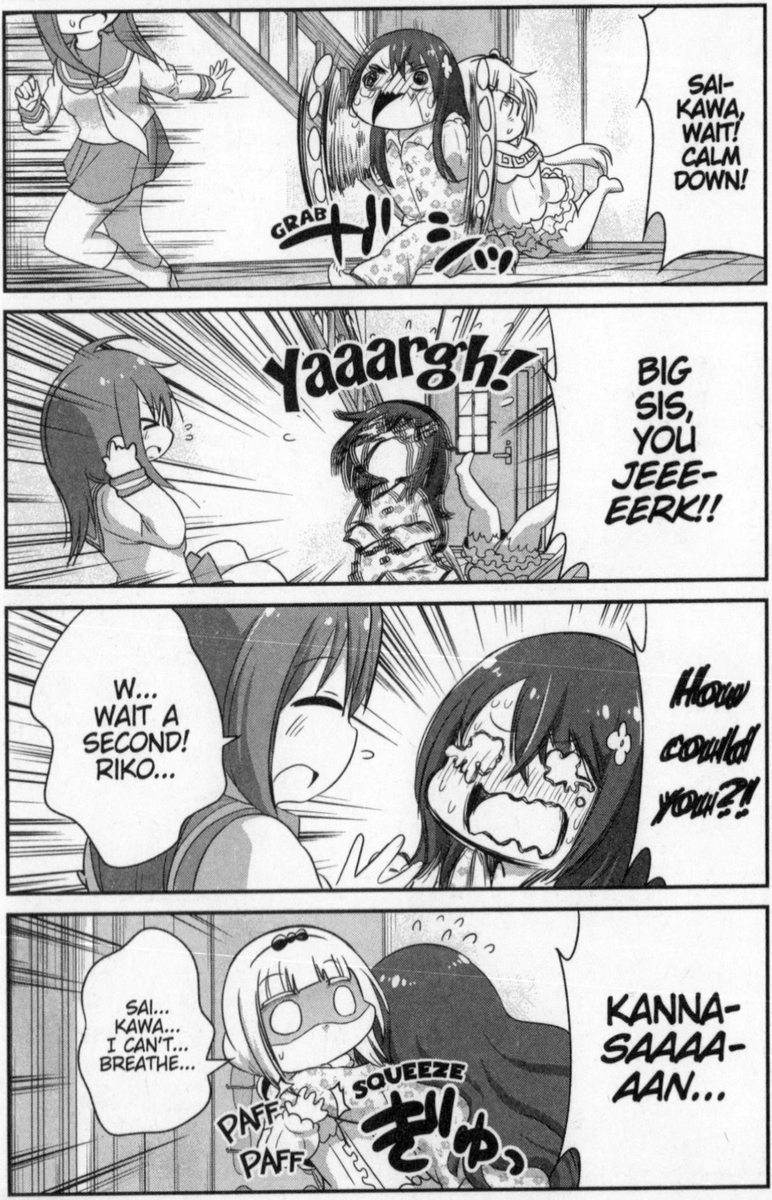
SAI-KAWA, WAIT! CALM DOWN!
GRAB
BIG SIS, YOU JEEE-EERK!!
Yaaargh!
How could you?!!
W... WAIT A SECOND! RIKO...
KANNA-SAAAAA-AAN...
SQUEEZE
SAI... KAWA... I CAN'T... BREATHE...
PAFF
PAFF

PRIORITIES

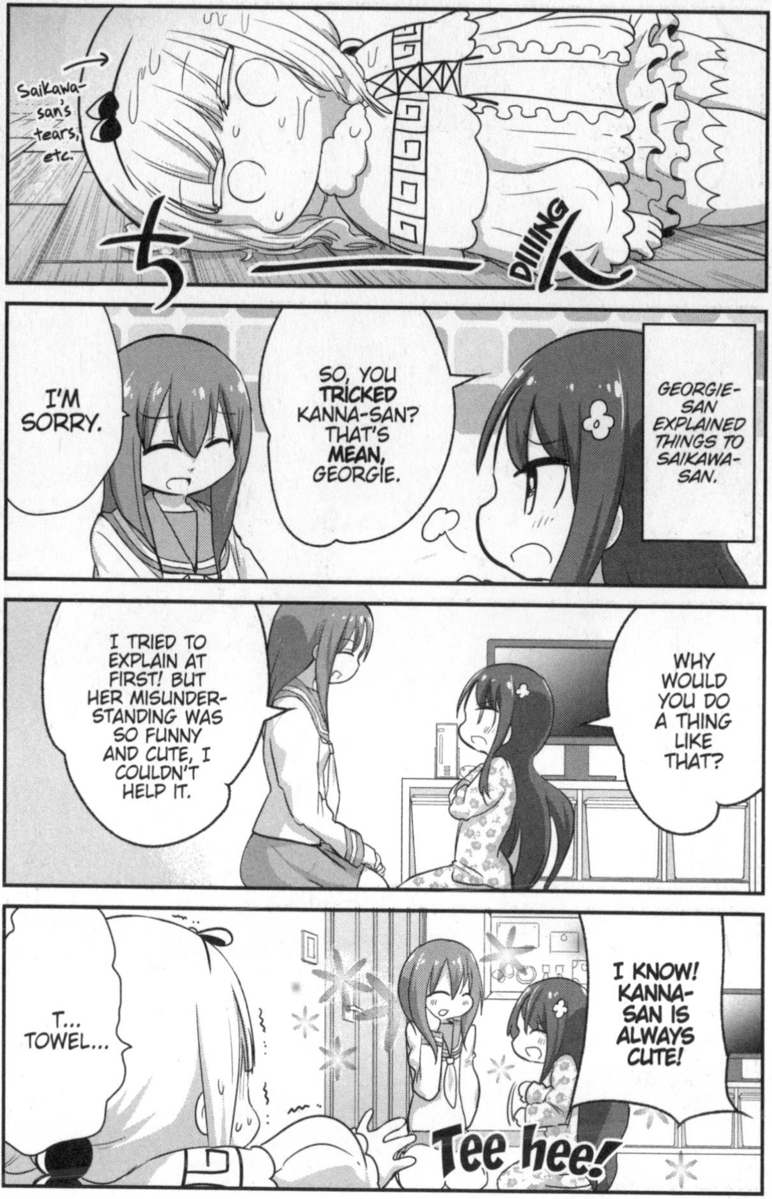
Saikawa-san's tears, etc.
DIIIING
GEORGIE-SAN EXPLAINED THINGS TO SAIKAWA-SAN.
SO, YOU TRICKED KANNA-SAN? THAT'S MEAN, GEORGIE.
I'M SORRY.
WHY WOULD YOU DO A THING LIKE THAT?
I TRIED TO EXPLAIN AT FIRST! BUT HER MISUNDER-STANDING WAS SO FUNNY AND CUTE, I COULDN'T HELP IT.
I KNOW! KANNA-SAN IS ALWAYS CUTE!
Tee hee!
T... TOWEL...

INSTANT FORGIVENESS

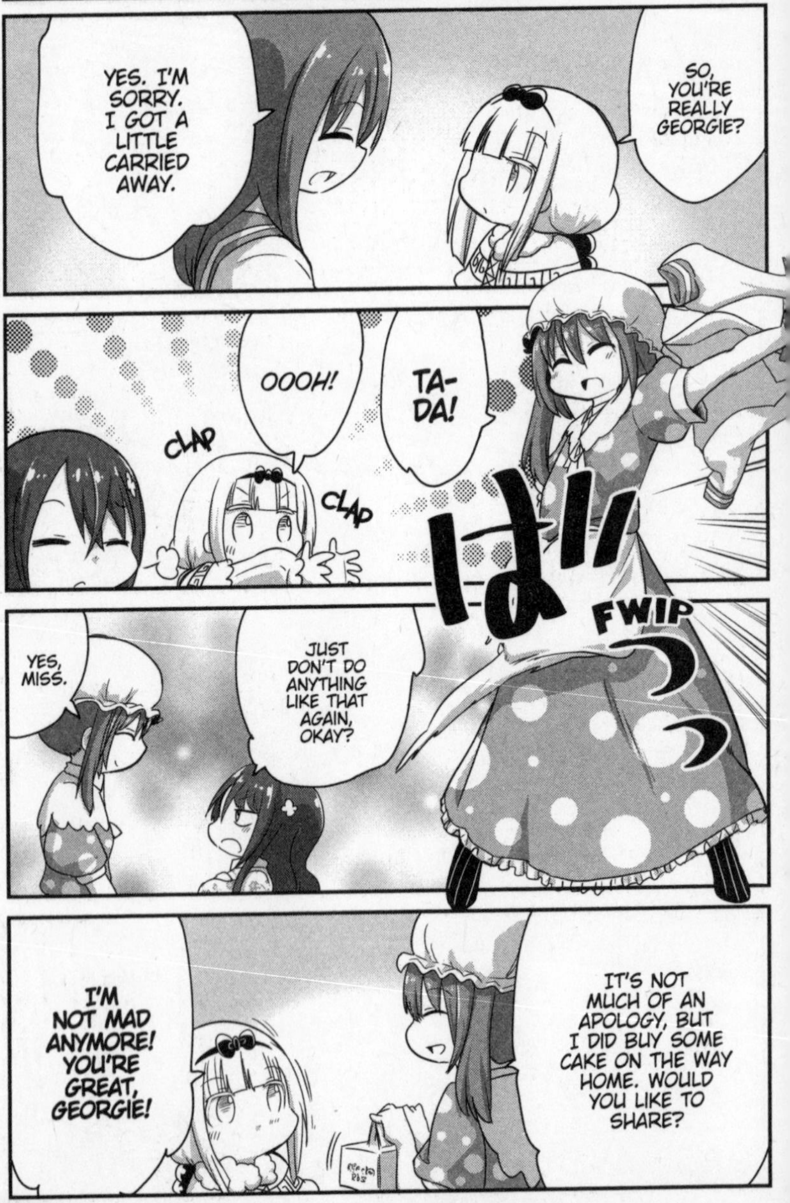

SO, YOU'RE REALLY GEORGIE?
YES. I'M SORRY. I GOT A LITTLE CARRIED AWAY.
TA-DA!
OOOH!
CLAP
CLAP
FWIP
JUST DON'T DO ANYTHING LIKE THAT AGAIN, OKAY?
YES, MISS.
IT'S NOT MUCH OF AN APOLOGY, BUT I DID BUY SOME CAKE ON THE WAY HOME. WOULD YOU LIKE TO SHARE?
I'M NOT MAD ANYMORE! YOU'RE GREAT, GEORGIE!

GEORGIE'S HAPPY, TOO

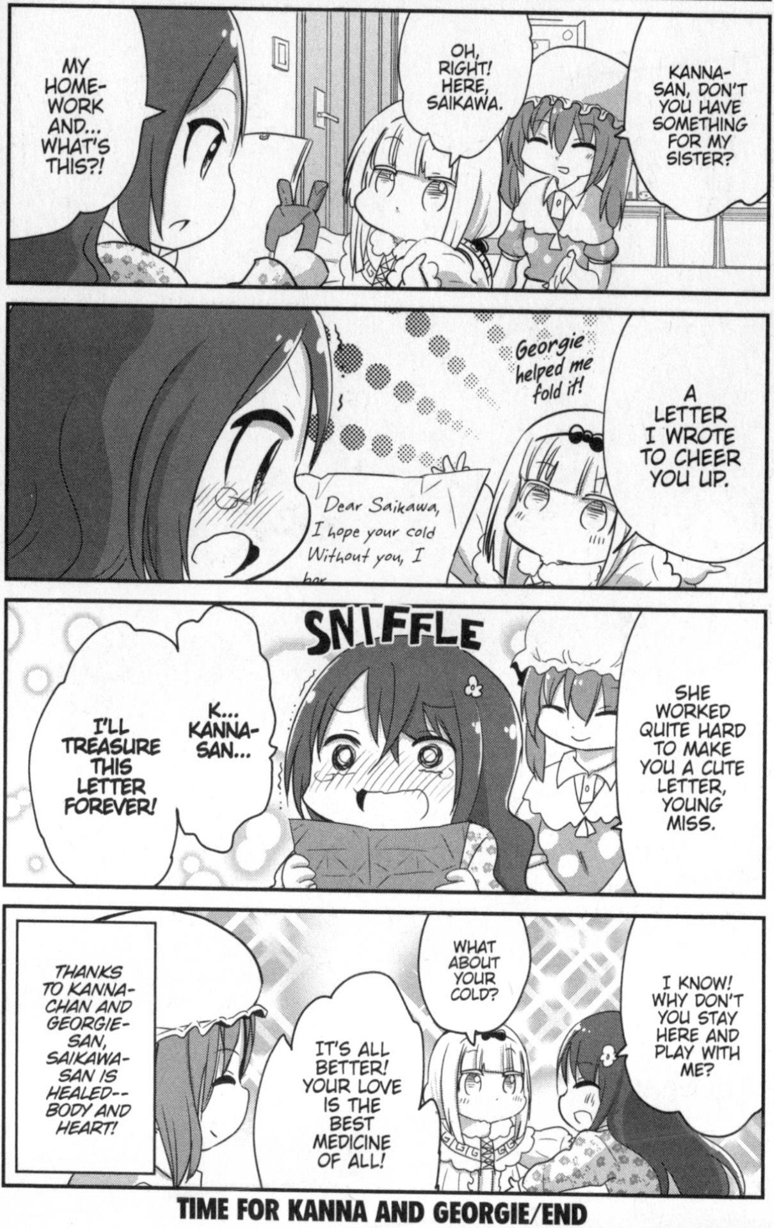
KANNA-SAN, DON'T YOU HAVE SOMETHING FOR MY SISTER?
OH, RIGHT! HERE, SAIKAWA.
MY HOMEWORK AND... WHAT'S THIS?!
A LETTER I WROTE TO CHEER YOU UP.
Georgie helped me fold it!
Dear Saikawa, I hope your cold Without you, I
SHE WORKED QUITE HARD TO MAKE YOU A CUTE LETTER, YOUNG MISS.
SNIFFLE
K... KANNA-SAN...
I'LL TREASURE THIS LETTER FOREVER!
I KNOW! WHY DON'T YOU STAY HERE AND PLAY WITH ME?
WHAT ABOUT YOUR COLD?
IT'S ALL BETTER! YOUR LOVE IS THE BEST MEDICINE OF ALL!
THANKS TO KANNA-CHAN AND GEORGIE-SAN, SAIKAWA-SAN IS HEALED--BODY AND HEART!

TIME FOR KANNA AND GEORGIE/END

BRINGS BACK (BAD) MEMORIES

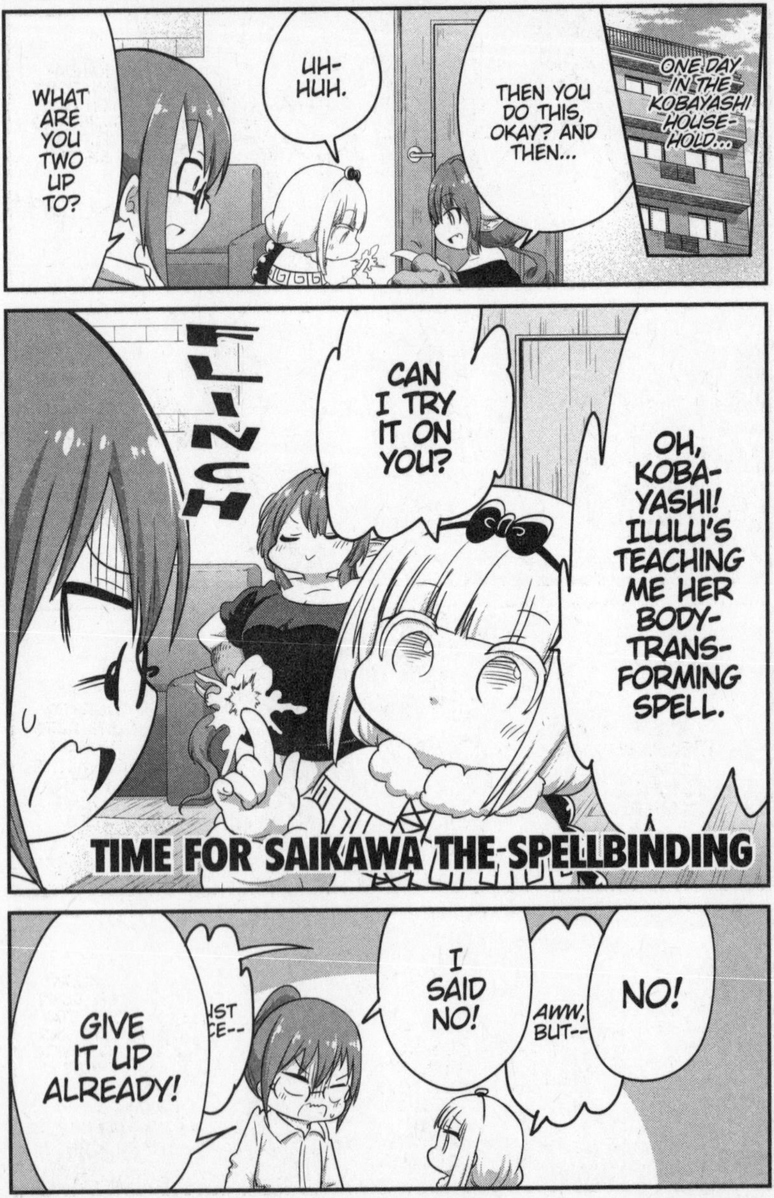
ONE DAY IN THE KOBAYASHI HOUSEHOLD...
THEN YOU DO THIS, OKAY? AND THEN...
UH-HUH.
WHAT ARE YOU TWO UP TO?
OH, KOBAYASHI! ILULU'S TEACHING ME HER BODY-TRANSFORMING SPELL.
CAN I TRY IT ON YOU?
FLINCH
TIME FOR SAIKAWA THE SPELLBINDING
NO!
AWW, BUT--
I SAID NO!
UST CE--
GIVE IT UP ALREADY!

OOPSIE-DAISY!

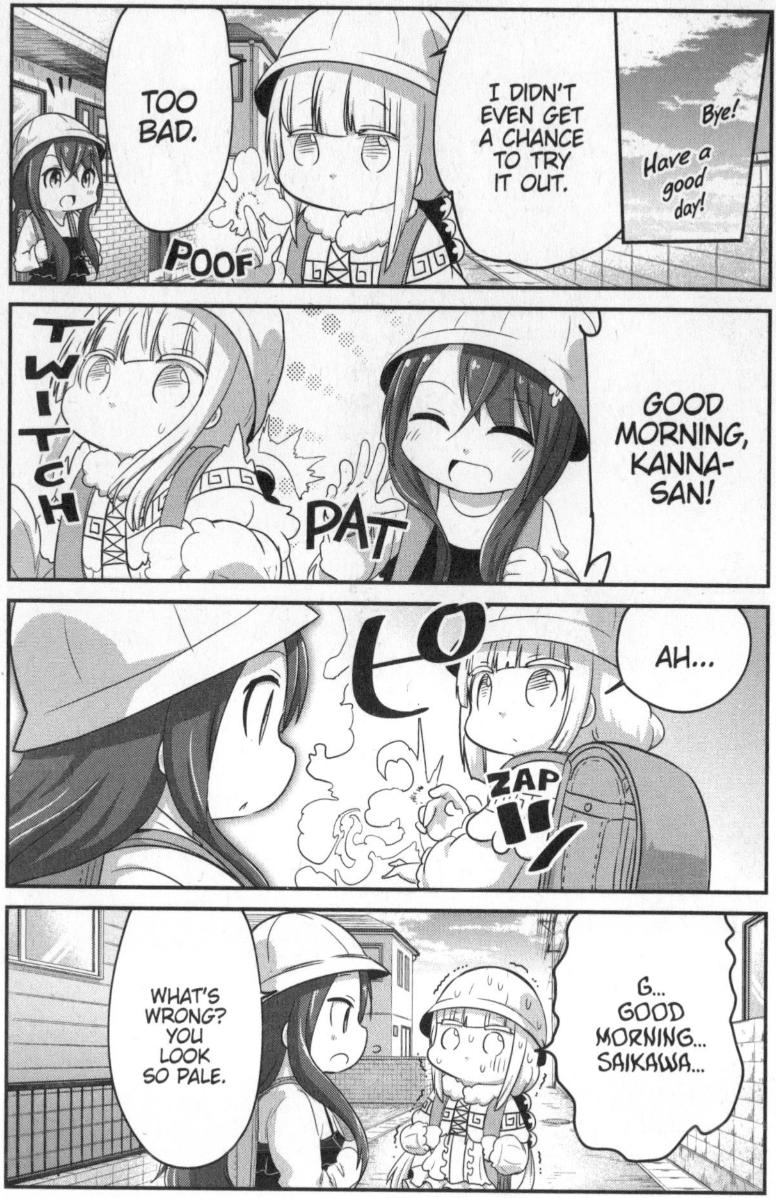

Bye!
Have a good day!
I DIDN'T EVEN GET A CHANCE TO TRY IT OUT.
TOO BAD.
POOF
GOOD MORNING, KANNA-SAN!
PAT
TWITCH
AH...
ZAP
G... GOOD MORNING... SAIKAWA...
WHAT'S WRONG? YOU LOOK SO PALE.

THE JIG IS UP!!

U... UH-HUH...

COME ON, LET'S HURRY UP AND GET TO SCHOOL!

SLIIIDE

SORRY, KANNA-SAN! I NEED TO USE THE RESTROOM.

!

SHUDDER

BA-DUMP

BA-DUMP

?!

Eeeeek!

GENDER-NEUTRAL CHARM!

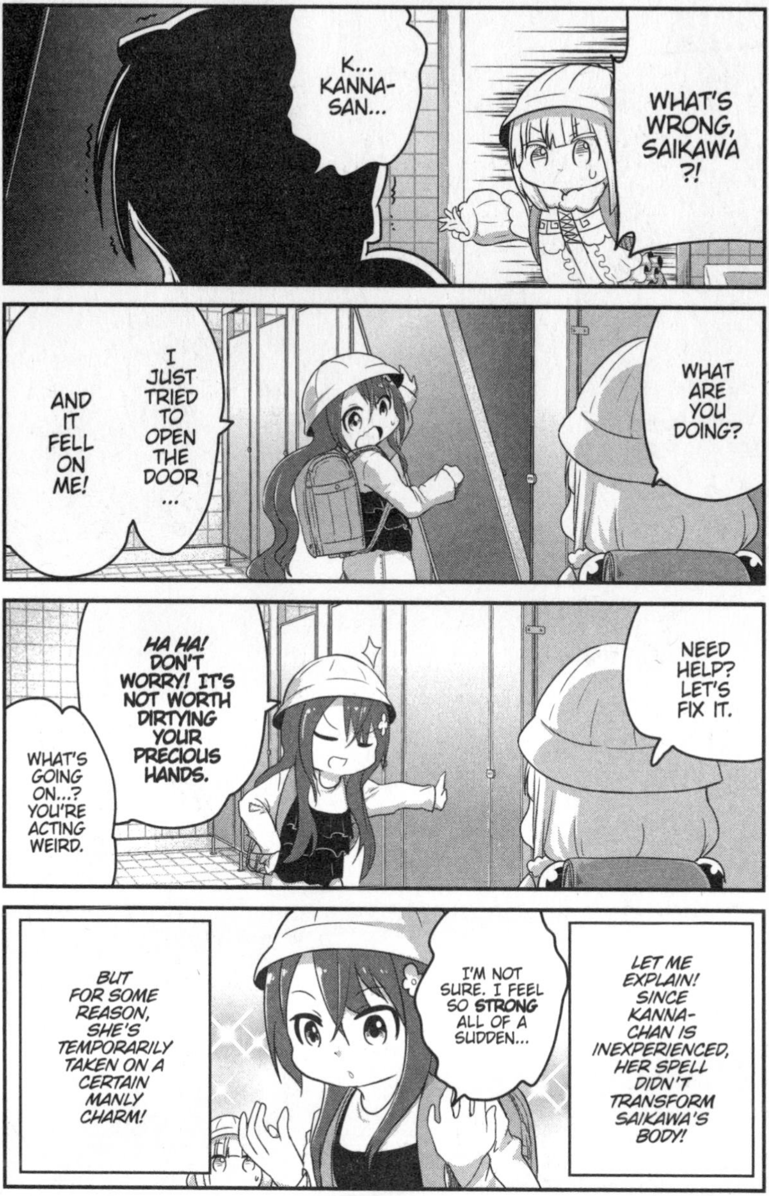
WHAT'S WRONG, SAIKAWA?!
K... KANNA-SAN...
WHAT ARE YOU DOING?
I JUST TRIED TO OPEN THE DOOR...
AND IT FELL ON ME!
NEED HELP? LET'S FIX IT.
HA HA! DON'T WORRY! IT'S NOT WORTH DIRTYING YOUR PRECIOUS HANDS.
WHAT'S GOING ON...? YOU'RE ACTING WEIRD.
LET ME EXPLAIN! SINCE KANNA-CHAN IS INEXPERIENCED, HER SPELL DIDN'T TRANSFORM SAIKAWA'S BODY!
I'M NOT SURE. I FEEL SO STRONG ALL OF A SUDDEN...
BUT FOR SOME REASON, SHE'S TEMPORARILY TAKEN ON A CERTAIN MANLY CHARM!

SAIKAWA THE GENTLEMAN

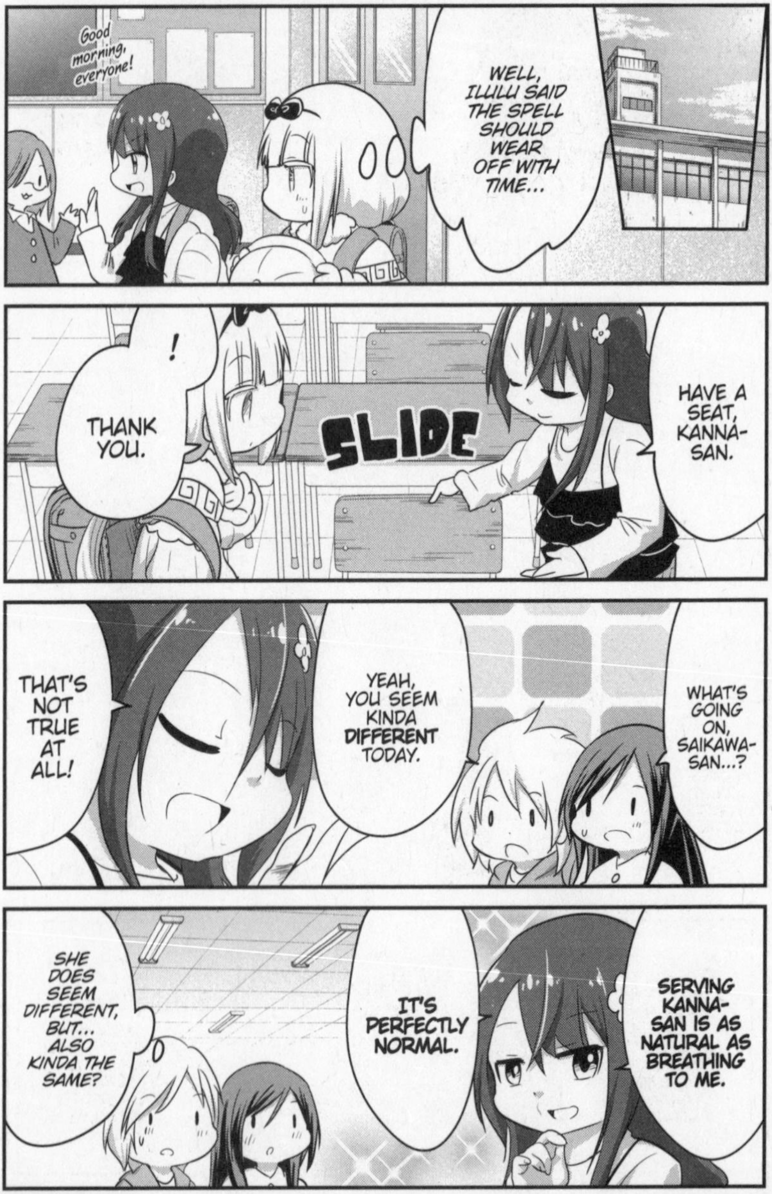
WELL, ILULU SAID THE SPELL SHOULD WEAR OFF WITH TIME...
Good morning, everyone!
HAVE A SEAT, KANNA-SAN.
SLIDE
!
THANK YOU.
WHAT'S GOING ON, SAIKAWA-SAN...?
YEAH, YOU SEEM KINDA DIFFERENT TODAY.
THAT'S NOT TRUE AT ALL!
SERVING KANNA-SAN IS AS NATURAL AS BREATHING TO ME.
IT'S PERFECTLY NORMAL.
SHE DOES SEEM DIFFERENT, BUT... ALSO KINDA THE SAME?

SO COOL...

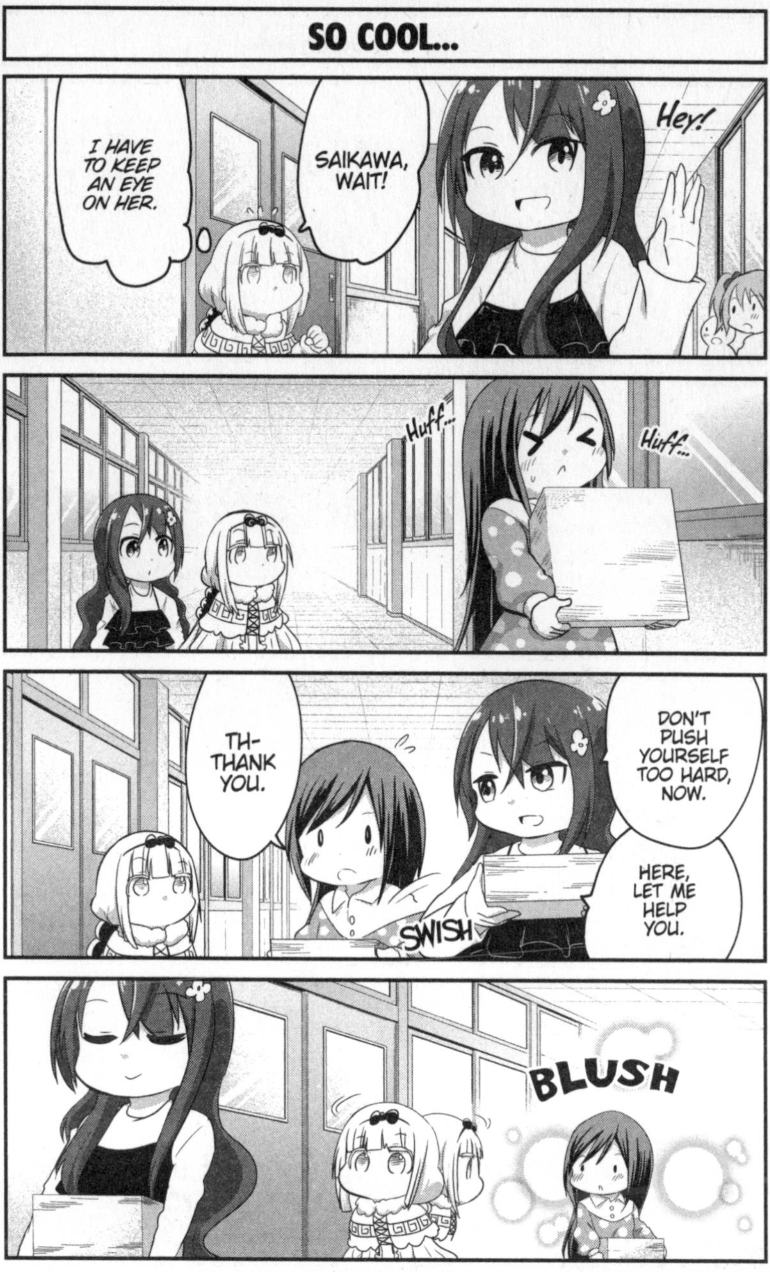
Hey!
SAIKAWA, WAIT!
I HAVE TO KEEP AN EYE ON HER.
Huff...
Huff...
DON'T PUSH YOURSELF TOO HARD, NOW.
HERE, LET ME HELP YOU.
SWISH
TH-THANK YOU.
BLUSH

HEART-POUNDING

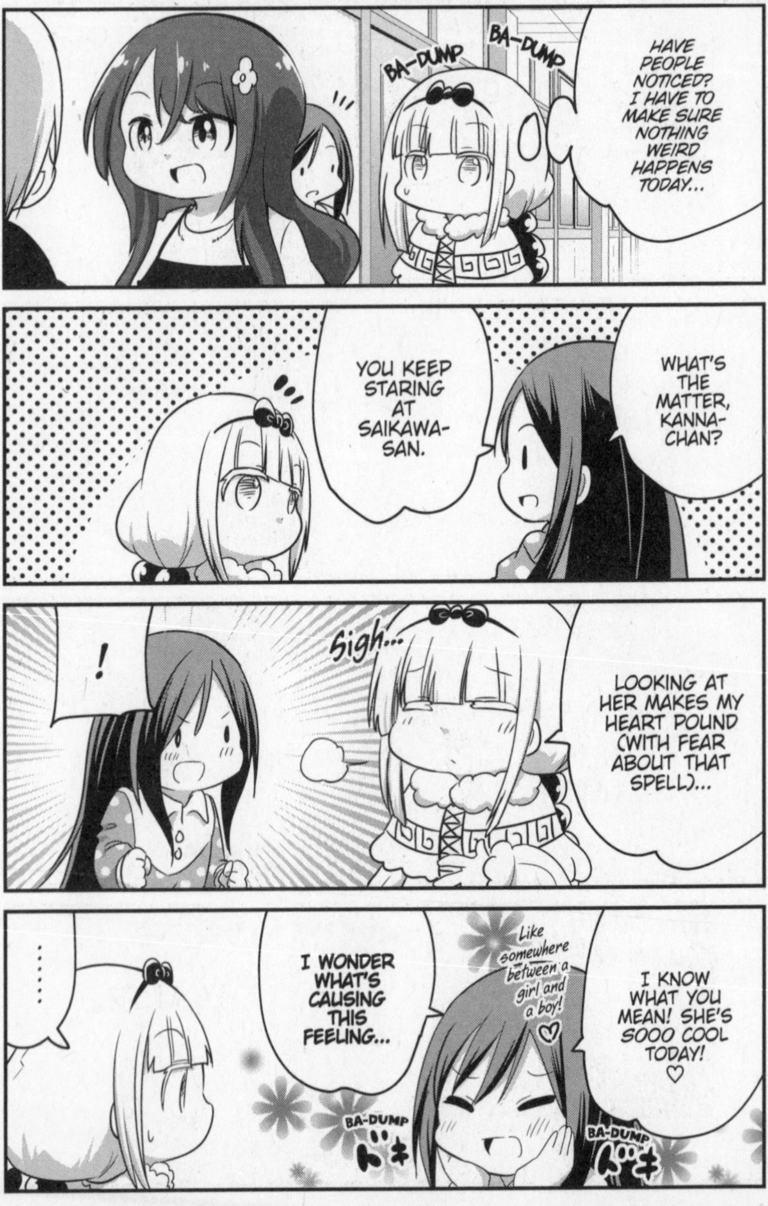

BA-DUMP
BA-DUMP
HAVE PEOPLE NOTICED? I HAVE TO MAKE SURE NOTHING WEIRD HAPPENS TODAY...
WHAT'S THE MATTER, KANNA-CHAN?
YOU KEEP STARING AT SAIKAWA-SAN.
LOOKING AT HER MAKES MY HEART POUND (WITH FEAR ABOUT THAT SPELL)...
Sigh...
!
I KNOW WHAT YOU MEAN! SHE'S SOOO COOL TODAY! ♡
Like somewhere between a girl and a boy! ♡
BA-DUMP
I WONDER WHAT'S CAUSING THIS FEELING...
BA-DUMP
......

SWEPT AWAY

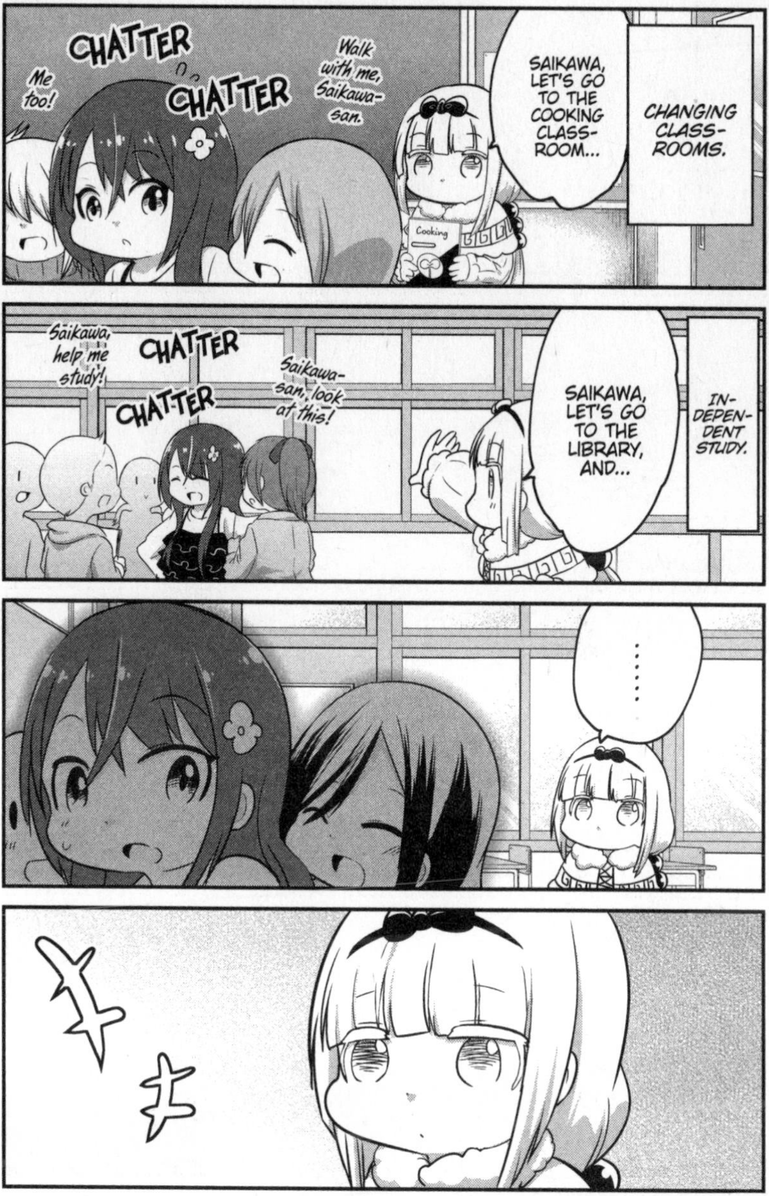
CHANGING CLASS-ROOMS.
SAIKAWA, LET'S GO TO THE COOKING CLASS-ROOM...
Walk with me, Saikawa-san.
CHATTER
CHATTER
Me too!
Cooking
IN-DEPEN-DENT STUDY.
SAIKAWA, LET'S GO TO THE LIBRARY, AND...
Saikawa-san, look at this!
CHATTER
CHATTER
Saikawa, help me study!
......

QUEEN OF THE CLASS!

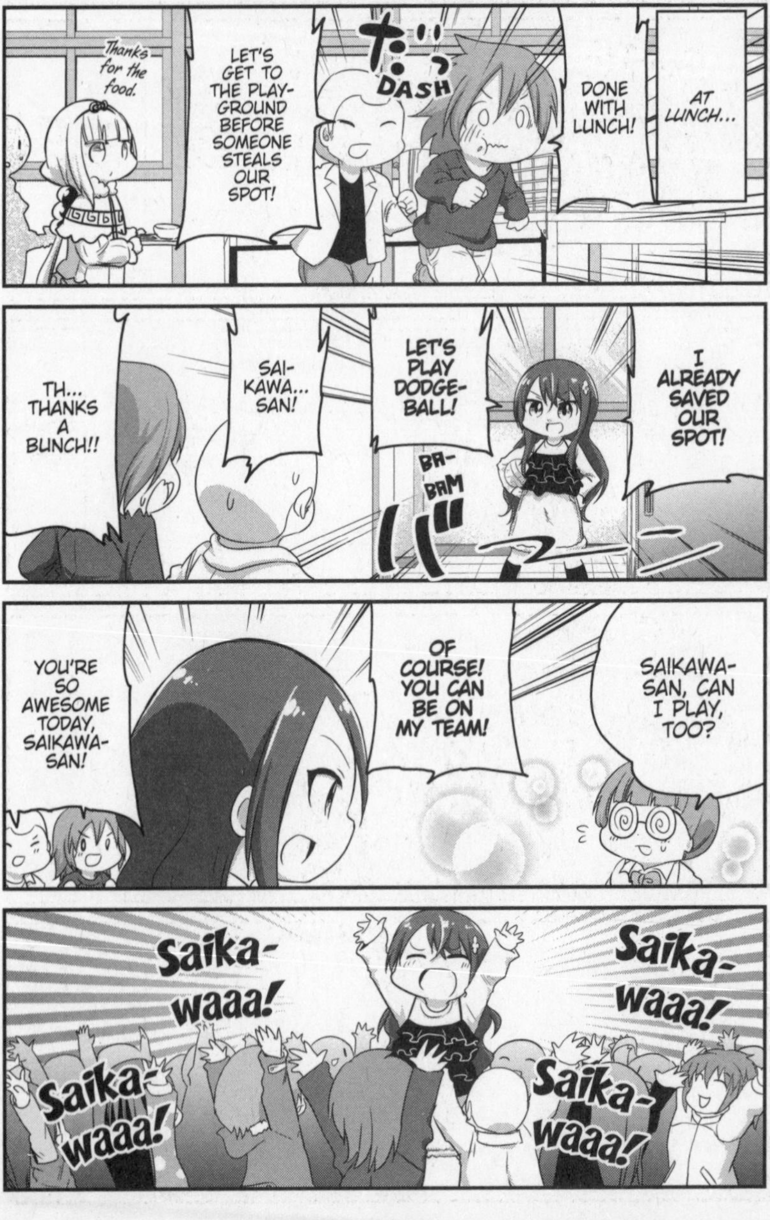
AT LUNCH...
DONE WITH LUNCH!
DASH
LET'S GET TO THE PLAY-GROUND BEFORE SOMEONE STEALS OUR SPOT!
Thanks for the food.
I ALREADY SAVED OUR SPOT!
BA-BAM
LET'S PLAY DODGE-BALL!
SAI-KAWA... SAN!
TH... THANKS A BUNCH!!
SAIKAWA-SAN, CAN I PLAY, TOO?
OF COURSE! YOU CAN BE ON MY TEAM!
YOU'RE SO AWESOME TODAY, SAIKAWA-SAN!
Saika-waaa!
Saika-waaa!
Saika-waaa!
Saika-waaa!

THE HEROINE ALWAYS SHOWS UP LATE!

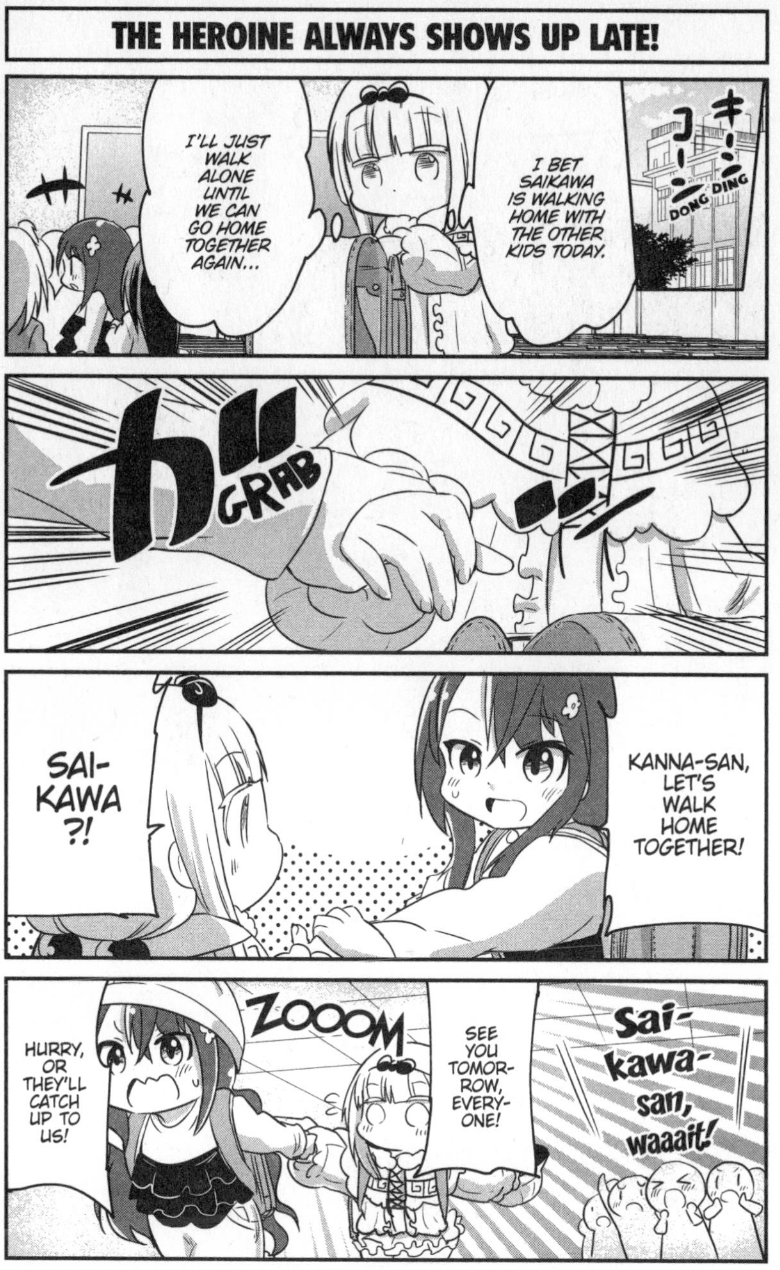
DING DONG
I BET SAIKAWA IS WALKING HOME WITH THE OTHER KIDS TODAY.
I'LL JUST WALK ALONE UNTIL WE CAN GO HOME TOGETHER AGAIN...
GRAB
KANNA-SAN, LET'S WALK HOME TOGETHER!
SAI-KAWA?!
Sai-kawa-san, waaait!
SEE YOU TOMOR-ROW, EVERY-ONE!
ZOOOM
HURRY, OR THEY'LL CATCH UP TO US!

A FRIENDLY WALK HOME

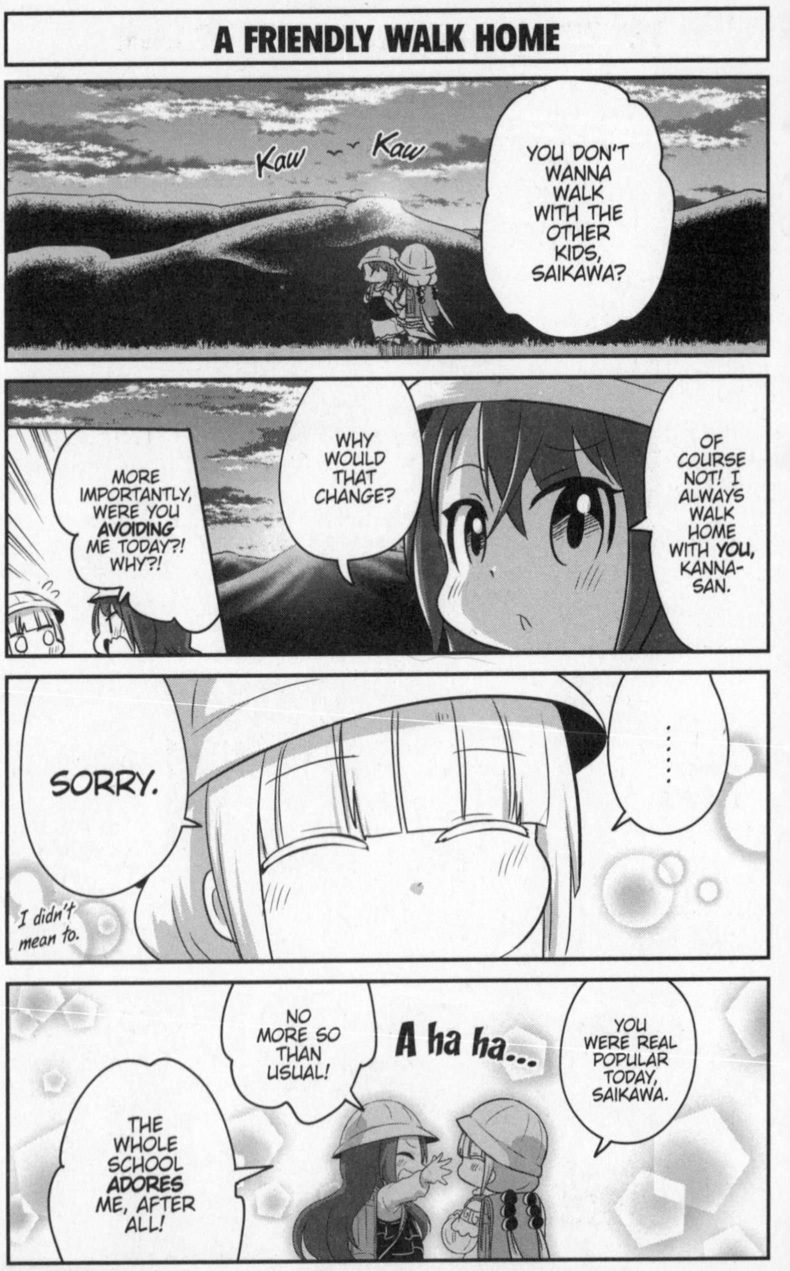
YOU DON'T WANNA WALK WITH THE OTHER KIDS, SAIKAWA?
Kaw Kaw
OF COURSE NOT! I ALWAYS WALK HOME WITH YOU, KANNA-SAN.
WHY WOULD THAT CHANGE?
MORE IMPORTANTLY, WERE YOU AVOIDING ME TODAY?! WHY?!
......
SORRY.
I didn't mean to.
YOU WERE REAL POPULAR TODAY, SAIKAWA.
A ha ha...
NO MORE SO THAN USUAL!
THE WHOLE SCHOOL ADORES ME, AFTER ALL!

BACK TO NORMAL!

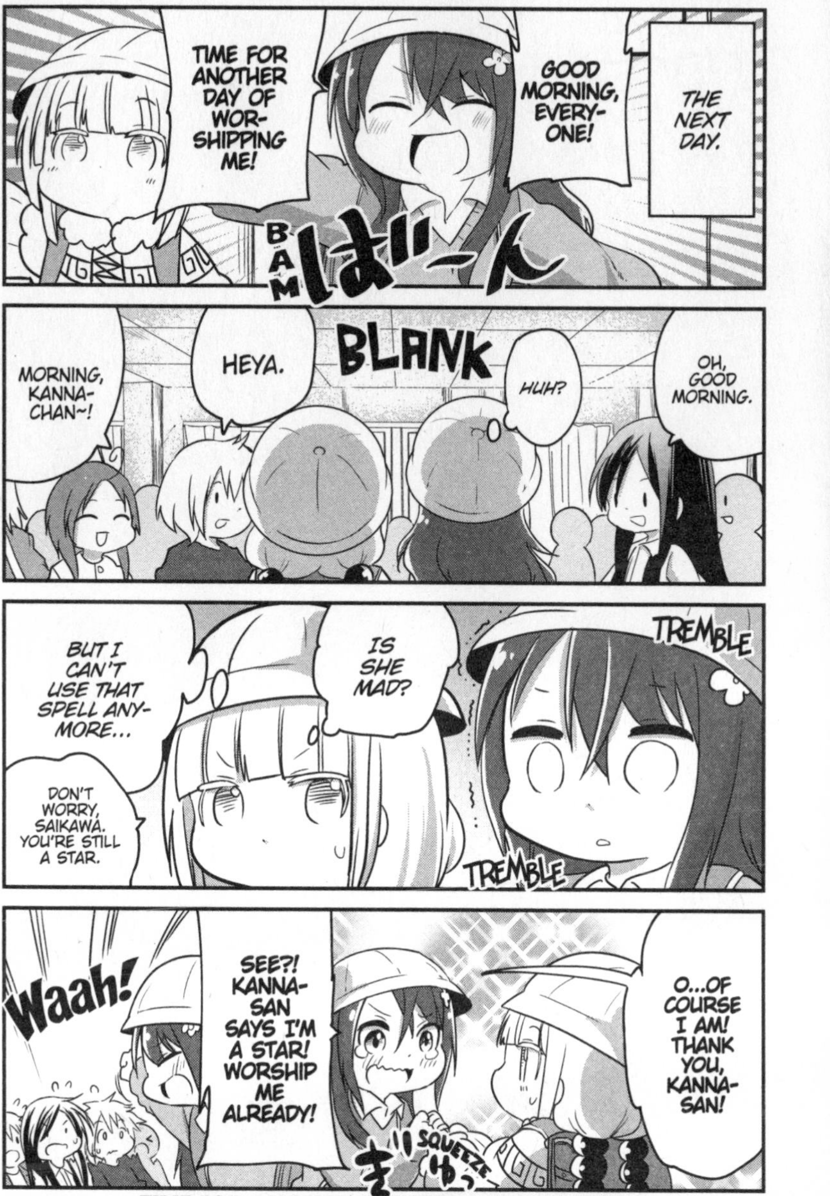
THE NEXT DAY.
GOOD MORNING, EVERYONE!
TIME FOR ANOTHER DAY OF WORSHIPPING ME!
BAM はばーん
OH, GOOD MORNING.
HUH?
BLANK
HEYA.
MORNING, KANNA-CHAN~!
TREMBLE
IS SHE MAD?
BUT I CAN'T USE THAT SPELL ANYMORE...
DON'T WORRY, SAIKAWA. YOU'RE STILL A STAR.
TREMBLE
O...OF COURSE I AM! THANK YOU, KANNA-SAN!
SEE?! KANNA-SAN SAYS I'M A STAR! WORSHIP ME ALREADY!
Waah!
SQUEEZE ぎゅっ

TIME FOR SAIKAWA THE SPELLBINDING/END

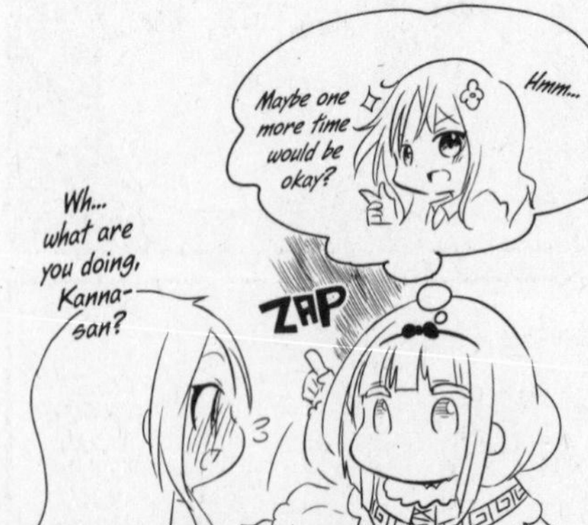
Hmm...
Maybe one more time would be okay?
Wh... what are you doing, Kanna-san?
ZAP
ZAP

Miss Kobayashi's Dragon Maid

Kanna's Daily Life

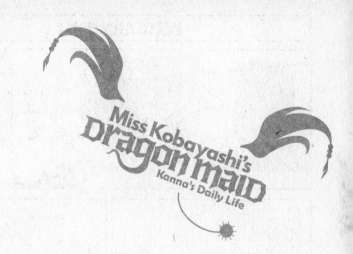

PEACE AND QUIET

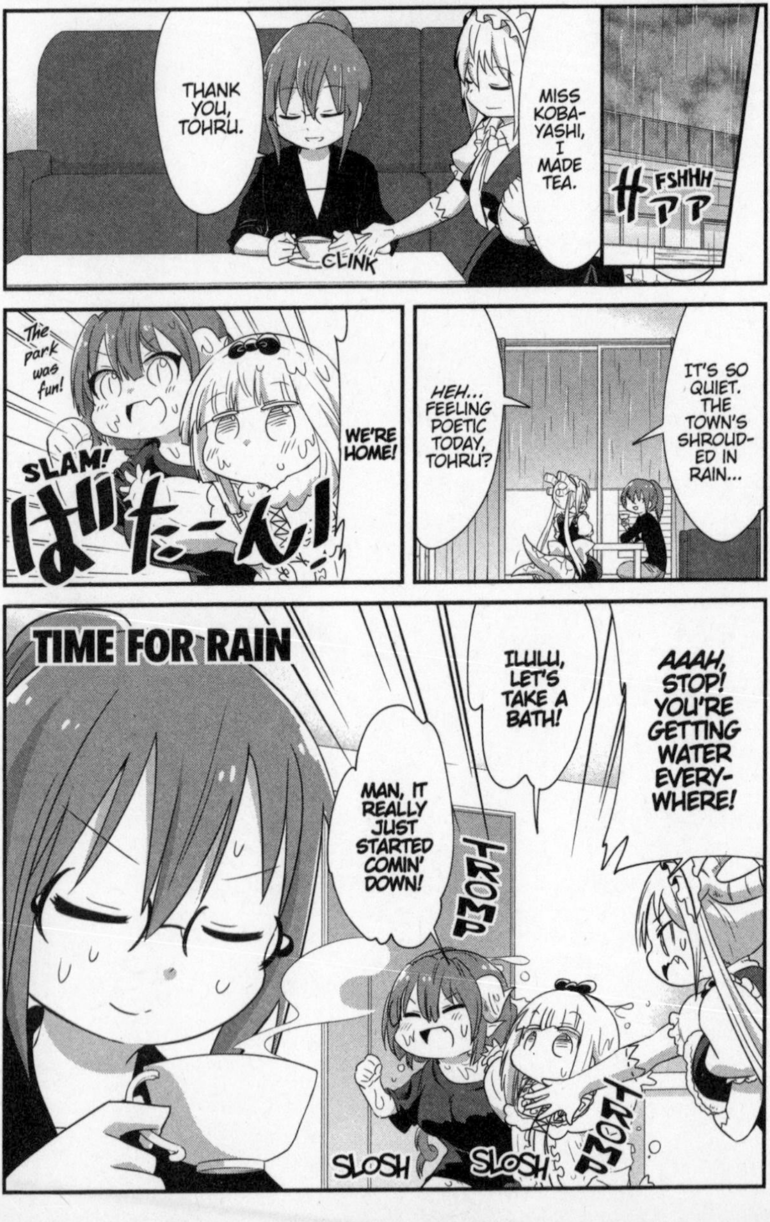
FSHHH
MISS KOBA-YASHI, I MADE TEA.
THANK YOU, TOHRU.
CLINK
IT'S SO QUIET. THE TOWN'S SHROUD-ED IN RAIN...
HEH... FEELING POETIC TODAY, TOHRU?
WE'RE HOME!
The park was fun!
SLAM!
ばたーん!
TIME FOR RAIN
AAAH, STOP! YOU'RE GETTING WATER EVERY-WHERE!
ILULU, LET'S TAKE A BATH!
MAN, IT REALLY JUST STARTED COMIN' DOWN!
TROMP
TROMP
SLOSH
SLOSH

DRAGONS AREN'T DOGS

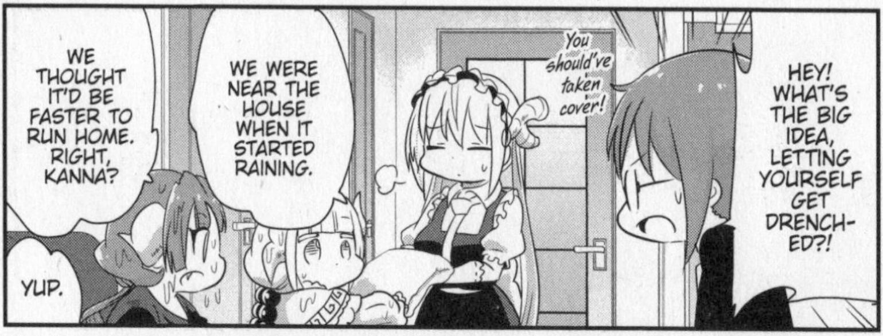
HEY! WHAT'S THE BIG IDEA, LETTING YOURSELF GET DRENCH-ED?!
You should've taken cover!
WE WERE NEAR THE HOUSE WHEN IT STARTED RAINING.
WE THOUGHT IT'D BE FASTER TO RUN HOME. RIGHT, KANNA?
YUP.

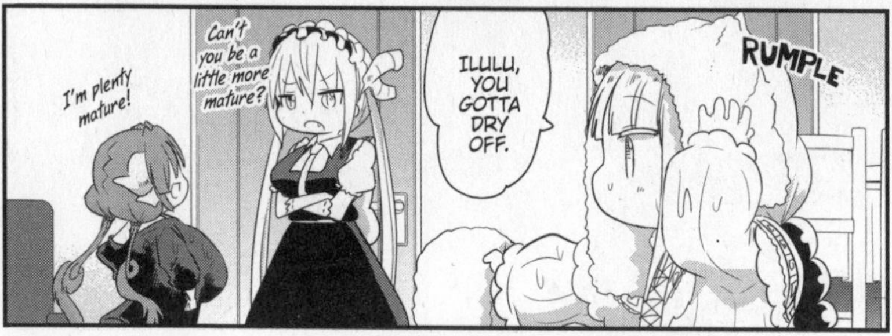
RUMPLE
ILULU, YOU GOTTA DRY OFF.
Can't you be a little more mature?
I'm plenty mature!

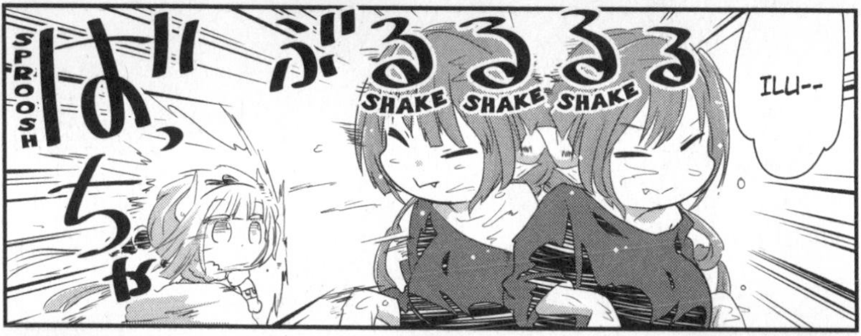
ILU--
ぶるるるる
SHAKE SHAKE SHAKE
SPROOSH

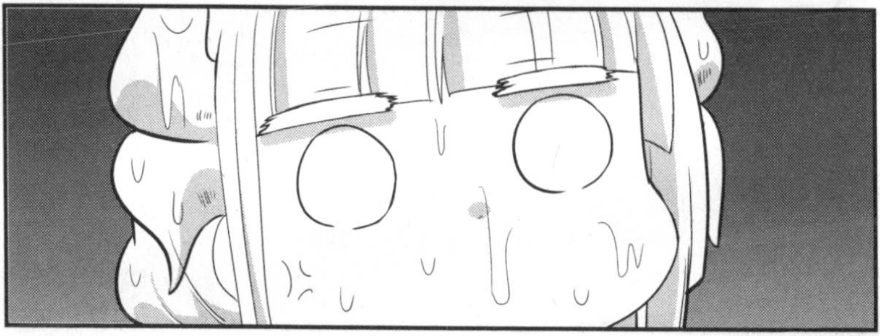

FITTING IN

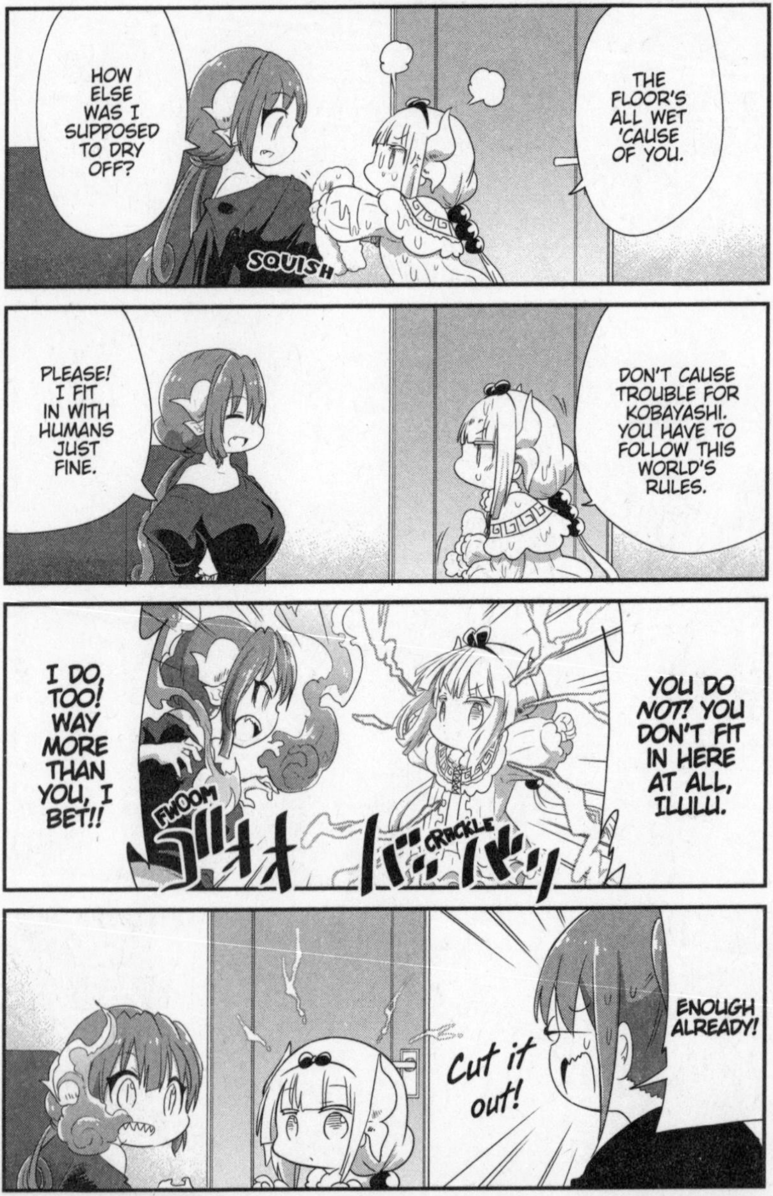
THE FLOOR'S ALL WET 'CAUSE OF YOU.
HOW ELSE WAS I SUPPOSED TO DRY OFF?
SQUISH
DON'T CAUSE TROUBLE FOR KOBAYASHI. YOU HAVE TO FOLLOW THIS WORLD'S RULES.
PLEASE! I FIT IN WITH HUMANS JUST FINE.
YOU DO NOT! YOU DON'T FIT IN HERE AT ALL, ILULU.
I DO, TOO! WAY MORE THAN YOU, I BET!!
CRACKLE
FWOOM
ENOUGH ALREADY!
Cut it out!

BIG SISTER TOHRU

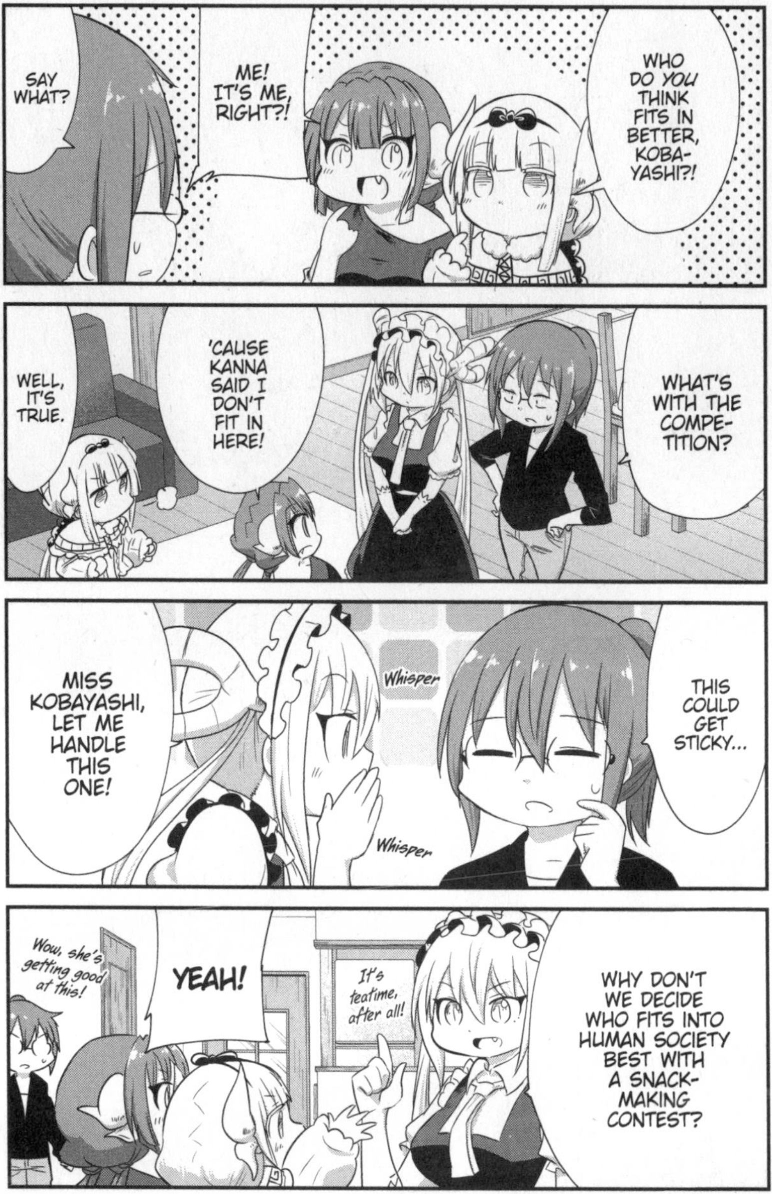
WHO DO YOU THINK FITS IN BETTER, KOBAYASHI?!
ME! IT'S ME, RIGHT?!
SAY WHAT?
WHAT'S WITH THE COMPETITION?
'CAUSE KANNA SAID I DON'T FIT IN HERE!
WELL, IT'S TRUE.
THIS COULD GET STICKY...
Whisper
MISS KOBAYASHI, LET ME HANDLE THIS ONE!
Whisper
WHY DON'T WE DECIDE WHO FITS INTO HUMAN SOCIETY BEST WITH A SNACK-MAKING CONTEST?
It's teatime, after all!
YEAH!
Wow, she's getting good at this!

PERSONAL PREFERENCES

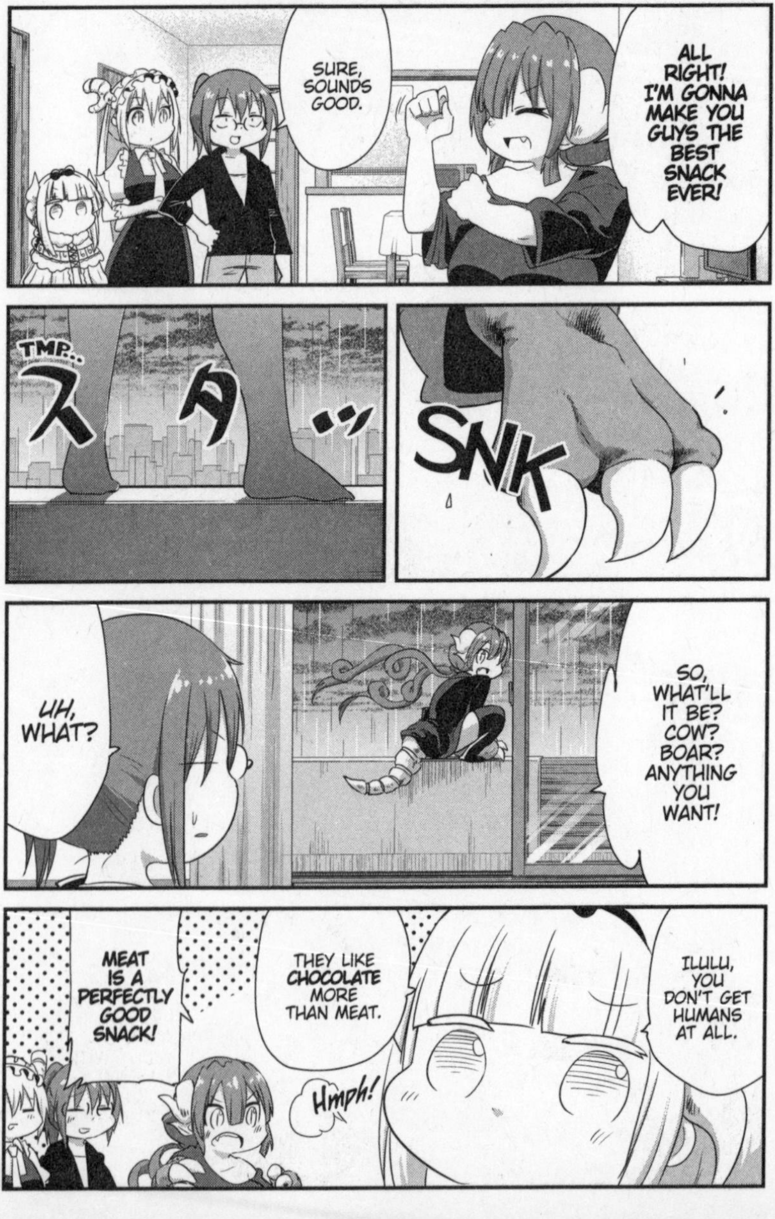
ALL RIGHT! I'M GONNA MAKE YOU GUYS THE BEST SNACK EVER!
SURE, SOUNDS GOOD.
SNK
TMP..
スタッ
SO, WHAT'LL IT BE? COW? BOAR? ANYTHING YOU WANT!
UH, WHAT?
ILULU, YOU DON'T GET HUMANS AT ALL.
THEY LIKE **CHOCOLATE** MORE THAN MEAT.
Hmph!
MEAT IS A PERFECTLY GOOD SNACK!

CRANKING UP THE HEAT

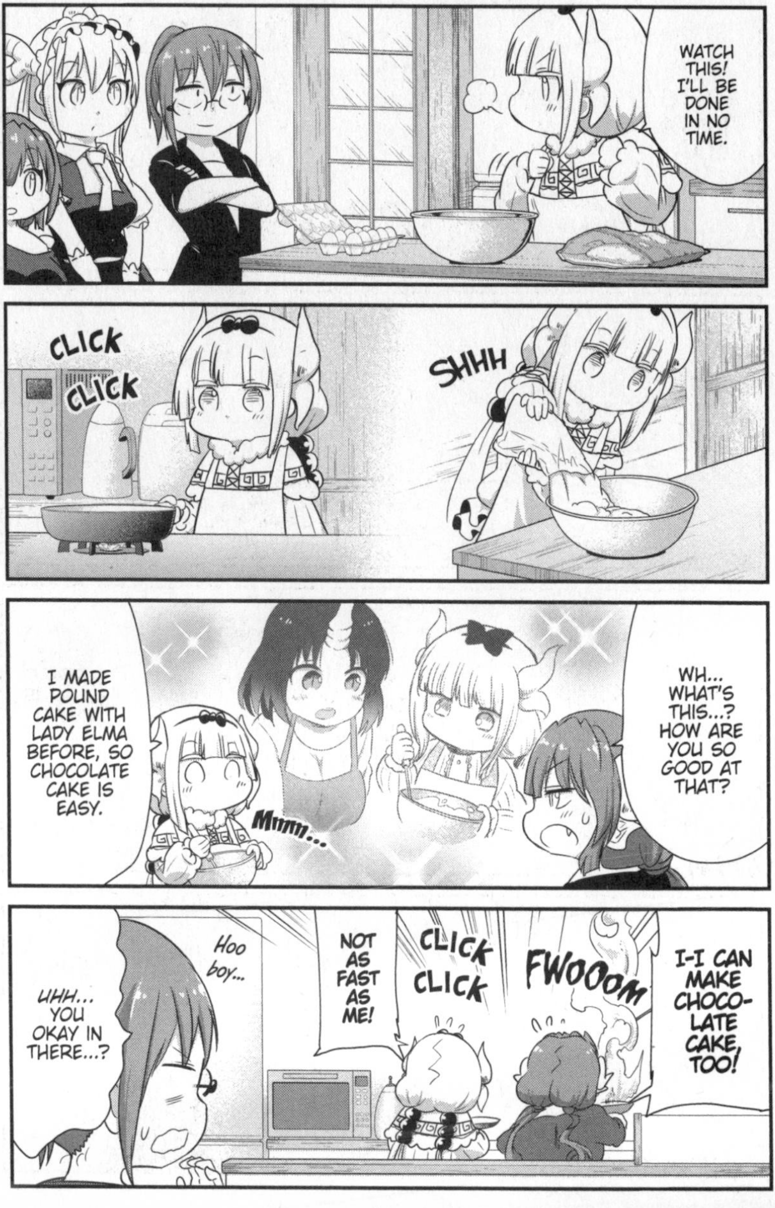
WATCH THIS! I'LL BE DONE IN NO TIME.
SHHH
CLICK CLICK
WH... WHAT'S THIS...? HOW ARE YOU SO GOOD AT THAT?
I MADE POUND CAKE WITH LADY ELMA BEFORE, SO CHOCOLATE CAKE IS EASY.
Mmm...
I-I CAN MAKE CHOCO-LATE CAKE, TOO!
FWOOOM
CLICK CLICK
NOT AS FAST AS ME!
Hoo boy...
UHH... YOU OKAY IN THERE...?

UNDERSTANDING HUMANITY

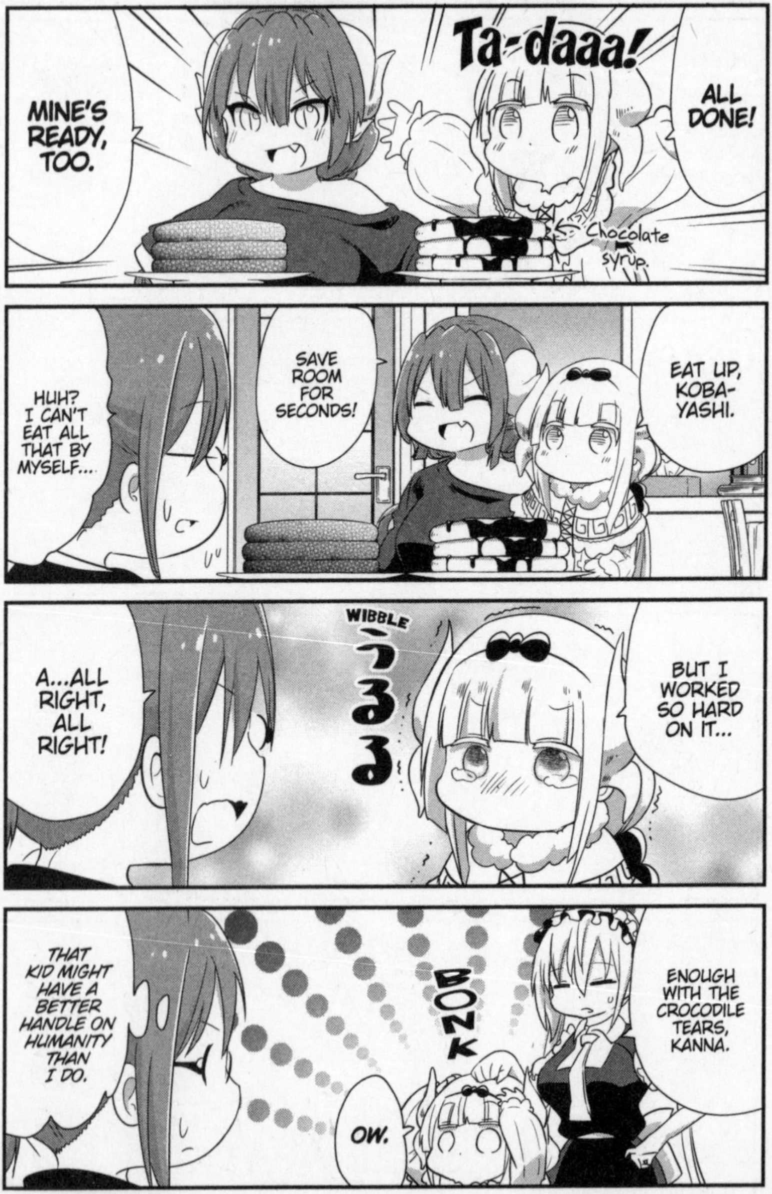
ALL DONE!
Ta-daaa!
Chocolate syrup.
MINE'S READY, TOO.
EAT UP, KOBA-YASHI.
SAVE ROOM FOR SECONDS!
HUH? I CAN'T EAT ALL THAT BY MYSELF....
BUT I WORKED SO HARD ON IT...
WIBBLE
うるる
A...ALL RIGHT, ALL RIGHT!
ENOUGH WITH THE CROCODILE TEARS, KANNA.
BONK
OW.
THAT KID MIGHT HAVE A BETTER HANDLE ON HUMANITY THAN I DO.

IT'S CHARCOAL!

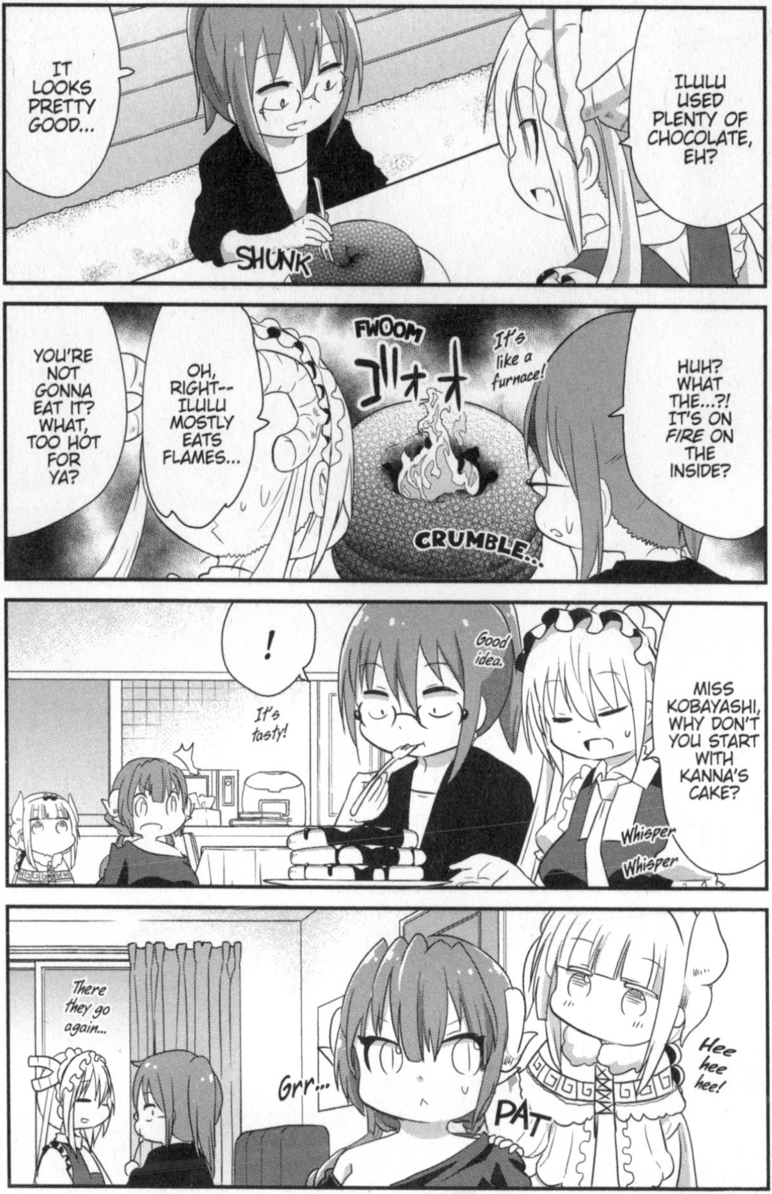
ILULU USED PLENTY OF CHOCOLATE, EH?
IT LOOKS PRETTY GOOD...
SHUNK
HUH? WHAT THE...?! IT'S ON *FIRE* ON THE INSIDE?
It's like a furnace!
FWOOM
ゴォォ
OH, RIGHT-- ILULU MOSTLY EATS FLAMES...
YOU'RE NOT GONNA EAT IT? WHAT, TOO HOT FOR YA?
CRUMBLE...
MISS KOBAYASHI, WHY DON'T YOU START WITH KANNA'S CAKE?
Whisper
Whisper
Good idea.
!
It's tasty!
Hee hee hee!
PAT
Grr...
There they go again...

SINCE THE DRAGONS CAME

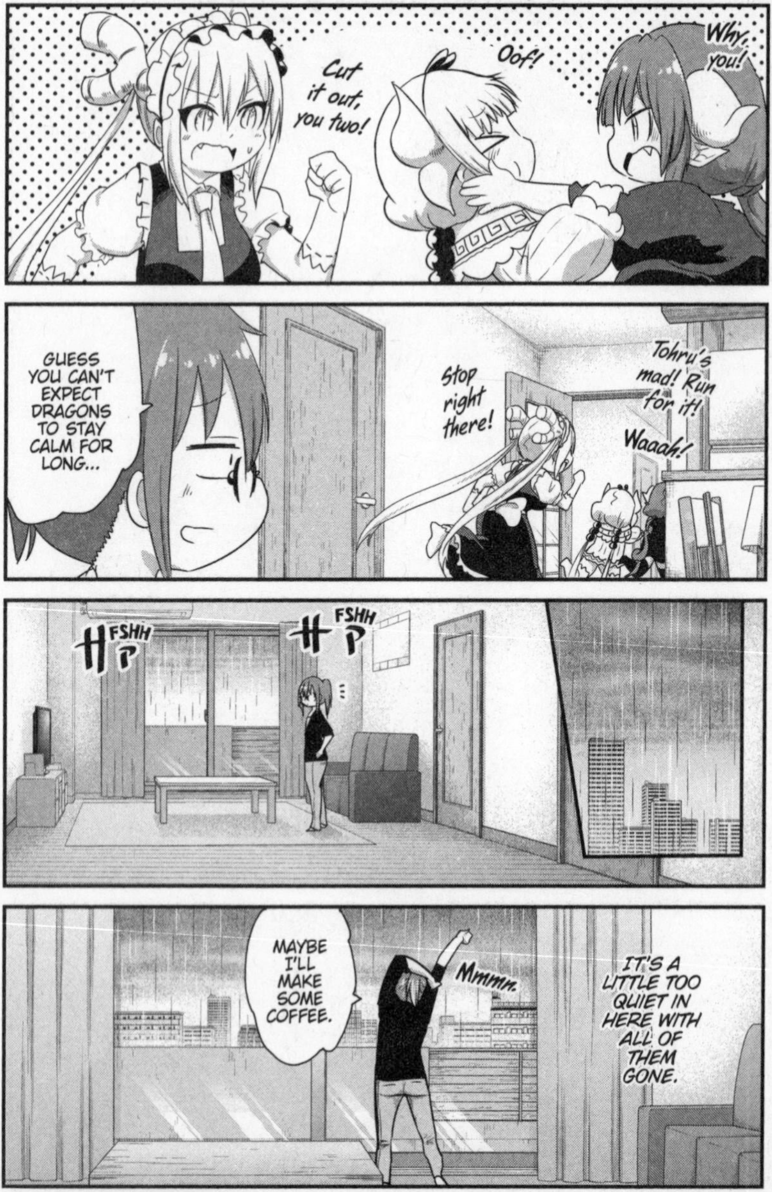
Why, you!
Oof!
Cut it out, you two!
Tohru's mad! Run for it!
Waaah!
Stop right there!
GUESS YOU CAN'T EXPECT DRAGONS TO STAY CALM FOR LONG...
FSHH
FSHH
IT'S A LITTLE TOO QUIET IN HERE WITH ALL OF THEM GONE.
Mmmm.
MAYBE I'LL MAKE SOME COFFEE.

ROLE REVERSAL

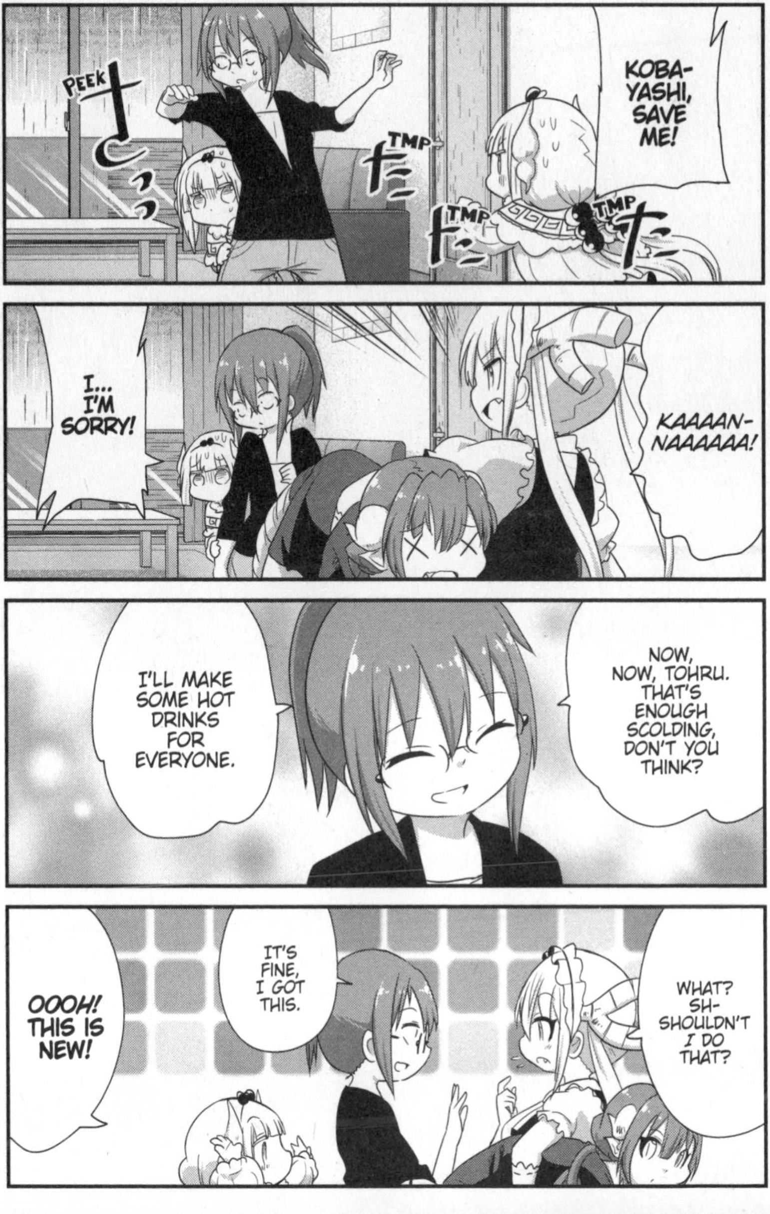
KOBA-YASHI, SAVE ME!
TMP
TMP
TMP
PEEK
KAAAAN-NAAAAAA!
I... I'M SORRY!
NOW, NOW, TOHRU. THAT'S ENOUGH SCOLDING, DON'T YOU THINK?
I'LL MAKE SOME HOT DRINKS FOR EVERYONE.
WHAT? SH-SHOULDN'T *I* DO THAT?
IT'S FINE, I GOT THIS.
OOOH! THIS IS NEW!

SIP AND MAKE UP

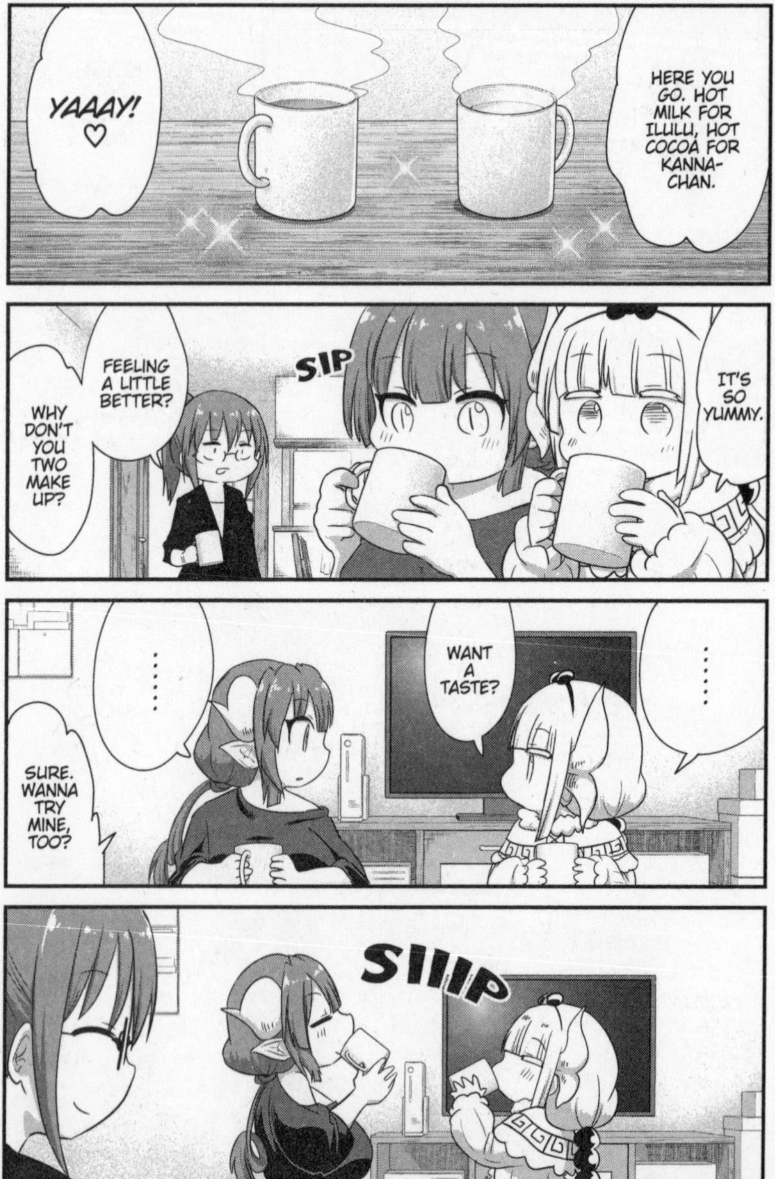
HERE YOU GO. HOT MILK FOR ILULU, HOT COCOA FOR KANNA-CHAN.
YAAAY! ♡
IT'S SO YUMMY.
SIP
FEELING A LITTLE BETTER?
WHY DON'T YOU TWO MAKE UP?
......
WANT A TASTE?
......
SURE. WANNA TRY MINE, TOO?
SIIIP

RAINY DAY

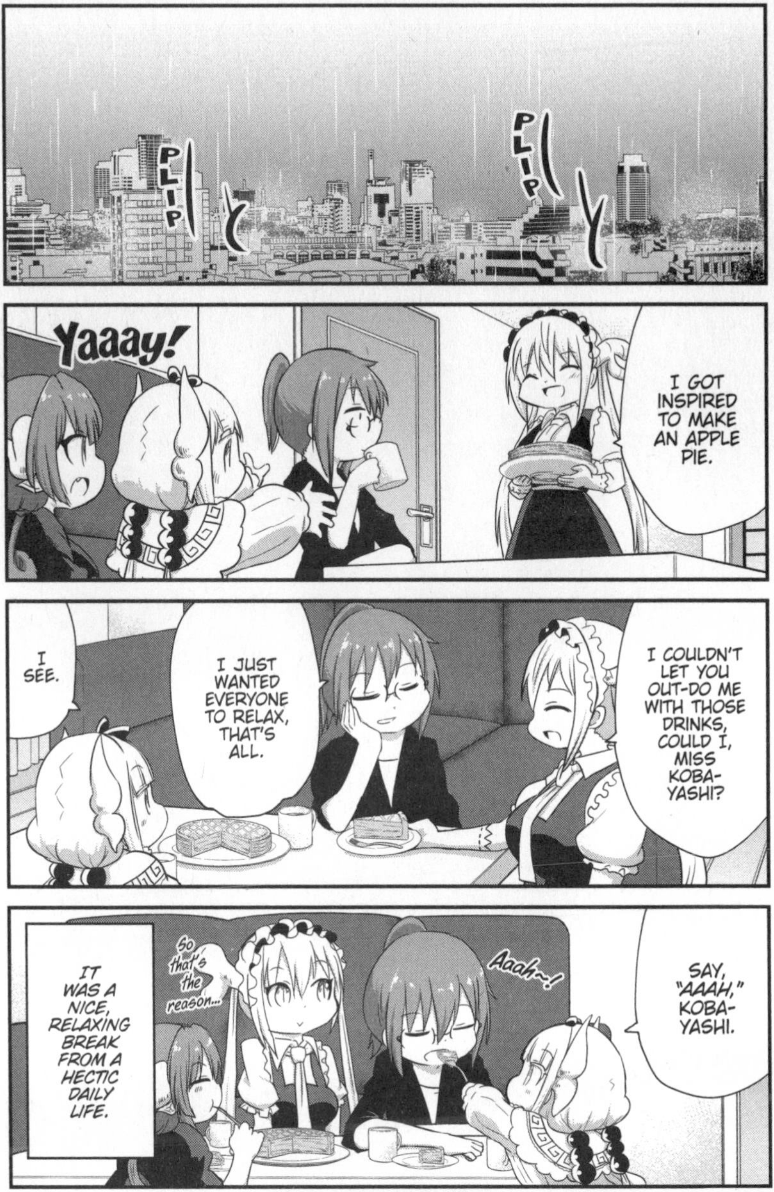
PLIP
PLIP
I GOT INSPIRED TO MAKE AN APPLE PIE.
Yaaay!
I COULDN'T LET YOU OUT-DO ME WITH THOSE DRINKS, COULD I, MISS KOBA-YASHI?
I JUST WANTED EVERYONE TO RELAX, THAT'S ALL.
I SEE.
SAY, "AAAH," KOBA-YASHI.
Aaah~!
So that's the reason...
IT WAS A NICE, RELAXING BREAK FROM A HECTIC DAILY LIFE.

TIME FOR RAIN/END

Miss Kobayashi's Dragon Maid
Kanna's Daily Life

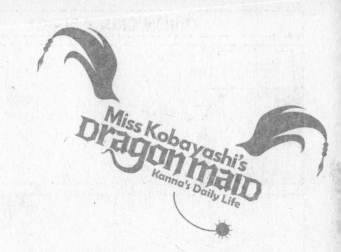

OTHERWORLDLY BEAUTY

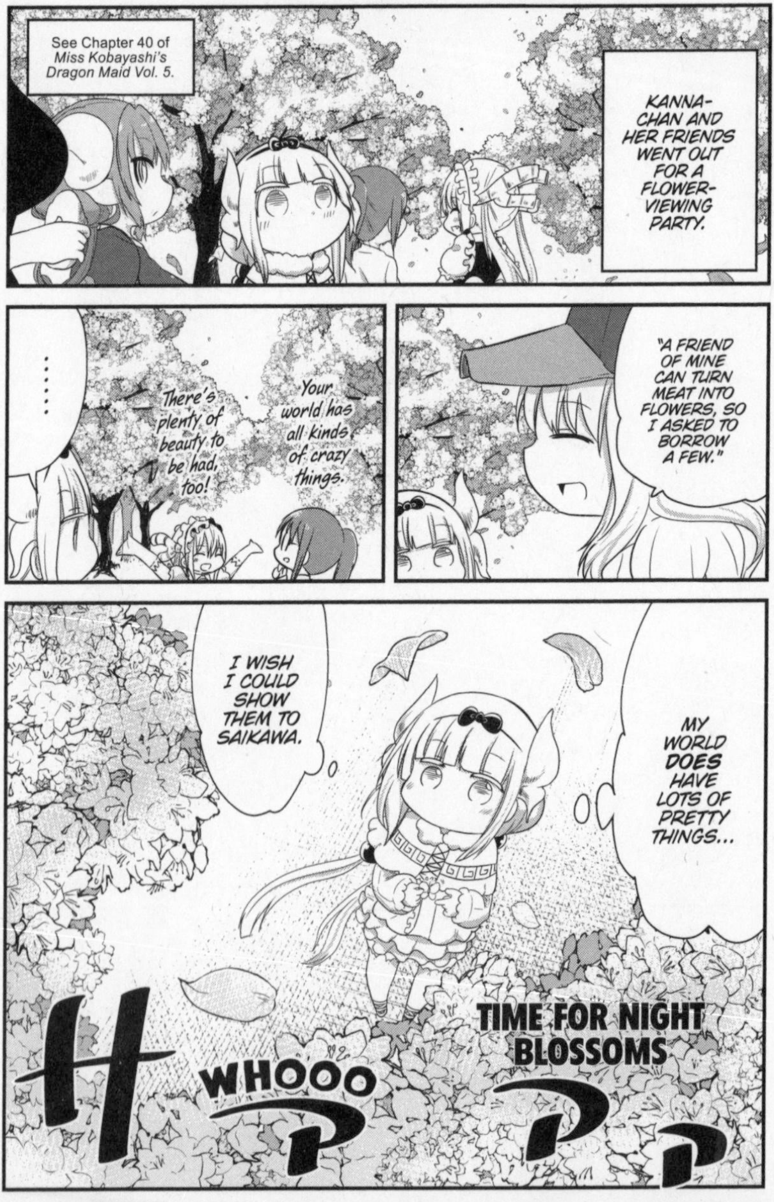
KANNA-CHAN AND HER FRIENDS WENT OUT FOR A FLOWER-VIEWING PARTY.
See Chapter 40 of *Miss Kobayashi's Dragon Maid Vol. 5.*
"A FRIEND OF MINE CAN TURN MEAT INTO FLOWERS, SO I ASKED TO BORROW A FEW."
Your world has all kinds of crazy things.
There's plenty of beauty to be had, too!
......
MY WORLD DOES HAVE LOTS OF PRETTY THINGS...
I WISH I COULD SHOW THEM TO SAIKAWA.
WHOOO
TIME FOR NIGHT BLOSSOMS

TOMORROW? THE NEXT DAY?

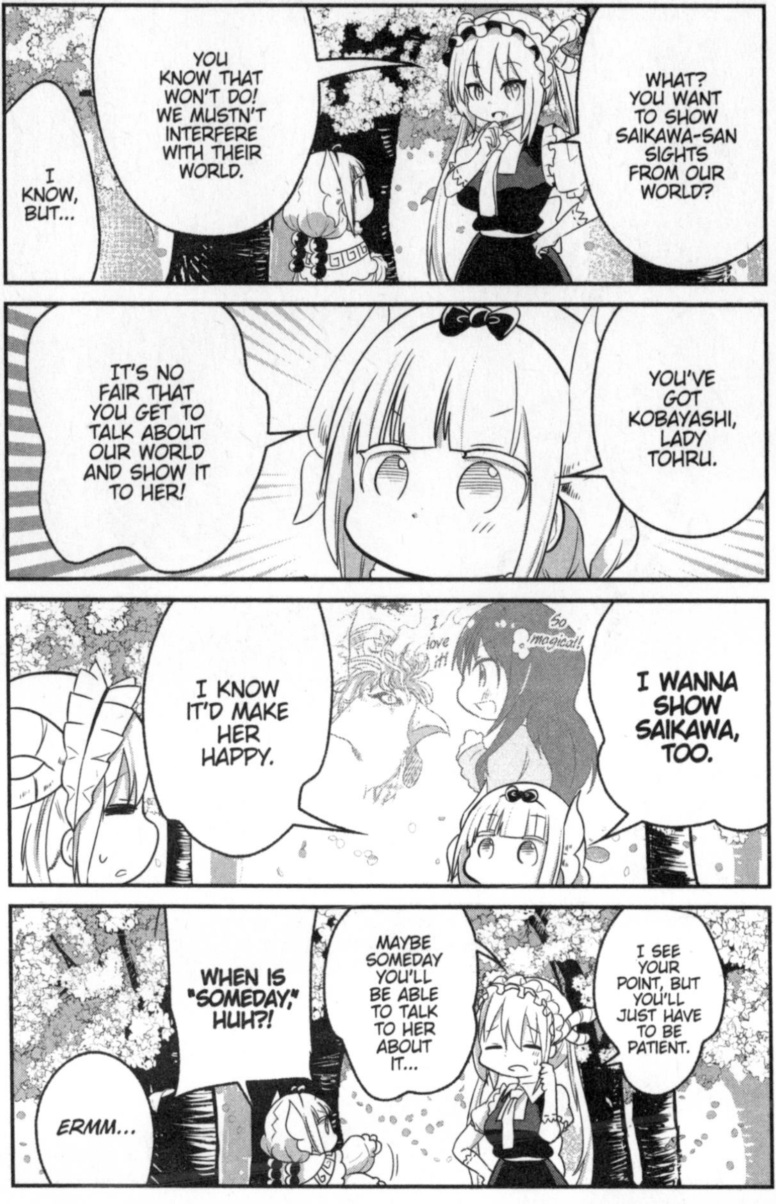
WHAT? YOU WANT TO SHOW SAIKAWA-SAN SIGHTS FROM OUR WORLD?
YOU KNOW THAT WON'T DO! WE MUSTN'T INTERFERE WITH THEIR WORLD.
I KNOW, BUT...
YOU'VE GOT KOBAYASHI, LADY TOHRU.
IT'S NO FAIR THAT YOU GET TO TALK ABOUT OUR WORLD AND SHOW IT TO HER!
I WANNA SHOW SAIKAWA, TOO.
So magical!!
I love it!!
I KNOW IT'D MAKE HER HAPPY.
I SEE YOUR POINT, BUT YOU'LL JUST HAVE TO BE PATIENT.
MAYBE SOMEDAY YOU'LL BE ABLE TO TALK TO HER ABOUT IT...
WHEN IS "SOMEDAY," HUH?!
ERMM...

I WAS RIGHT!

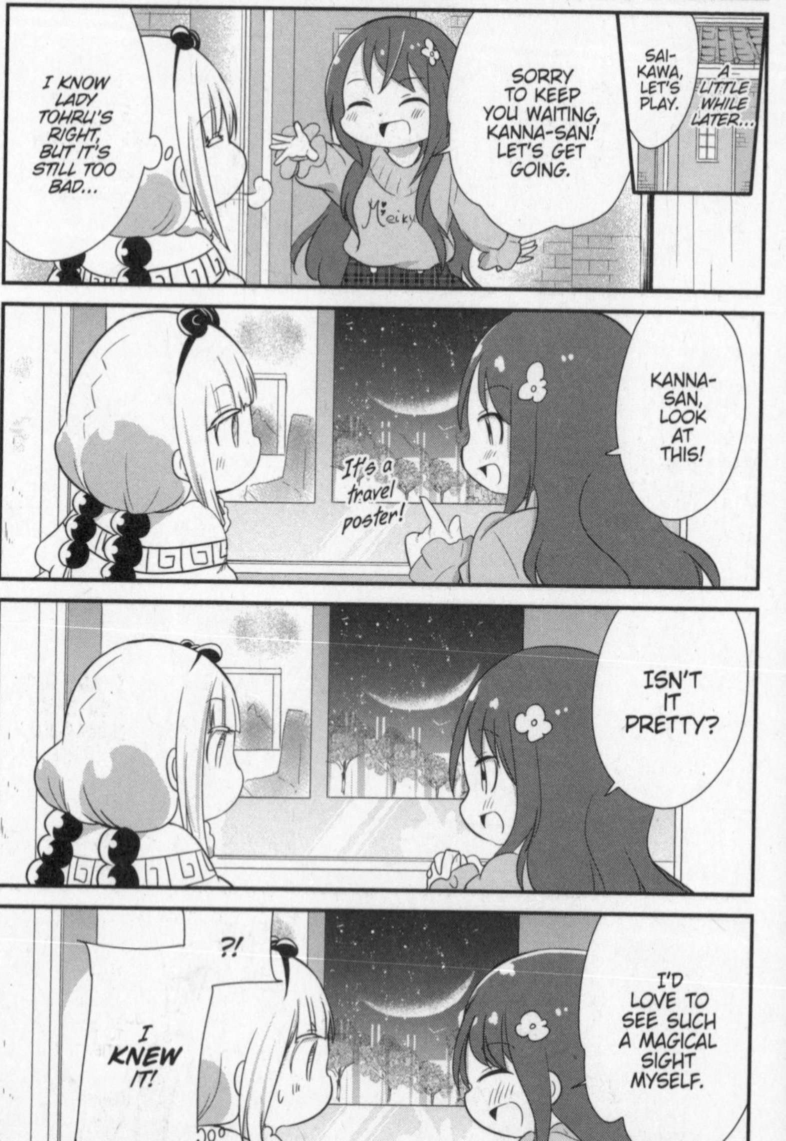
A LITTLE WHILE LATER...
SAI-KAWA, LET'S PLAY.
SORRY TO KEEP YOU WAITING, KANNA-SAN! LET'S GET GOING.
I KNOW LADY TOHRU'S RIGHT, BUT IT'S STILL TOO BAD...
KANNA-SAN, LOOK AT THIS!
It's a travel poster!
ISN'T IT PRETTY?
I'D LOVE TO SEE SUCH A MAGICAL SIGHT MYSELF.
?!
I KNEW IT!

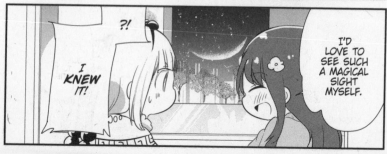

PROMISES

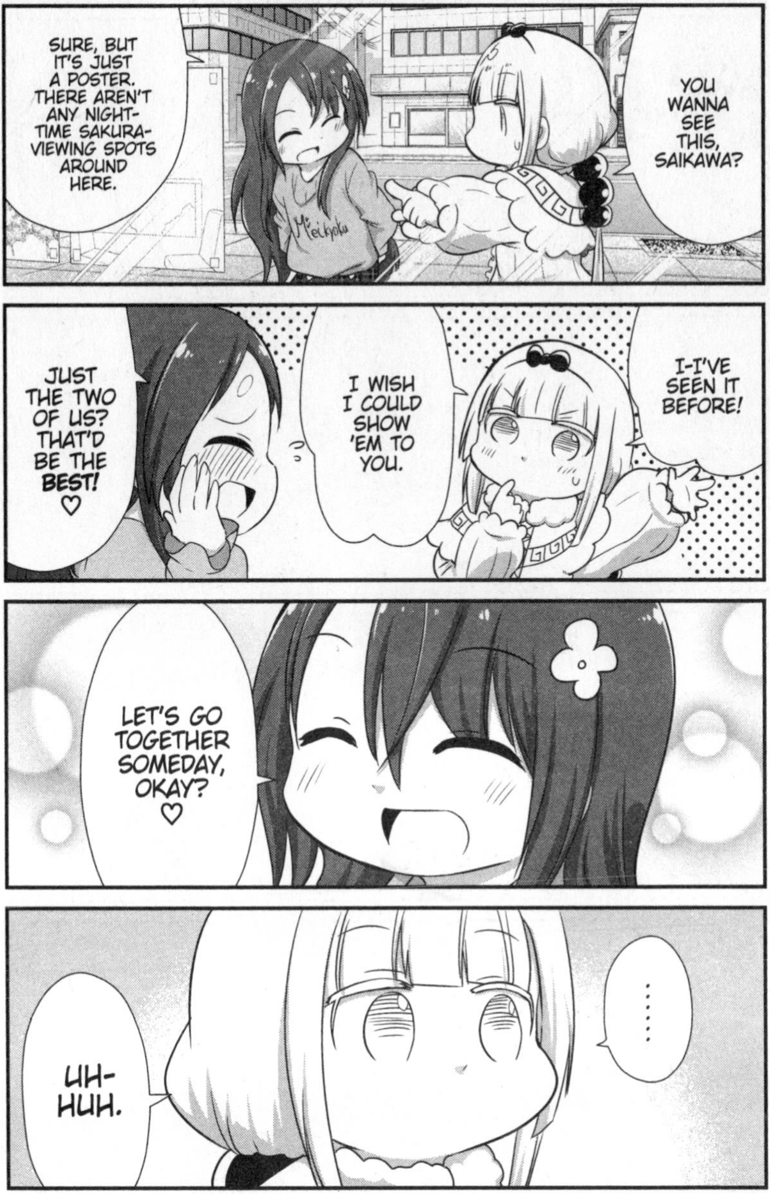
YOU WANNA SEE THIS, SAIKAWA?
SURE, BUT IT'S JUST A POSTER. THERE AREN'T ANY NIGHT-TIME SAKURA-VIEWING SPOTS AROUND HERE.
I-I'VE SEEN IT BEFORE!
I WISH I COULD SHOW 'EM TO YOU.
JUST THE TWO OF US? THAT'D BE THE BEST! ♡
LET'S GO TOGETHER SOMEDAY, OKAY? ♡
......
UH-HUH.

DRACONIC CHANGE OF HEART

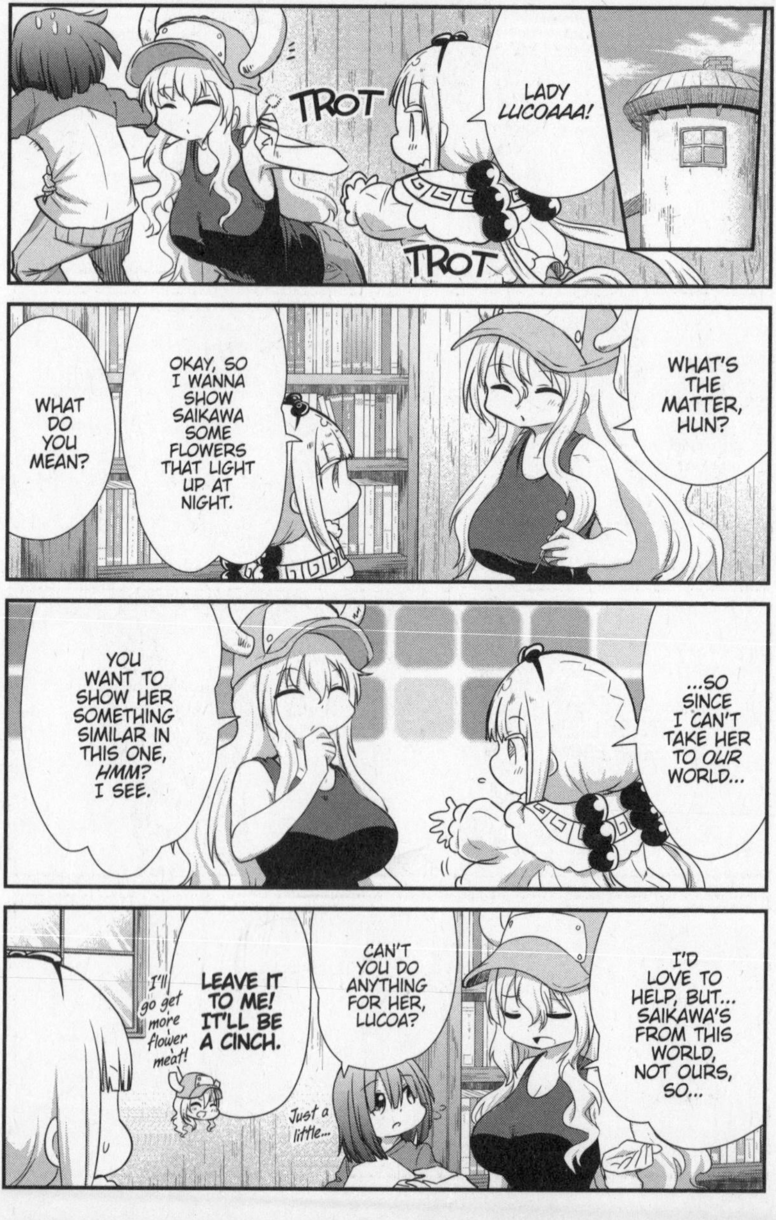
LADY LUCOAAA!
TROT
TROT
WHAT'S THE MATTER, HUN?
OKAY, SO I WANNA SHOW SAIKAWA SOME FLOWERS THAT LIGHT UP AT NIGHT.
WHAT DO YOU MEAN?
...SO SINCE I CAN'T TAKE HER TO *OUR* WORLD...
YOU WANT TO SHOW HER SOMETHING SIMILAR IN THIS ONE, *HMM?* I SEE.
I'D LOVE TO HELP, BUT... SAIKAWA'S FROM THIS WORLD, NOT OURS, SO...
CAN'T YOU DO ANYTHING FOR HER, LUCOA?
Just a little...
LEAVE IT TO ME! IT'LL BE A CINCH.
I'll go get more flower meat!

LEAVE IT TO LUCOA

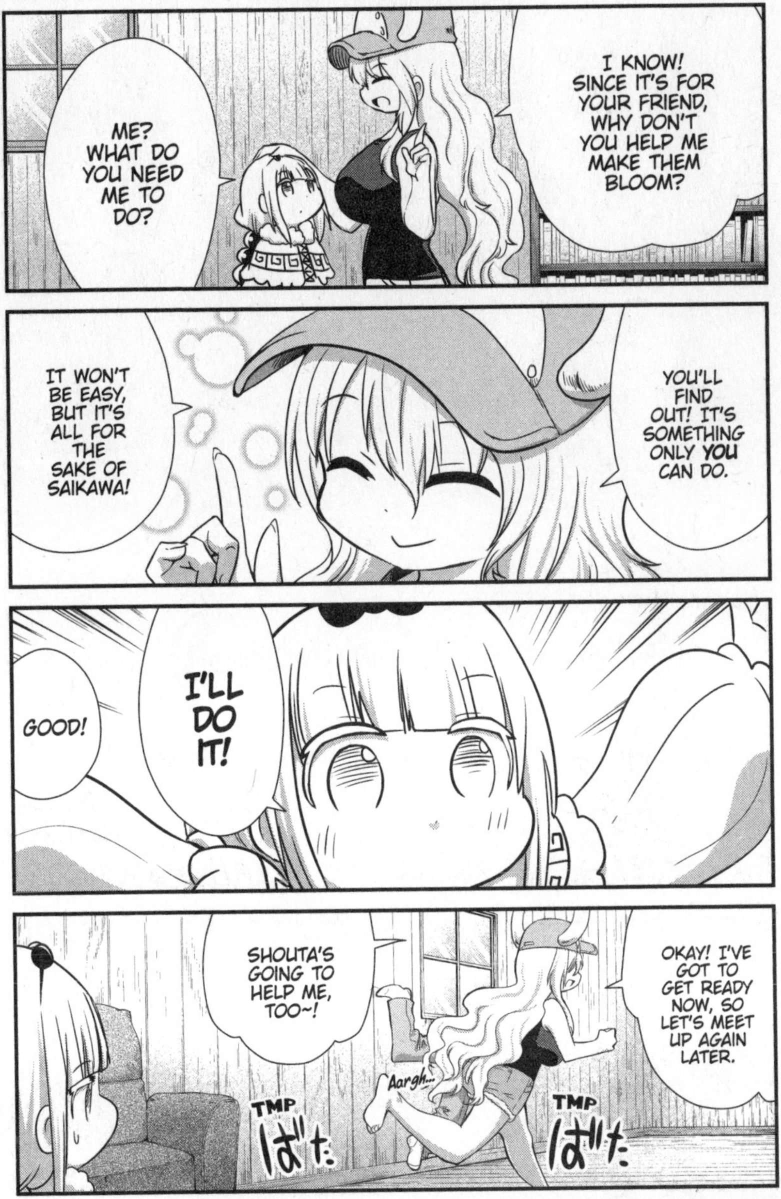
I KNOW! SINCE IT'S FOR YOUR FRIEND, WHY DON'T YOU HELP ME MAKE THEM BLOOM?
ME? WHAT DO YOU NEED ME TO DO?
YOU'LL FIND OUT! IT'S SOMETHING ONLY YOU CAN DO.
IT WON'T BE EASY, BUT IT'S ALL FOR THE SAKE OF SAIKAWA!
I'LL DO IT!
GOOD!
OKAY! I'VE GOT TO GET READY NOW, SO LET'S MEET UP AGAIN LATER.
SHOUTA'S GOING TO HELP ME, TOO~!
TMP
ばた
Aargh...
TMP
ばた

SURPRISE

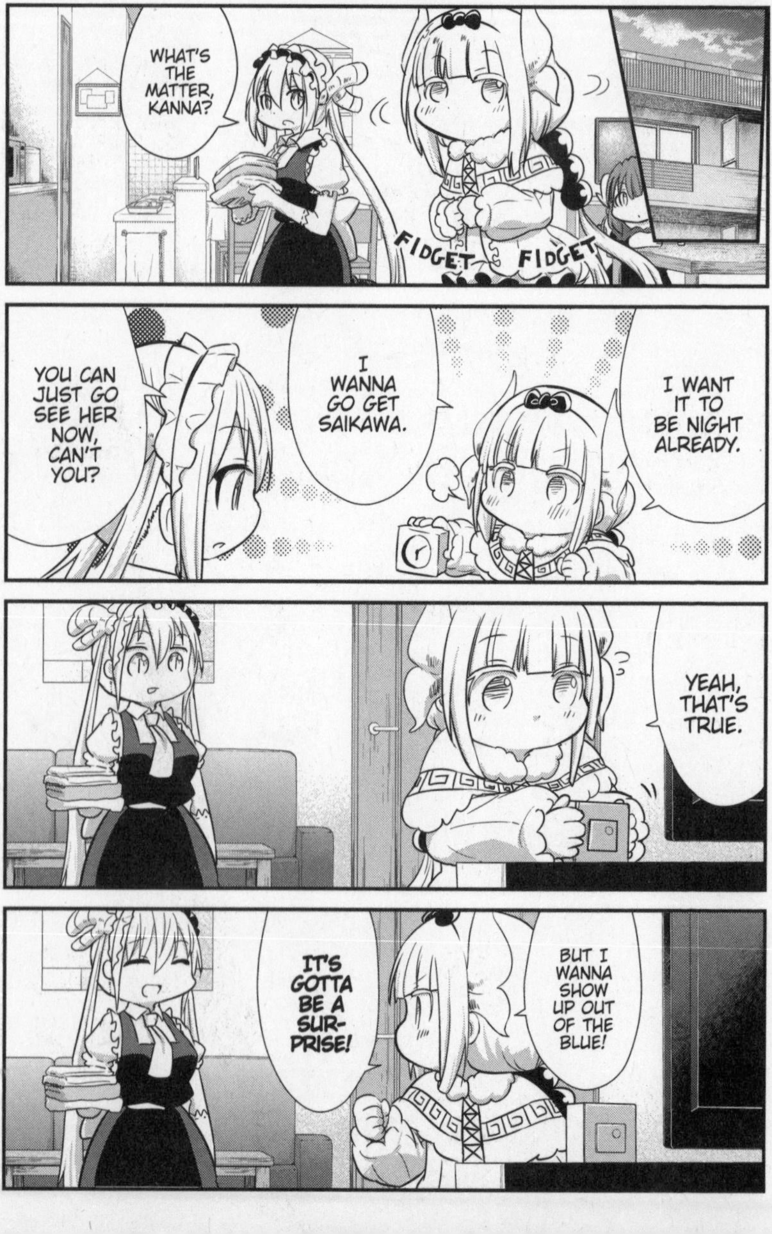
WHAT'S THE MATTER, KANNA?
FIDGET
FIDGET
I WANT IT TO BE NIGHT ALREADY.
I WANNA GO GET SAIKAWA.
YOU CAN JUST GO SEE HER NOW, CAN'T YOU?
YEAH, THAT'S TRUE.
BUT I WANNA SHOW UP OUT OF THE BLUE!
IT'S GOTTA BE A SUR-PRISE!

NIGHTTIME DATE

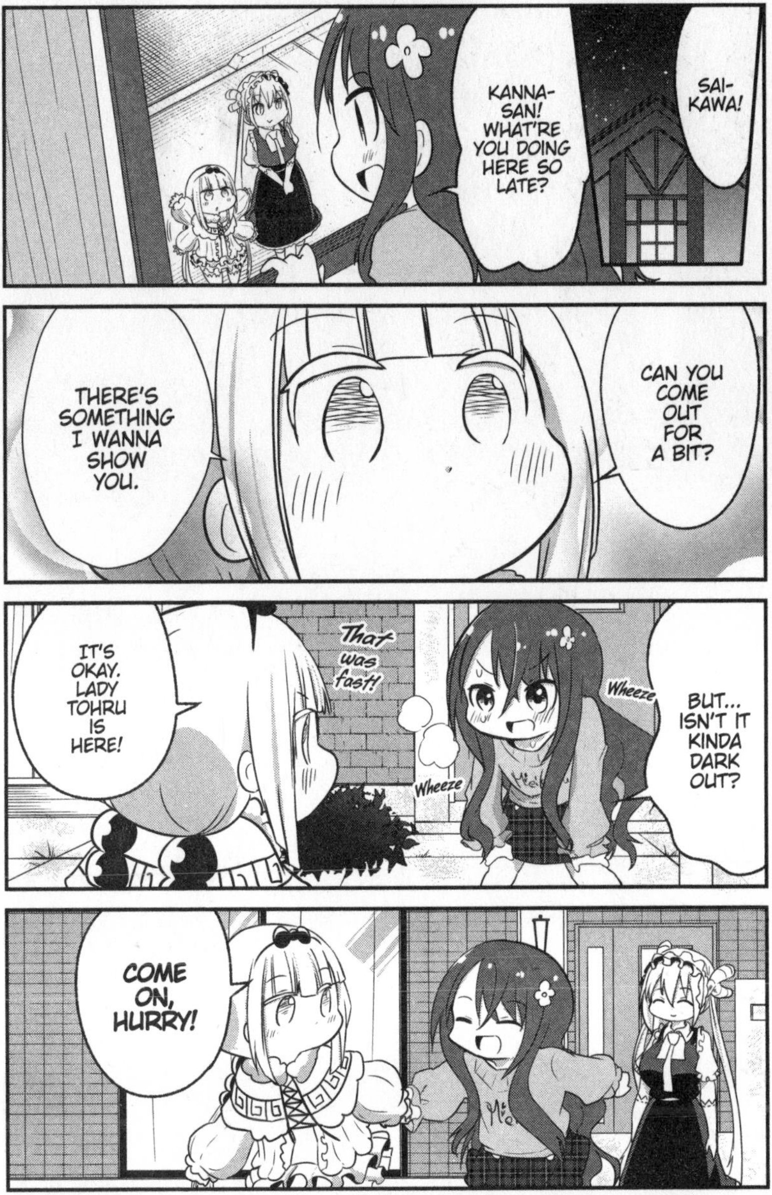
SAI-KAWA!
KANNA-SAN! WHAT'RE YOU DOING HERE SO LATE?
CAN YOU COME OUT FOR A BIT?
THERE'S SOMETHING I WANNA SHOW YOU.
BUT... ISN'T IT KINDA DARK OUT?
Wheeze
Wheeze
That was fast!
IT'S OKAY. LADY TOHRU IS HERE!
COME ON, HURRY!

A LADY LUCOA INVENTION!

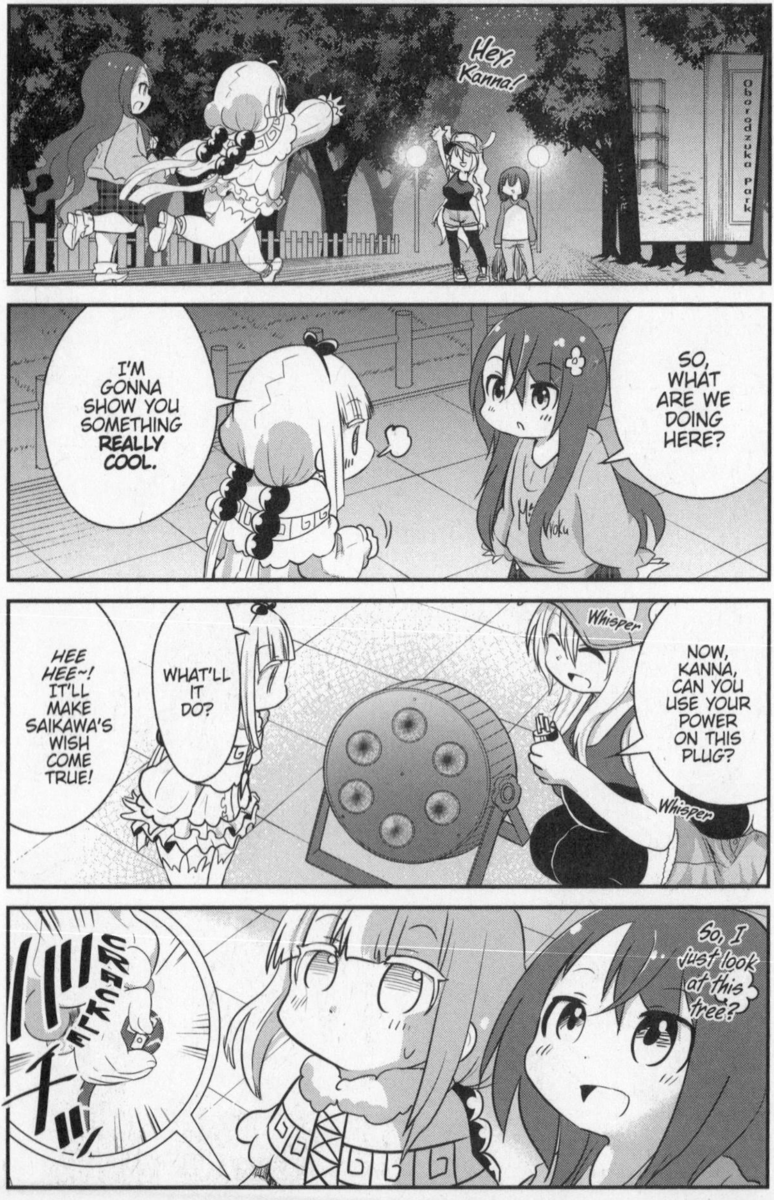
Oborodzuka Park
Hey, Kanna!
SO, WHAT ARE WE DOING HERE?
I'M GONNA SHOW YOU SOMETHING **REALLY COOL.**
Whisper
NOW, KANNA, CAN YOU USE YOUR POWER ON THIS PLUG?
Whisper
WHAT'LL IT DO?
HEE HEE~! IT'LL MAKE SAIKAWA'S WISH COME TRUE!
So, I just look at this tree?
CRACKLE

A WORLD OF MYSTERY

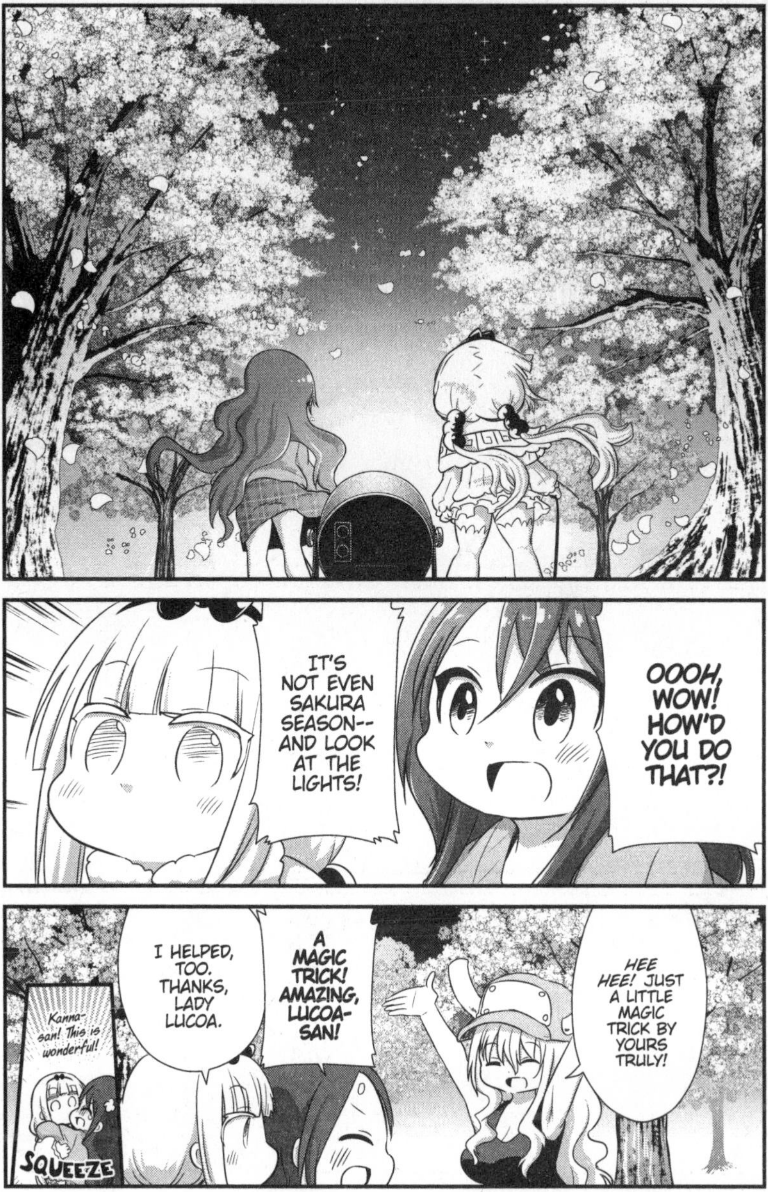
OOOH, WOW! HOW'D YOU DO THAT?!
IT'S NOT EVEN SAKURA SEASON-- AND LOOK AT THE LIGHTS!
HEE HEE! JUST A LITTLE MAGIC TRICK BY YOURS TRULY!
A MAGIC TRICK! AMAZING, LUCOA-SAN!
I HELPED, TOO. THANKS, LADY LUCOA.
Kanna-san! This is wonderful!
SQUEEZE

A PROMISE IS A PROMISE

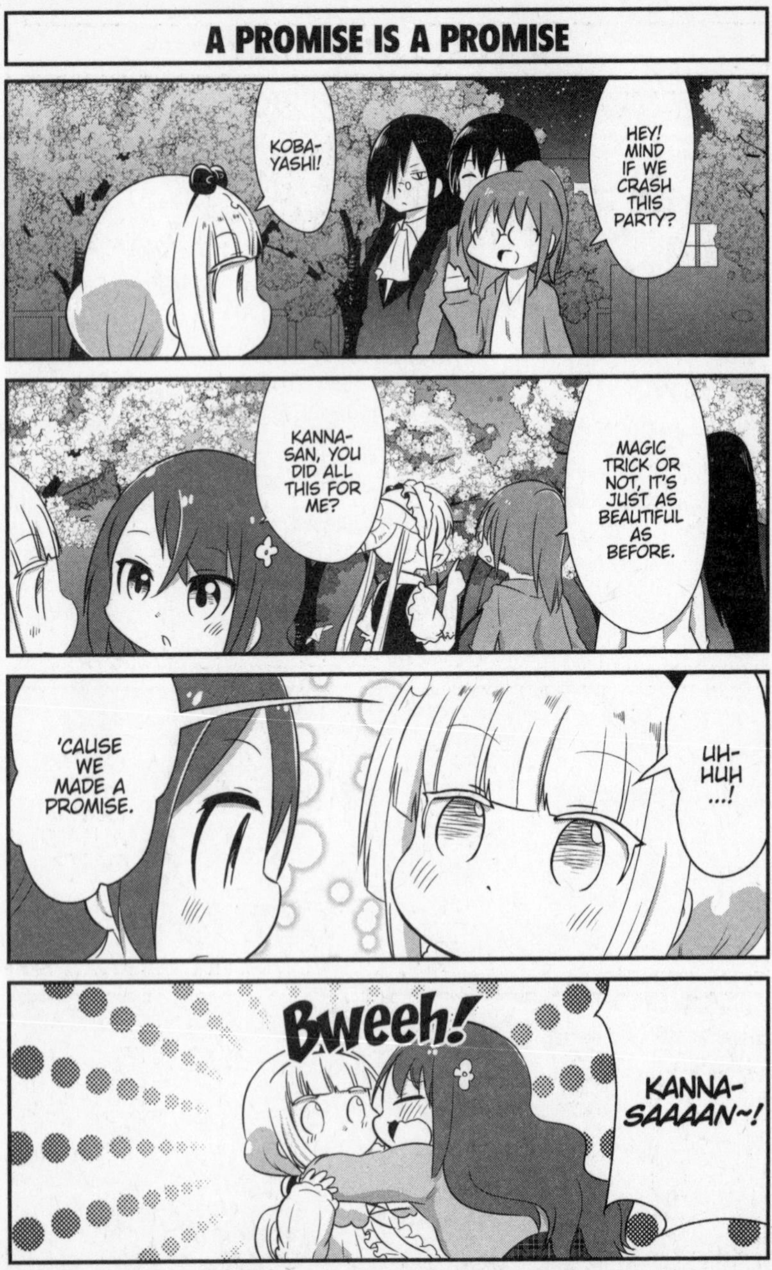
KOBA-YASHI!
HEY! MIND IF WE CRASH THIS PARTY?
KANNA-SAN, YOU DID ALL THIS FOR ME?
MAGIC TRICK OR NOT, IT'S JUST AS BEAUTIFUL AS BEFORE.
'CAUSE WE MADE A PROMISE.
UH-HUH ...!
Bweeh!
KANNA-SAAAAN~!

A WISH FOR TWO WORLDS

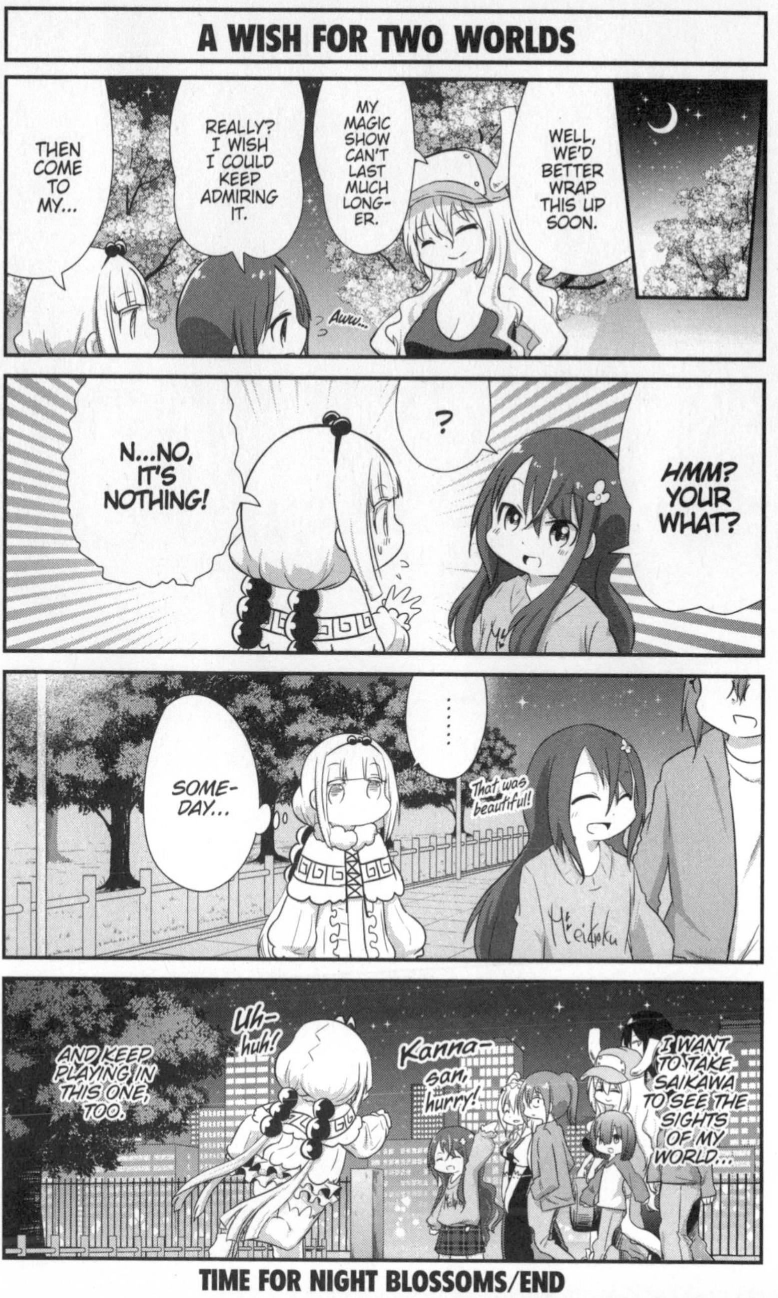
WELL, WE'D BETTER WRAP THIS UP SOON.
MY MAGIC SHOW CAN'T LAST MUCH LONGER.
REALLY? I WISH I COULD KEEP ADMIRING IT.
Awu...
THEN COME TO MY...
HMM? YOUR WHAT?
?
N...NO, IT'S NOTHING!
......
That was beautiful!
SOME-DAY...
I WANT TO TAKE SAIKAWA TO SEE THE SIGHTS OF MY WORLD...
Kanna-san, hurry!
Uh-huh!
AND KEEP PLAYING IN THIS ONE, TOO.

TIME FOR NIGHT BLOSSOMS/END

Miss Kobayashi's Dragon Maid

Kanna's Daily Life

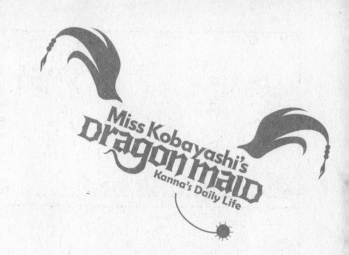

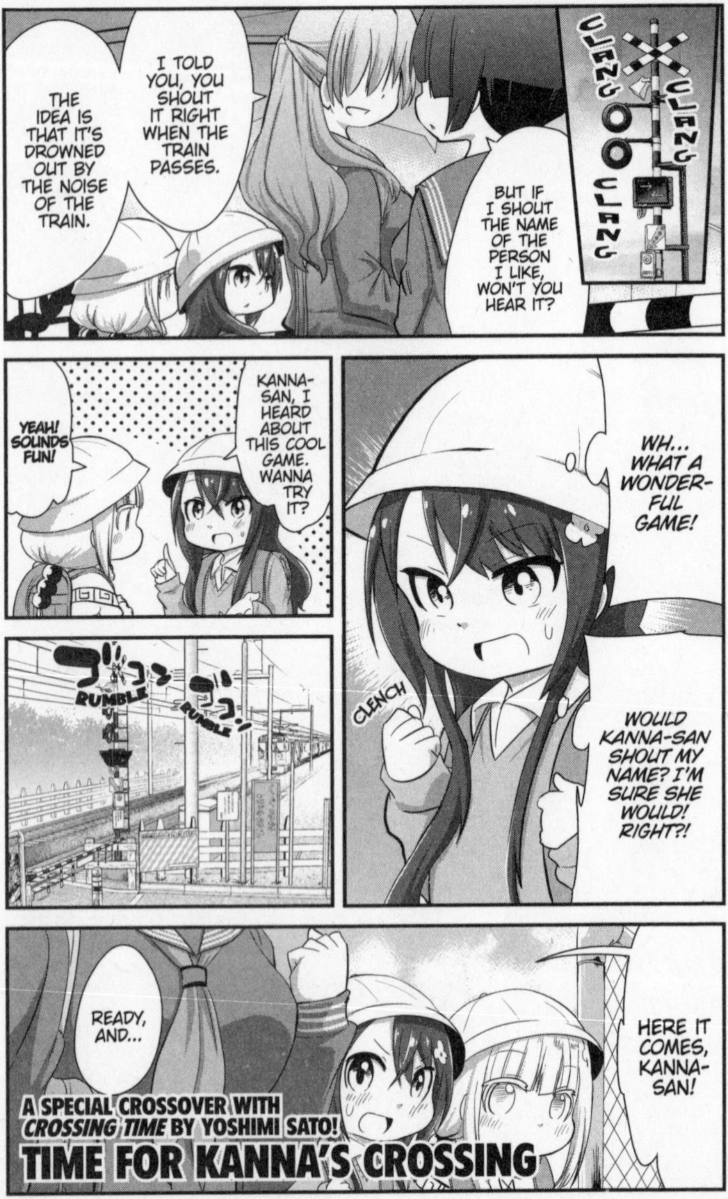
CLANG CLANG CLANG CLANG
BUT IF I SHOUT THE NAME OF THE PERSON I LIKE, WON'T YOU HEAR IT?
I TOLD YOU, YOU SHOUT IT RIGHT WHEN THE TRAIN PASSES.
THE IDEA IS THAT IT'S DROWNED OUT BY THE NOISE OF THE TRAIN.
WH... WHAT A WONDERFUL GAME!
CLENCH
WOULD KANNA-SAN SHOUT MY NAME? I'M SURE SHE WOULD! RIGHT?!
KANNA-SAN, I HEARD ABOUT THIS COOL GAME. WANNA TRY IT?
YEAH! SOUNDS FUN!
RUMBLE RUMBLE
HERE IT COMES, KANNA-SAN!
READY, AND...

A SPECIAL CROSSOVER WITH *CROSSING TIME* BY YOSHIMI SATO!

TIME FOR KANNA'S CROSSING

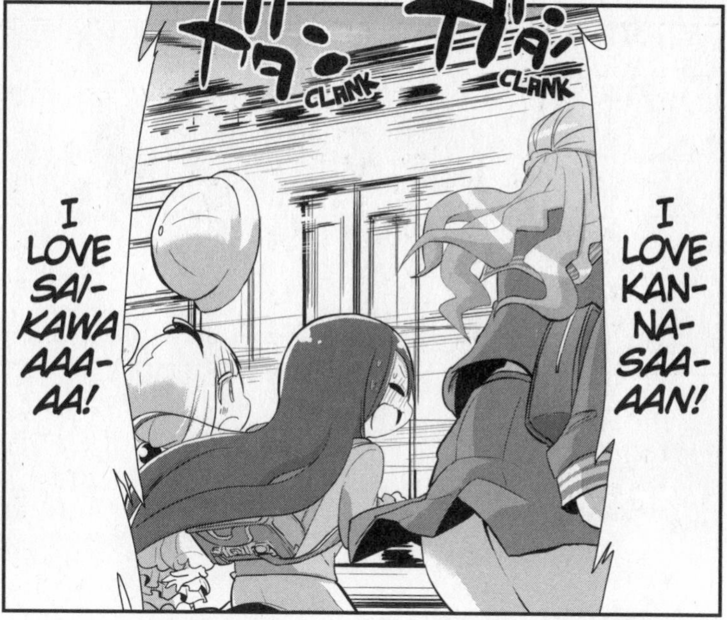
CLANK
CLANK
I LOVE KAN-NA-SAA-AAN!
I LOVE SAI-KAWA AAA-AA!
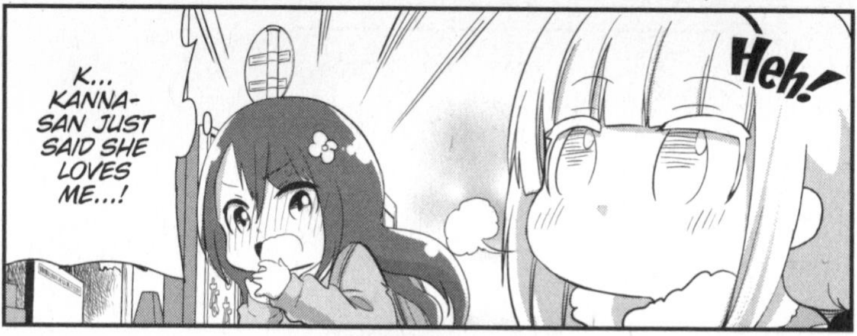
Heh!
K... KANNA-SAN JUST SAID SHE LOVES ME...!
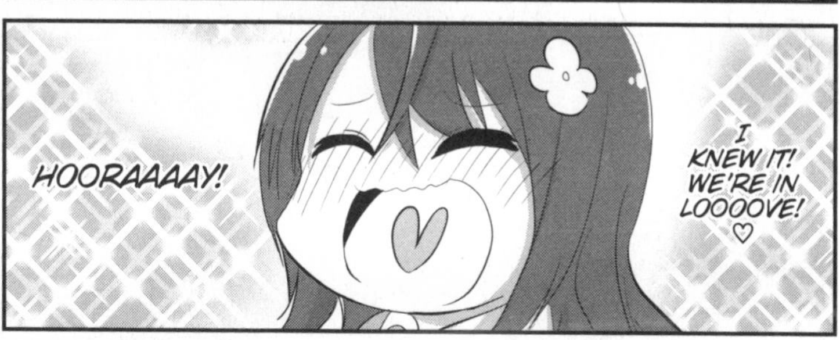
I KNEW IT! WE'RE IN LOOOOVE! ♡
HOORAAAAY!

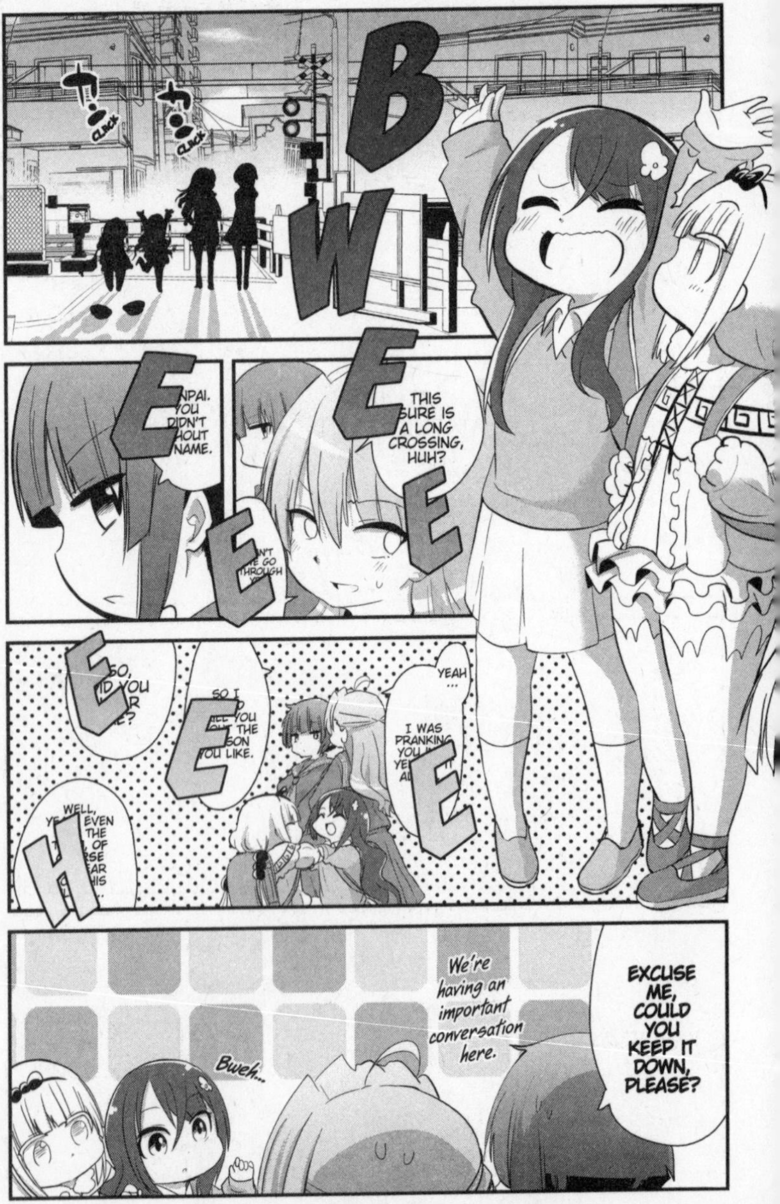
CLACK
CLACK
BWEEEEEEEH
THIS SURE IS A LONG CROSSING, HUH?
YOU DIDN'T
YEAH ...
I WAS PRANKING
YOU LIKE.
WELL,
EXCUSE ME, COULD YOU KEEP IT DOWN, PLEASE?
We're having an important conversation here.
Bweh...

TIME FOR KANNA'S CROSSING/END

That felt great!

Afterword Manga

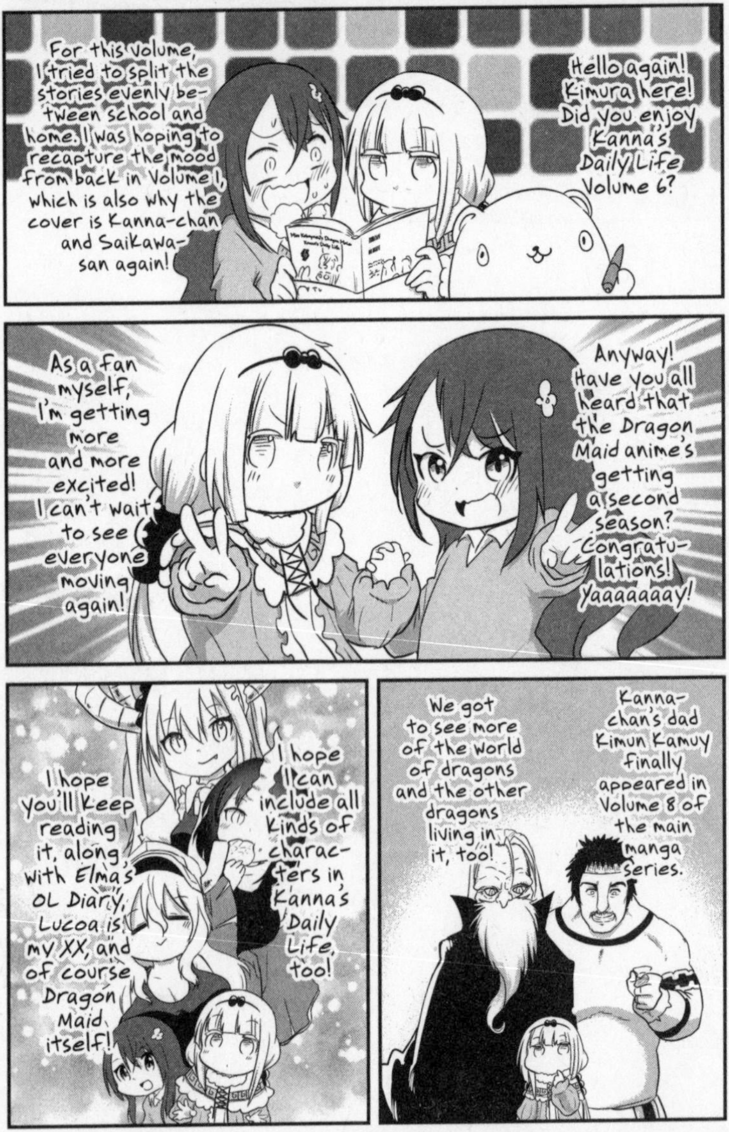
Hello again! Kimura here! Did you enjoy Kanna's Daily Life Volume 6?
For this volume, I tried to split the stories evenly be-tween school and home. I was hoping to recapture the mood from back in Volume 1, which is also why the cover is Kanna-chan and Saikawa-san again!
Anyway! Have you all heard that the Dragon Maid anime's getting a second season? Congratu-lations! Yaaaaaaay!
As a fan myself, I'm getting more and more excited! I can't wait to see everyone moving again!
Kanna-chan's dad Kimun Kamuy finally appeared in Volume 8 of the main manga series.
We got to see more of the world of dragons and the other dragons living in it, too!
I hope I can include all kinds of charac-ters in Kanna's Daily Life, too!
I hope you'll keep reading it, along with Elma's OL Diary, Lucoa is my XX, and of course Dragon Maid itself!

A 4-Panel Manga Called "The Afterword"

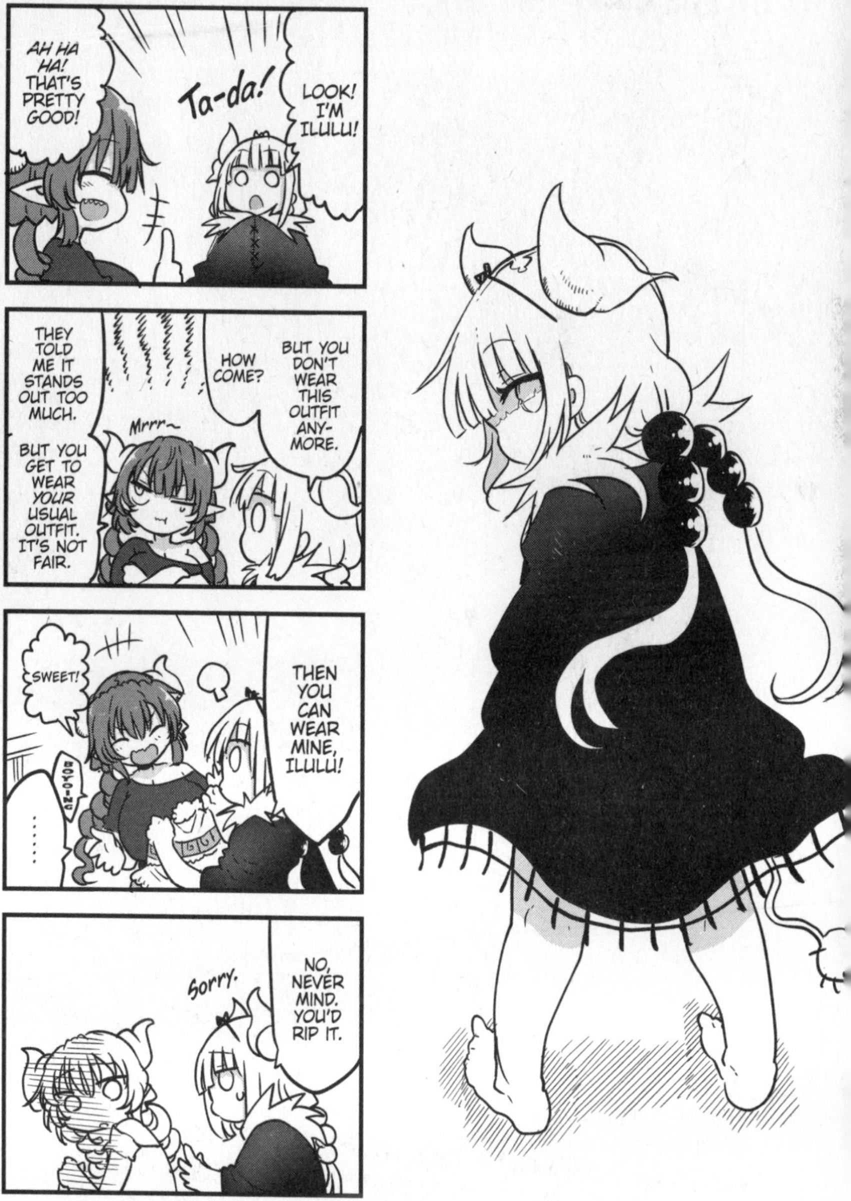
LOOK! I'M ILULU!
Ta-da!
AH HA HA! THAT'S PRETTY GOOD!
BUT YOU DON'T WEAR THIS OUTFIT ANYMORE.
HOW COME?
THEY TOLD ME IT STANDS OUT TOO MUCH.
Mrrr~
BUT YOU GET TO WEAR *YOUR* USUAL OUTFIT. IT'S NOT FAIR.
THEN YOU CAN WEAR MINE, ILULU!
SWEET!
BOYOING
......
NO, NEVER MIND. YOU'D RIP IT.
Sorry.

coolkyousinnjya

SEVEN SEAS ENTERTA

Miss Kobayashi's Dragon Maid
Kanna's Daily Life VOL.6

original story by **coolkyousinnjya** story and art by **Mitsuhiro Kimura**

[redacted]

TRANSLATION
Jenny McKeon

ADAPTATION
Shanti Whitesides

LETTERING
Jennifer Skarupa

LOGO DESIGN
KC Fabellon

COVER DESIGN
Nicky Lim

PROOFREADING
Stephanie Cohen

PRODUCTION MANAGER
Lissa Pattillo

MANAGING EDITOR
Julie Davis

EDITOR-IN-CHIEF
Adam Arnold

PUBLISHER
Jason DeAngelis

MISS [redacted]I'S DRAGON MAID: KANNA'S DAILY LIFE VOL. 6

First published in Japan in 2019 by Futabasha Publishers Ltd., Tokyo.
English version published by Seven Seas Entertainment.
Under license from Futabasha Publishers Ltd.

Seven Seas press and purchase enquiries can be sent to Marketing Manager Lianne Sentar at press@gomanga.com. Information regarding the distribution and purchase of digital editions is available from Digital Manager CK Russell at digital@gomanga.com.

ISBN: 978-1-64275-749-1

Printed in Canada

First Printing: December 2019

10 9 8 7 6 5 4 3 2 1

[redacted]

FOLLOW US ONLINE: ***www.sevenseasentertainment.com***

READING DIRECTIONS

This book reads from ***right to left***, Japanese style. If this is your first time reading manga, you start reading from the top right panel on each page and take it from there. If you get lost, just follow the numbered diagram here. It may seem backwards at first, but you'll get the hang of it! Have fun!!

1
2
3
4
5
6
7
8
9

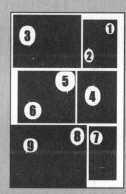